From Lament to Advocacy

BLACK RELIGIOUS EDUCATION AND PUBLIC MINISTRY

Anne E. Streaty Wimberly
Nathaniel D. West
Annie Lockhart-Gilroy

General Editors

From Lament to Advocacy: Black Religious Education and Public Ministry

The General Board of Higher Education and Ministry leads and serves The United Methodist Church in the recruitment, preparation, nurture, education, and support of Christian leaders—lay and clergy—for the work of making disciples of Jesus Christ for the transformation of the world. Its vision is that a new generation of Christian leaders will commit boldly to Jesus Christ and be characterized by intellectual excellence, moral integrity, spiritual courage, and holiness of heart and life. The General Board of Higher Education and Ministry of The United Methodist Church serves as an advocate for the intellectual life of the church. The Board's mission embodies the Wesleyan tradition of commitment to the education of laypersons and ordained persons by providing access to higher education for all persons.

Wesley's Foundery Books is named for the abandoned foundery that early followers of John Wesley transformed, which later became the cradle of London's Methodist movement.

From Lament to Advocacy: Black Religious Education and Public Ministry

ISBN 978-1-945935-749

GBHEM Publishing is an affiliate member of the Association of University Presses.

Manufactured in the United States of America

In honor and gratitude for all who are teaching, leading, striving, and advocating for justice.

Contents

vii Preface

xiii Introduction Black Religious Education and Public Ministry: The Time Is Now
Anne E. Streaty Wimberly

1 Chapter 1 Religious Education and Lament: Inviting Cries from the Heart, Guiding the Way Forward
Anne E. Streaty Wimberly

31 Chapter 2 Religious Educators as Public Ministry Leaders
Nathaniel D. West

59 Chapter 3 Religious Education and Communities of Learning and Practice: Inspiring Advocacy in Public Ministry
Mary H. Young

89 Chapter 4 Religious Education in Response to Black Lives Matter: A Case for Critical Pedagogy
Joseph V. Crockett

117 Chapter 5 Religious Education and Womanist Formation: Mothering and the Reinterpretation of Body Politics
Nancy Lynne Westfield

139 Chapter 6 Religious Education and Prison Ministry: Where Public Theology and Public Pedagogy Meet
Sarah F. Farmer

169 Chapter 7 Religious Education and the Public Role of the Sister's Keeper: A Historical Correlational Method
Richelle B. White

199 Chapter 8 Religious Education for Making It Out of "Da Hood": Spiritual Retreat Encounters for Youth and Young Adult Resilience and Spiritual Formation
Cynthia P. Stewart

229 Epilogue Religious Education, the Black Church, and the Future of Public Ministry: A Village Encounter
Annie Lockhart-Gilroy

239 Contributors

Preface

This book is about a vision of what must happen now and into the unfolding future of Black religious education that takes seriously the demand for attention to public ministry centered on justice. It is a call for leaders, those associated with and in support of educational endeavors within and beyond the church, to consider and join an agenda that empowers advocacy for change amid the continuing challenging realities of Black life in the nation we call home. Each chapter reveals key themes for critical reflection and recommendations for action that are undergirded by a view of God's presence as Advocate and Liberator along life's journey.

The process of writing has been a personal and up-close experience for the authors. Each author had a reason to join this collaborative effort. The chapters come from very real encounters and teaching endeavors. It is, then, appropriate to say that what is included in the forthcoming pages conveys not simply inquiries and reflections on the role of religious education in public ministry but concerns of the heart and desires for religious educators to invite one another and whole communities into conversation.

Mary H. Young: Young speaks of seeing the "coordinated effort [of this book] as a representation of the voices of religious educators who care deeply about the Black Church and the role it serves in nurturing leaders and learners in communities. It is my belief that religious education should equip people of faith to live their belief in the public square–to bear witness to the transforming nature of a faith that extends beyond hearing and finds expression as public witness. My desire is to contribute to this endeavor."

Nathaniel D. West: The role of the religious educator is central to West's thoughts that "historically, religious educators (including myself) have been champions of nurturing people in the faith through various educational programs and activities within our faiths/religions. However, I became dissatisfied with teaching and preaching that only seemed to engage the 'spiritual' lives of individuals while the social and economic ills of society remained unattended. I realized that faith has to be engaged in the public sphere because faith as a private entity allows believers to ignore social, political, and economic challenges. As a professor and practitioner of religious education, I feel I have a responsibility to engage faith in ways that also address numerous challenges individuals, institutions, and communities encounter daily. To add, I feel strongly that religious educators are called to be more than just 'in-house' faith nurturers. We are called to provide leadership as public theologians."

Joseph V. Crockett: As Crockett says, "It is important to me that Black religious educators give voice to their experiences, knowledge, and wisdom on concerns that reside in the public sphere. These conversations matter! Black religious educators share the scars of institutional racism. They, along with many other people of color, regularly face racial prejudice and discrimination. They also know the joys of racial pride. Their experiences make Black religious educators uniquely poised to provide indispensable perspectives on issues that shape and are shaped by us all."

Richelle B. White: In response to her longstanding ministry with and on behalf of young Black girls, White has a clear understanding of her role as writer, stating that "there is need for a framework that builds character, pursues identity, transforms character, and strengthens self-esteem of Black girls who confront negative encounters in the public sphere. It is critical to affirm Black girls as creations of the 'imago Dei.'"

Nancy Lynne Westfield: Out of her own experience and observations of others in privatized education, Westfield tells of the importance of her writing that "opposes privatized education that dampens moral courage, disempowers values of equity, and considers the work of justice as optional. Religious education in the public sphere must be about reclaiming and reconceiving acknowledged and unacknowledged power through teaching that nurtures persons' ability to pursue genuine change in our world. In conversations between my mother and me, I discovered the power of African American mothers as teachers. They have the ability and audacity to reinterpret the politics of hatred, inferiority, and required mediocrity foisted upon girl children. Their interpretation of the distorted reality is to make more possible the lives of girl children, as well as the entire community."

Sarah F. Farmer: From a personal perspective, Farmer claims that "as a religious educator who sees the prison as a site of learning, it was critical for me to think through what it means to be faithful to the task of ministry and theological reflection in the prison. Amid current challenges, we, as people of faith, must know how to navigate issues related to the criminal justice system. Really, this occasion to write has offered me an opportunity to share ideas about prison ministry that I've been thinking for quite some time. It's opened connections with others that I hope will open for the readers to the end that there is greater awareness that religious education is not just about information but about transformation of people and the world."

Cynthia P. Stewart: "I grew up on the South Side of Chicago," says Stewart, "and when I drive through my old neighborhood as an adult, I see boarded-up homes, vacant lots, abandoned buildings, as well as hear on the news countless reports of senseless gun violence. However, growing up in Englewood in a single-parent household, I was privileged to attend the neighborhood Catholic grammar school and church. They were the foundation of the neighborhood. The Catholic priest of the church was known as Papa Smurf because of his paternal nature. He was the father figure in my life that exposed the gift of ministry inside me as a young child. He chose me, at age fourteen, to represent my church at a retreat for African American youth called Kujenga Catholic Leadership Youth Retreat. Through these retreats, I broke the stereotype of growing up in an impoverished neighborhood and single-parent household to matriculate to college, achieve advanced degrees, study abroad, and maintain a successful professional career. The retreats provided space for me to share my story, manage my emotions, and gain a closer relationship with God. Because of the door that was opened for me, I want to provide the same opportunity for others. It gave me reason to write."

Annie Lockhart-Gilroy: "To be honest, as this collective effort was developing, I became intrigued, because the relationship between religious education and public theology was emphasized throughout my education as a minister and scholar. Then I entered as teacher in theological education after Donald Trump was elected president, and I witnessed a wide range of emotions. Questions emerged from students and faculty: What are we supposed to do now? How will we live differently as individuals and Christian leaders? How do we lead congregations in this reality that, for many, is new? How do we address various political issues in our churches? Should we? As time went on, the concerns of these Christians became less about the personality in the White House and more about the policies coming out of the White House. My intrigue became a passion sparked by the reminder of just how desperate the need is for transforming action. I am reminded that religious education that deals with advocacy and public ministry is needed. As religious educators, we are not dealing with simply interesting theories. We are dealing with real people."

Anne E. Streaty Wimberly: On the unfolding contents of the book and the process of writing, Wimberly recounts the famed words of the Negro National Anthem, "We have come over a way that with tears has been watered."[1] "But, we've got a ways more to go that demands willpower for change even as we wail amid continuing deleterious circumstances. This way forward requires prodigious efforts of religious educators to refuse to go it alone but instead place ourselves squarely in and of the community, stay aware of present challenges, create spaces that allow ourselves and others to grieve and lament hardships and setbacks, discover and act on our own advocacy role, and foster and be in conversation with others–young and

---

1 James Weldon Johnson, "Lift Every Voice and Sing," *African American Heritage Hymnal* (Chicago: GIA Publications, 2001), #540.

old, church leaders and laity, community leaders and residents, societal organizations and structures–and surely in conversation with God. It requires a religious education that helps people move from lament to advocacy by embracing a public ministry responsibility."

Conversation partners: Along the way, a number of colleagues and students have already joined in the conversation by reading, reflecting on, raising pertinent and challenging questions about, and posing affirming and encouraging comments on the material shared with them. These enormously helpful and gracious individuals include Dr. Darius M. Benton, community leader and assistant professor of communication studies, Department of Arts and Communication, College of Humanities and Social Science at the University of Houston Downtown, Houston, Texas; Bishop Sedgwick Daniels, Church of God in Christ, Prelate in the Wisconsin and Northern Illinois districts; Rev. Dr. Rebecca Davis, associate professor of Christian education, Union Presbyterian Seminary, Charlotte, North Carolina; Rev. Dr. Tammie Grimm, assistant professor of congregational formation at Indiana Wesleyan University in Marion, Indiana; Dr. Archie Smith Jr., professor emeritus, pastoral psychology and counseling at Pacific School of Religion and Graduate Theological Union, Berkeley, California, and Diplomate in the American Association of Pastoral Counseling; Rev. Richard Stewart, youth director, Beulahland Bible Church, South Campus, Warner Robins, Georgia; Rev. Susan Warren, United Methodist pastor, prison ministry leader, and doctor of ministry student focused on incarcerated women; Dr. Indonesia Wilson, program coordinator, Youth Hope-Builders Academy and the Connecting with Hope Innovation Hub Black Millennials Ministry Initiative at Interdenominational Theological Center, Atlanta, Georgia; and Dr. Edward P. Wimberly, ninth president and professor emeritus of pastoral psychology and care at Interdenominational Theological Center.

Anne E. Streaty Wimberly
Nathaniel D. West
Annie Lockhart-Gilroy

Introduction

Black Religious Education and Public Ministry
The Time Is Now

Anne E. Streaty Wimberly

> As we have watched our heroes falling over the years, . . . our own small stone of activism, which might not seem to measure up to the rugged boulders of heroism we have so admired, is a paltry offering toward the building of an edifice of hope. . . . We can do nothing substantial toward changing our course on the planet . . . without rousing ourselves, individual by individual, and bringing our small imperfect stones to the pile.
>
> —Alice Walker, *Anything We Love Can Be Saved*

A Call to Act

The impassioned cry of "What should we do?" resounded during a gathering of Black religious educators at the November 2015 Religious Educators Association meeting in Atlanta, Georgia. There was good reason for the urgent tone of the question and the conversation that followed. At the time of the meeting, we were reeling with deep emotions. We could not avoid our thoughts about difficult events in recent years: the death of seventeen-year-old Trayvon Martin in February 2012 by a White neighborhood watchman, who considered him out of place in the community, and the acquittal of his killer in July 2013; the July 2014 killing of Eric Garner in Staten Island, New York, by a White police officer's illegal choke hold; the August 2014 death of eighteen-year-old Michael Brown in Ferguson, Missouri; the November 2014 police killing of twelve-year-old Tamir

Rice in Cleveland, Ohio, over a toy gun; and the June 2015 attack on parishioners at the historic Emanuel African Methodist Episcopal (AME) Church in Charleston, South Carolina. These incidents were paralleled by the recollection of Black church arson and personal experiences of other types of aggression and wide-ranging social issues and disparities.

As Black people, we struggled with our own grief about all that had taken place and pondered how long we must continue to sing the song "We Shall Overcome." We felt deep concern for the safety and future of Black people. We grappled with who we are and our role as religious educators, and wrestled with what is needed to fulfill a relevant and credible religious education function in present turbulent times. Emerging group sentiments highlighted a quandary about what to do that could possibly address the plethora of challenges faced by Black communities. The thought surfaced: It's hard to know where to begin or even move churches beyond simply being safe spiritual havens without action in the world. In response, a wide range of religious educational efforts, including some centered on social concerns and justice issues, were recognized. But overall, there appears to be limited attention to applying faith to social justice issues and its impact on major life issues. Most important, the group said in clearest terms that public ministry and advocacy on behalf of justice and human well-being are critically needed aspects of religious education within and beyond today's and tomorrow's Black churches.

This book emerged specifically out of recognition that Black religious education is at a crossroads and that now is a decisive time for renewing the direction, experiences, and resources needed to meet current challenges in Black life. Moving forward entails taking seriously a public ministry emphasis in religious education focused on personal, sociocultural, political, and spiritual crises. We recognize, too, that young people especially are calling for the Church to speak of and act out of a faith that can sustain and guide them as they experience up-close threats to their lives and are told to "go back to where [they] came from," as though they are orphans or aliens in the land of their birth. Youth and adults, for that matter, wonder what justice looks like in particular situations and how to attain it. They see images of the struggle for it in movies and in remembrance of the civil rights movement and the history of slavery that began the sojourn of Black people in this country. They also see that past and present struggles for justice are tricky and complex. Guilt, innocence, punishment, and fairness for whom, when, where, what, and decided by whom all too often comprise a strange discomforting state of affairs. Often, justice seems far off, and when it comes, the question arises of whether the wrong has been fully redressed. At other times, justice does not seem to come at all, and a new struggle emerges in the form of questions about how to deal with grief, anger, thoughts of revenge, and the notion of forgiveness that lies at the center of the Christian faith. Amid it all, young people are clear, as noted in such statements: "Churches should discuss community situations." "Talk more about the political in the community." "Try to connect on a more personal level about problems we're facing in today's society." "Get involved!" "Help us fix the problems." "Try your hardest to fix the issues!" "There's a lot of stuff going on. Help get us young people involved by allowing us and teaching us to lead."[1]

Of course, there is no mistaking that the requirement of connecting religious education and public ministry is not new! We recall revered Black religious educator Grant Shockley's admonition for a new direction in Black religious education, drawing on the liberation theological perspectives of James Cone and other

1 These thoughts of young Black people were shared in a research project led by principal investigator Anne E. Streaty Wimberly, titled "The Church's Role in Reaching Disconnected Black Youth," undertaken from 2014 to 2016 by the Youth Hope-Builders Academy (YHBA) of Interdenominational Theological Center, Atlanta, Georgia, with 435 respondents ages thirteen to eighteen from across the four regions of the United States. A pivotal part of the project focused on obtaining the youths' ideas, attitudes, and expectations of the Church in their lives.

liberation theologians.[2] Shockley challenged the Black Church and religious education to focus on a public agenda, reconstruct a new ministry paradigm, direct teaching and learning processes toward justice and a new humanity, and center programmatic efforts on people's experiences. Theologically, Shockley maintained that religious education is about connecting Black people with a socially active and political God who affirms their "somebodyness" and is present with and sustains them. This view instructs the very nature of religious educational content "centering around the experiences, relationships, and situational dilemmas that Black people face in their day-to-day struggle to survive, develop, and progress in an often hostile, uncaring, majority-dominated society . . . [and] practices, methods, and techniques that embody, complement, and reinforce this principle."[3] Shockley confirms that religious education is about public engagement. In fact, he adroitly raises the questions, "Why have Christian education in the Black Church at all? What are the guidelines?" In response, he maintains that Christian education must provide the tools to empower Black people's engagement in civil rights activity.[4] It is interesting to note that a parallel to Shockley's call for Black religious education as a public ministry endeavor emerged in 1990 research on effective Christian education. It revealed that "Christian education in a majority

2 Grant S. Shockley, "Black Theology and Religious Education," in *Theologies of Religious Education*, ed. Randolph Crump Miller (Birmingham, AL: Religious Education Press, 1995), 317–21.

3 Shockley, "Black Theology and Religious Education," 321.

4 Grant S. Shockley, "Christian Education and the Black Church," in *Christian Education Journey of Black Americans: Past, Present, Future*, ed. Charles Foster, Ethel R. Johnson, and Grant S. Shockley (Nashville: Discipleship Resources, 1985), 1–18. Additional information on Shockley's emphasis on a liberation theology and agenda in Black religious education appears in Grant S. Shockley, "Liberation Theology, Black Theology, and Religious Education," in *Foundations for Christian Education in an Era of Change*, ed. Marvin J. Taylor (Nashville: Abingdon Press, 1976), 80–95; and Shockley, "Black Theology and Religious Education," 314–35.

of congregations is a tired enterprise in need of reform."[5] The outcomes pointed to a necessary emphasis on faith formation that includes content emphasizing major life issues of adults and adolescents and processes that build understanding of faith applied to political and social issues, oppression, and injustice.[6]

Even as we recognize the call for a public sensibility in religious education in the years leading to the twenty-first century and the present call for it, we need not forget earlier examples of Black religious education that connect with social and community issues, faith, and action. Indeed, a review whence we have come is helpful in revealing forerunners in religious education who set the ground for proposals, public actions, and pedagogical processes appearing in this book. Thus, we turn now to a brief historical recall or looking back before turning to a way forward that stresses current meanings of religious education as public ministry, the necessity of lament, importance of advocacy, and theological underpinnings.

Looking Back

Black religious education has a history of developing people's social consciousness and empowering them "to act for social transformation in line with the prophetic witness of the gospel."[7] The role and vision of religious educators were pivotal in this regard and adeptly modeled predominantly by Black women into the early decades of the twentieth century, providing an informative basis

5 Peter L. Benson and Carolyn H. Eklin, *Effective Christian Education: A National Study of Protestant Congregations* (Minneapolis: Search Institute, 1990), 58.

6 Benson and Eklin, *Effective Christian Education*, 54-55, 65-66.

7 An overview of this model appears in Kenneth H. Hill, *Religious Education in the African American Tradition* (St. Louis: Chalice Press, 2007), 121, 130-31; and Stacey Floyd-Thomas, Juan Floyd-Thomas, Carol B. Duncan, Stephen C. Ray Jr., and Nancy Lynne Westfield, "Christian Education in the Black Church Tradition," in *Black Church Studies: An Introduction* (Nashville: Abingdon Press, 2007), 151-76, esp. 167-73.

for current-day model building; this appears in Richelle B. White's chapter in this resource.

Black Women at the Forefront of Religious Education as Public Ministry

In the early twentieth century, religious educator and activist Mary McLeod Bethune clearly affirmed, "If we accept and acquiesce in the face of discrimination, we accept the responsibility ourselves. We should, therefore, protest openly everything . . . that smacks of discrimination or slander."[8] Educating children and adults for self-help and to become agents of social change was integral to her understanding of the unity of spiritual, social, and political dimensions of life guided by Scripture and following the life of Jesus Christ.[9] She aptly pointed to faith as "the first factor in a life devoted to service. Without it, nothing is possible. With it, nothing is impossible."[10] The religious educational efforts of another leader, Nannie Burroughs, centered on Black students' moral values alongside the promotion of political mobilization. Her pedagogical approach enabled students' agency in accomplishing personal and communal uplift. At the same time, she modeled the role of social and moral change agent through her own advocacy for equal rights in public services such as education and public transportation.[11]

---

8 Mary McLeod Bethune, "Certain Unalienable Rights," in *What the Negro Wants*, ed. Rayford W. Logan (South Bend, IN: University of Notre Dame Press, 1944, 2001), 256.

9 Clarence G. Newsome, "Mary McLeod Bethune in Religious Perspective: A Seminal Essay" (PhD diss., Duke University, 1982), 217.

10 Mary McLeod Bethune, Audrey Thomas McCluskey, and Elaine M. Smith, *Mary McLeod Bethune: Building a Better World: Essays and Selected Documents* (Bloomington: Indiana University Press, 2001), 60.

11 Burroughs's educational efforts over a particular period of time are described in National Training School for Women and Girls, "Special Aims," *Circular of Information for the Seventeenth Annual Session of the National Training School for Women and Girls Incorporated* (Washington, DC: Lincoln Heights, 1925–1926).

The religious educational efforts of the Black Women's Movement and Baptist Women's Convention Auxiliary beginning in the late nineteenth century and continuing through the opening decades of the twentieth century responded to intensified racism. Led by Black women, including Nannie Burroughs, primarily on behalf of Black women and girls, these endeavors utilized biblical teaching and church involvement to develop leadership for political organizing and empowerment to confront oppressive realities.[12] These religious education leaders were activists who modeled the decisive and indispensable role of women, which predated womanist approaches to religious education. Their efforts blended secular and religious concerns and moved religious education beyond the walls of the church.

It is important to note that the instructional models of early religious educators invariably incorporated skills-building methods for personal and cultural uplift and were therefore identified as accommodationist. That is, the critique is that their perceived purpose was "to indoctrinate Blacks with middle-class Victorian values—now referred to as 'the politics of respectability'—in order to defy messages of the cultural and intellectual inferiority of Blacks."[13] However, this view evades the more truthful view that education for racial uplift functions as a resistance strategy centered on Black people in general and Black women in particular as "equals rather than subordinate to Whites."[14] Moreover, it must not be forgotten that the

12 The history and work of the movement appears in Prathia L. Hall, "The Religious and Social Consciousness of African American Baptist Women" (PhD diss., Princeton University, 1997). Ann Arbor: UMI, 1997. ATT 9730183; Cheryl T. Gilkes, *If It Wasn't for the Women: Black Women's Culture and Womanist Culture in Church and Community* (Maryknoll, NY: Orbis Books, 2001).

13 Kendra H. Barber, "Whither Shall We Go? The Past and Present of Black Churches and the Public Sphere," in "Solidarities and Separations," special issue, *Religions* 6, no. 1 (March 2015): 252, https://doi.org/10.3390/rel6010245.

14 Barber, "Whither Shall We Go?," 252.

early religious educators' personal advocacy efforts affirmed the importance of the modeling role of leaders and that movements for change require leaders.

Religious Education for Health and Well-Being

Early evidence of what Mary Young calls in her chapter a "community of learning and action" appeared in the early twentieth-century National Negro Health Movement (NNHW), which connected community mobilization efforts with religious education. This endeavor was a campaign to improve community health through collaborative involvement of churches along with schools, clinics, and in community settings. This movement exemplifies what it means to form a comprehensive arena in which vital conversations and needed action on behalf of people's well-being occur. The effort featured "a heavy focus on sermons about health during church services and popular mass meetings."[15] The church played a pivotal educational role in addressing the often-neglected issue of Black health by hosting conferences, lectures, sermons, and exhibits on health issues. Health essays, songs, and games for children; providing educational brochures; and promoting attendance at health clinics and community health events were added vehicles of public education.[16]

Continuing Public Ministry Orientation in Religious Education

Alongside the efforts largely led by women, Carter Woodson's initiation of Black history celebration in 1926 served as a model leading to an ongoing focus of churches and schools on learning and celebrating Black American history. Yet the intent was also to inspire young people's leadership and social activism through stories of

---

15 Stephen B. Thomas and Sandra Crouse Quinn, "Closing the Gap," in *Health Issues in the Black Community*, 2nd ed., ed. Ronald L. Braithwaite and Sandra E. Taylor (San Francisco: Jossey-Bass Publishers, 2001), 553.

16 Thomas and Quinn, "Closing the Gap," 553–57.

the journey of Black people and Black leaders.[17] Later twentieth-century religious education efforts that followed continued to respond to painful social-cultural and political issues, as noted in the advocacy efforts of religious educator Olivia Pearl Stokes, to address stereotypical views of Black people. During the civil rights era, she also "challenged religious educators to analyze and critique disparaging images, teaching practices, and social structures. She further challenged them to engage in honest dialogue, to address community concerns, and to develop programs that would allow them and their students to bring about transformation and change in their individual lives and communities."[18] Stokes's leadership paralleled the earlier-mentioned emphasis of Grant Shockley on the indispensable relationship between Black liberation theology and religious education.

Truthfully, much of what happened in religious education in institutionalized Black Churches from Emancipation forward reflected a pietistic-oriented approach patterned after White Protestant models of Bible study, sermons, and Sunday school, emphasizing Christian values, stewardship, and responsibility in personal, family, church, and social relationships.[19] By the end of the twentieth century, it is fair to say that religious education functioned in three types of churches. They included conservative churches that centered on spiritual matters and ignored social crises; minimally involved churches that addressed social and community issues only slightly; and activist churches, mostly headed by activist pastors, that gave vigorous attention to the wider range of social issues.[20]

---

17 See "National Fraternal Council of Negro Churches in America, Wilberforce, Ohio," in *The Negro Journal of Religion* 1, no. 2 (March 1935): 14.

18 Yolanda Y. Smith, "Olivia Pearl Stokes," Christian Educators of the 20th Century Database, Biola University, accessed January 8, 2020, www.biola.edu/talbot/ce20/database/olivia-pearl-stokes.

19 See Kenneth H. Hill, *Religious Education in the African American Tradition: A Comprehensive Introduction* (St. Louis: Chalice Press, 2007), 25.

20 Andrew Billingsley, *Mighty Like a River: The Black Church and Social Reform* (New York: Oxford University Press, 1999), 185.

A study of the role of religious education into the twenty-first century further shows a wide range of educational models. They include (1) kerygmatic education focused on disclosure of the gospel in teaching and preaching; (2) holiness education centered on biblical understandings of the work of the Holy Spirit, the spiritual disciplines, and life empowered by both; (3) Afrocentric education emphasizing discovery of African history, culture, and religious history as pathways to personal and collective cultural identity and pride; (4) contemplative education focused on the spiritual disciplines, forming and living out of a relationship with God; (5) confessional education directed toward transmitting the tradition represented by a particular faith community; and (6) liberation education occurring through attention on sociopolitical realities and the implication of these for transforming action in society. In truth, however, the liberation model is tied with the holiness approach as the least emphasized (7 percent) among the study sample.[21] Moreover, respondents in the study indicated a greater desire for Afrocentric and contemplative models with no mention of the liberation model.[22]

A Way Forward: Religious Education and Public Ministry

The journey of Black people has continued to be one of struggle amid oppressive circumstances. In light of the continuation of this journey, Billingsley raises a pertinent question that is quite instructive for religious educators. He says, "The question for the future is this: Can the Black Church garner enough strength from its rich, fruitful past and its struggles in the present against widespread

21 The study showed the following emphases in churches: kerygmatic education, 88 percent; confessional education, 88 percent; contemplative, 37 percent; Afrocentric, 25 percent; Holiness, 7 percent; and liberation, 7 percent. See Hill, *Religious Education in the African American Tradition*, 121–34.

22 Hill, *Religious Education in the African American Tradition*, 134.

social turmoil to lead the African American community into a viable future?"[23] In response to the question, our position as religious educators is that there is no question that the effort must be made. As in the past, a public ministry emphasis in religious education is considered here to be a mandate.

The Present Public Ministry Mandate in Religious Education

A twenty-first-century public emphasis on religious education derives from a renewed and mandated vision for social action and change–justice–that not only recognizes but ensures the human dignity, worth, and well-being of Black people, who are God's creations. This vision acknowledges the reality of little change since the advent of the liberation orientation set forth by Grant Shockley. It sustains the relevant theological pivot on setting people–both the oppressed and the oppressor–free from injustices, inequalities, and differential power relations and structures based on a belief in the activity of a political God who is on the side of the oppressed. But it also holds to five key theological assumptions: (1) God's creation is socially constructed; (2) Christian living patterned after the ministry of Jesus requires attention to justice on behalf of those who, even though present in society, are not valued and are treated as orphans or aliens; (3) God, whom Black people identify as "mother to the motherless" and "father to the fatherless," redefines the orphaned or alien by declaring them God's treasured children and ones for whom God has a future and a vocation; (4) God is present as the Advocate whom Jesus promised would give them the life-force or God's Spirit of love, truth, comfort, and counsel needed to situate them beyond an orphaned or alien circumstance and to enable their advocacy on behalf of justice and righteousness in society (John 14:15-19); and (5) practical Christianity enacted through advocacy

23 Billingsley, *Mighty Like a River*, 187.

and justice-seeking efforts may inconvenience people or call for sacrifice.[24]

The focus on advocacy and justice on behalf of alienated and oppressed people in the theological assumptions is intentional and pivotal because it connects with what is heard, especially from present generations of young people, that extends beyond the language of liberation. They do not yell, "Liberate us!" Rather, their thunderous plea is, "We want, we demand justice–justice for those brutally killed; justice in the criminal justice system; economic justice; social, educational, political justice!" And they want to know by what means justice will become a concrete reality. Interestingly, one answer to the question does not appear in the institutional Church but rather in what is known as the Black Lives Matter movement, which was inspired by the 1960s civil rights movement's call for freedom. Yet, as Joseph Crockett reminds us in his chapter in this resource, while fighting for freedom and liberation, the present movement is self-identified as a justice campaign set to train community residents to organize, activate, and press on for justice revealed in the transformation and restoration of all that makes for injustice.[25] In short, the multivalent vision presented here points to a religious education that is rightly identified as justice education.

24 Aspects of these theological assumptions appear in Elizabeth Conde-Frazier, "From Hospitality to Shalom," in *A Many Colored Kingdom: Multicultural Dynamics for Spiritual Formation*, ed. Elizabeth Conde-Frazier, S. Steve Kang, and Gary A. Parrett (Grand Rapids, MI: Baker Academic, 2004), 167-201, esp. 205; Walter Brueggemann, *The Bible Makes Sense*, rev. ed. (Louisville, KY: Westminster John Knox, 2001), 75-79; Jamie Phelps, "Black Spirituality," in *Spiritual Traditions for the Contemporary Church*, ed. Robin Maas and Gabriel O'Donnell (Nashville: Abingdon Press, 1990), 332-51, esp. 343-45; James H. Cone, *Black Theology and Black Power* (New York: Seabury Press, 1969), 56-61; and *The Wesley Study Bible, NRSV* (Nashville: Abingdon Press, 2009), 1312.

25 See "About," Black Lives Matter, accessed January 8, 2020, https://Blacklivesmatter.com/about.

Justice Education: What Is It?

Justice education centers on understandings, critiques, and practices of the ethical standard of a just society that assures respectful treatment of people and unbiased access to benefits and opportunities that are supposed to be available to all. Moreover, it includes examination of meanings and functions of justice and righteousness in the Christian faith and a vision for living in public life. Justice education proceeds to practices of being present with and hearing people's narratives of encroachments on the ethical and spiritual principles of justice and discerning what is needed and how to advocate for just responses. Justice education is about advocacy as the practice of promoting and enacting the prophetic command to "let justice roll down like waters, and righteousness like an ever-flowing stream" (Amos 5:24, NRSV) and the gospel vision of people in right or just relationship with God and one another set forth in the Great Commandment.

Justice education includes a necessary holistic orientation, which means attention is given to truth-telling and potential action on the following:

- A *relational component* centered on persons' receiving respectful, nonhumiliating, and nondiscriminatory attitudes and behaviors in public spaces in everyday life.
- A *physical component* focused on assuring accessible and affordable resources for bodily health, insisting on safe living spaces and security in public places, and demanding justice following life-threatening and life-taking violence.
- A *psychological component* that sheds light on biases against Black appearance, color, physique, body size, language, and cultural artifacts in media and public spaces that attack inner peace and positive self-view.
- An *economic and vocational component* emphasizing fairness in accessing and attaining economic, educational, and occupational resources and supports or employment needed to sustain life for self and others for whom one is responsible materially.

- A *spiritual component* centered on public spaces, networks, and activities appending in-church functions for forming religious knowledge, nurturing spiritual enrichment, and empowering life practices and justice-promoting competencies.[26]

In this resource, the contributors pay particular attention to these aspects of justice education in Nancy Lynne Westfield's focus on body politics, Sarah Farmer's attention to unequal and retributive treatment of Black people in the criminal justice system, and the impact of and way out of disparaging circumstances in inner cities, pejoratively referred to as "da hood," described in the chapter by Cynthia Stewart.

Central to the view of religious education as justice education is the understanding of the larger public sphere or societal ethos as enactors of governing rules, political decisions, opportunities to participate, access to resources, and treatment of people that affect the human spirit, well-being, and ability not simply to survive but thrive. The nature and quality of life experienced by Black people in this wider societal sphere matter! Thus, teaching and learning as central undertakings in religious education are not immune from public involvement. Religious education is not socially or politically neutral.

The Practice of Advocacy

From a social action perspective, advocacy is a skill that is used to correct an injustice or harmful circumstance affecting an individual or a group. From an ethical standpoint, advocacy is understood as those efforts occurring in the public sphere that are directed toward upholding people's sense of human dignity and worth, empowering experiences of their human rights, and enhancing their human

26 These dimensions are presented as multidimensional aspects of well-being in Anne E. Streaty Wimberly and Sarah Frances Farmer, *Raising Hope: 4 Paths to Courageous Living for Black Youth* (Nashville: Wesley's Foundery Books, 2017), 38–44.

wholeness or a way of being that is life giving, life affirming, and life sustaining. It may be directed toward government, public policy makers, educational institutions, businesses or corporations, or other agencies affecting people's health and well-being. It addresses an identified problem and promotes a cause or principle. It has a goal or intended outcome and strategies directed toward goal achievement. In religious education, advocacy is about consciousness-raising but proceeds to gaining knowledge and skills to pursue activities and decisions on action—called *ethical decision-making*—that address social, economic, educational, healthcare, and political issues that impede or obstruct people's rights and well-being.[27] In this current era of continuing attacks against the human dignity of Black people, struggle amid oppressive circumstances, and the threat and reality of death, we assert that the public role of religious education is carried through these understandings of advocacy.

The importance of advocacy is further heralded by those who identify a pivotal need to rely on the private sector, including efforts of faith communities to address gaps, prepare activists, and support existing justice-seeking networks.[28] Religious education is needed to provide race-specific services and educational information that the government has either refused to offer or has done so minimally while at the same time pressing to fill the gaps. Frankly, religious education has a pivotal role in advocating for justice, revealing knowledge about systems and structures that allow injustice, engaging people in critical reflection on the nature of policies and practices affecting daily life, determining practices that influence policy-making and promote justice, and teaching the practices of advocacy.

This understanding of Black religious education that addresses the human rights of Black people further builds on what may be called a *spirituality of advocacy*. It evolves from the view of God's Spirit in all that is done in religious education to comfort, strengthen, and guide people in ways they themselves may become a spirit-filled

27 Wimberly and Farmer, *Raising Hope*, 246.

28 Barber, "Whither Shall We Go?," 246, 254.

body or family of God who acts on their own and others' behalf to bring attention to injustice and press for the imperative of justice mirrored in the life and teaching of Jesus Christ. From a Christian perspective, advocacy formation as an integral aspect of public ministry is about educating and inspiring people to be partners with God and agents of Jesus on behalf of the oppressed, including in their own situation of oppression. It is about engendering in people the commitment and know-how to live out the Christian faith in faithful action. It is important to note, however, that we propose that religious education becomes an evocative trigger for people's advocacy only insofar as it functions as

- a nurturing agent that recognizes and assists people's grief and their learning ways to lament losses incurred by experiences thwarting their lives and well-being;
- a promoting agent that assists people's formation of a valued identity based on an understanding of themselves as valuable creations of God; and
- an empowering agent that prepares people to bring about or influence positive change.

The Religious Educator and a Teaching, Learning, Acting Community

The narrative emphasis in justice education requires religious educators' efforts of tending to their own and nurturing others' passion for making happen in the public sphere what is sorely needed as an expression of their faith. Nathaniel West's chapter in this resource on the role of the religious educator makes clear that movements for change do not happen without leaders. Leaders are required who seek out, see, feel, and want to change the tough stuff that is happening in the community and larger society. These leaders have what is called a *disruptive awareness.*[29] They may be pastors, church school or Bible study teachers, young people's group leaders, women's

29 See Wimberly and Farmer, *Raising Hope*, 86–87.

and men's organization heads, discipleship ministry guides, community outreach heads, and faculty in higher education and seminary who consider themselves called by God to participate in God's activity on behalf of justice. In addition, it must not be forgotten that parents and family members are not simply needed but are, in fact, on the front lines of being the caring presence, advocate, and justice educator, as noted by Nancy Lynne Westfield in her chapter focused on a womanist formation of religious education and public ministry. Educational guides may also be community activists who have taken the lead in advocacy and justice-seeking efforts. The chapter by Joseph Crockett presents as a case in point the rise and impact of the Black Lives Matter movement, which began outside the bounds of institutional religion and yet embraces a spiritual foundation as well as connects and collaborates with churches in fulfilling a mission of advocacy and activism.

The call is not for loner leaders. Rather, the requirement is for those who see themselves as partners with religious education participants and others in the tasks of discerning, learning, and becoming "boots on the ground" in the forward movement for advocacy and change. It is also understood that leaders of religious education focused on justice in the public sphere see the locus of activity not simply within but beyond the church building. The ministry of the Christian Church, in following the teachings of Jesus Christ, must necessarily respond to people wherever need arises. Also warranted is an underlying contextualized approach that draws on Afrocentric understandings of positive interdependent relationships that form the vision of justice and guide ethical attitudes and actions needed for transforming alternatives to marginalization and discrimination. Mary Young proposes, in fact, that a public ministry orientation in religious education requires communities of learning and communities of action.

The Necessity of Lament

There is an assertion that in a "justice-centered model of education, the curricular starting points are the wounds of a community, particularly those that people are passionate about."[30] Those of us who contributed to this volume and others with whom we have interacted are aware of something new in current circumstances that evokes deep grief and mourning. Today's situation is rife with forms of oppression threatening Black people in ways that appear to overtake the effectiveness of formerly used approaches such as boycotts and public protests. Immigration and globalization add a kind of complexity to the racist identity politics of this country that the Black Church has yet to address.[31] This situation is compounded by complex racial identity politics that attach new stigmatization to being Black informed by an increasingly multicultural society.[32] For example, Alexander describes the more pernicious assignment of the social meaning of "being Black" that for Black youth "often begins with the first police stop, interrogation, search, or arrest" and is felt in experiences of being "'pushed out' of schools through racially biased school discipline policies."[33] A wide range of concerns in education, healthcare, and political processes continue to threaten people's health and holistic well-being.

Public ministry-oriented religious education as justice education must not deny the woundedness and deep feelings that epitomize people's grief emanating from the impact of Black people's experiences in a hostile world. An intentional embrace of a public sensibility is a necessary religious educational priority that requires attention to lament that is the self's and community's expression of grief. Clearly, there is already evidence of lamentation in response to senseless death. We have heard it in the cry of young people, "I can't breathe!" and in the shout, "Black lives matter!" And, as noted

30 Conde-Frazier, "From Hospitality to Shalom," 205.

31 See Floyd-Thomas et al., "Christian Education in the Black Church Tradition," 173.

32 See Floyd-Thomas et al., "Christian Education in the Black Church Tradition," 173.

33 Michelle Alexander, *The New Jim Crow: Mass Incarceration in the Age of Colorblindness*, rev. ed. (New York: New Press, 2010), 199.

in the forthcoming chapter on lament by Anne Wimberly, it has surfaced in silent prayers accompanied by marching feet, and by shrill cries to God: "Why?"

The realities of very present oppressive circumstances, racially motivated incidents, and death are evocative triggers of deep feelings, anger, grief, and mourning. The need for lament must not be ignored even in the prevailing "mourning-avoidant" culture.[34] Regardless of the recognized resilience of Black people, individual and collective trauma cannot be assuaged by the words "Somehow, you've got to keep on keeping on" or "It's not helpful to linger on what's happened." In fact, Aubrey Sampson's audacious claim is that "grief won't be contained. Grief won't stay hidden. Grief explodes."[35] From her perspective there is a louder song to be sung, a summons from God to accept the invitation to "create a pathway from pain to possibility."[36] But the question is, What responses may be given? Clearly, an essential role of religious education is one of hearing people's stories and tending to their loss and grief over difficult experiences in the larger societal sphere based on an awareness that "there can be gratitude that someone is asking about their narratives."[37]

Amid the disclosures of pain, however, what must emerge is a means of what Black people call "keeping on keeping on." The role of religious education is not simply to be the holding and listening space for persons who are devastated, hopeless, experiencing a sense of homelessness, and seeing God as failing them. It must

---

34 Reference to the prevailing mourning-avoidant culture appears in Alan D. Wolfelt, "Grieving vs. Mourning," accessed January 8, 2020, https://www.taps.org/articles/24-3/grieving-vs-mourning. The article is excerpted from his book, *Eight Critical Questions for Mourners: And the Answers That Will Help You Heal* (Fort Collins, CO: Companion Press, 2010).

35 Aubrey Sampson, *The Louder Song: Listening for Hope in the Midst of Lament* (Colorado Springs, CO: NavPress, 2019), 5.

36 Sampson, *The Louder Song,* 161.

37 Paul C. Rosenblatt and Beverly R. Wallace, *African American Grief,* Series in Death, Dying, and Bereavement (New York: Routledge, 2005), xx.

also provide an opening for people to discover where and how God may be found and what it means to continue in the walk of faith even through its ups and downs. As shown in the chapter on lament, inviting people into conversations with biblical passages from Lamentations and the psalms of lament is one means of creating this opening, while another is critique of and movement into the very acts of advocacy and activism as embodiments of the walk of faith and declaration of hope in God and joy that comes in the morning anyhow.

Challenges before Us

We do not profess that the task of infusing a public ministry orientation and advocacy in religious education is an easy one. Truthfully, even the contributors to this volume do not agree about how to address both public ministry and advocacy in church and religious education. Combining ministry and advocacy in varying degrees can conflict with critics who assert that a public role is inappropriate and that the responsibility rests more appropriately with contributions to people's individual spiritual lives.[38] Conversely, an envisioned public ministry direction is considered by others as a continuing part of the Black Church's historic dialectical orientation, which holds in dynamic tension its spiritual and secular roles or its religious piety and social consciousness emphasis.[39] Nonetheless, our appeal to religious education leaders is to make concrete a public ministry and advocacy emphasis. This is summed up in the words of Robert Franklin: "Now the burden rests on us."[40]

---

38 This view is explored in Anthony Pinn, *What Has the Black Church to Do with Public Life?* (New York: Palgrave Macmillan, 2013).

39 Lincoln and Mamiya describe dimensions of the Black Church's dialectical character in C. Eric Lincoln and Lawrence H. Mamiya, *The Black Church in the African American Experience* (Durham, NC: Duke University Press, 1991), 10–16.

40 Robert Franklin, *Crisis in the Village: Restoring Hope in African American Communities* (Minneapolis: Fortress Press, 2007), 239.

An Invitation to Read Further

The book is organized in eight chapters and begins with the chapter titled "Religious Education and Lament: Inviting Cries from the Heart, Guiding the Way Forward." Although Anne Wimberly, the author, recognizes that life is not without trials and tribulations, she asserts that intensifying situations of oppression of Black people in the present era call for attention to the human need to grieve and opportunities to lament. The assumption is that doing so prevents individuals and communities from becoming stuck in or creating "graveyards of woundedness" from which exit is limited or nonexistent, and it creates an opening for people to either envision their roles as agents of change or, in fact, inhabit forms of agentry in the process or as a form of grieving. While recognizing the mourning-avoidant culture in which we live, the chapter forthrightly describes societal incidents of injustice that evoke grief and lamentations, presents seven movements that describe people's experiences of grieving and lament, and sets forth specific ways in which religious education can provide both space and processes for engaging people in these movements.

In chapter 2, "Religious Educators Public Ministry Leaders," Nate West highlights participatory "crescive" leadership of religious educators designed to respond to the continuing demands for justice-seeking and social activism in consultation with a wide range of leaders within and beyond congregations. The chapter stresses the contrasting nature of this role to the oft-times loner orientation and top-down, linear-directed subject-matter transmission or information-giving approach. Attention is given to the religious educator as public theologian and how this function is activated on behalf of advocacy in public ministry utilizing Afrocentric and other race-oriented practices that emphasize partnering with community members to deal with community concerns. A concluding section presents a pedagogical approach called Prophetic Inquiry (PI), which encompasses strategic responsibilities of religious educators involved in political action and advocacy.

In chapter 3, "Religious Education and Communities of Learning and Practice: Inspiring Advocacy in Public Ministry," Mary Young turns to the role of religious education in forming and nurturing communities of learning and practice that respond to social and political realities affecting the lives of Black people. Beginning with a description of identified communities, she introduces the faith community as the primary context in which religious education occurs and its goal to teach the nature of speaking truth to power and to actually speak it in the public sphere. The chapter further claims the need for collaborative communities of learning and practice that connect the church with people and organizations in the public sphere. The central message is of politically empowering religious education that reaches beyond the church and invites disclosure and acknowledgment of sociopolitical circumstances requiring advocacy, engagement in critical reflection on them, and exploration of methods and guidance to act. The chapter presents examples of this form of education.

The Black Lives Matter movement is the central focus of Joseph Crockett's chapter 4, "Religious Education in Response to Black Lives Matter: A Case for Critical Pedagogy." The author proposes that religious education can be conceptualized in a variety of ways and approached from varying vantage points. After a review of several theories and approaches to education, and religious education in particular, a case is made for the use of critical pedagogy in teaching and learning for emancipator religious education. The argument is that words grounded in experience and animated by actions have the capacity–power–to reconstruct significations of "otherness" for framing and refreshing prophetic visions of teaching and learning. Five features of critical education–context, power, praxis, "otherness," and critical and religious literacy–are identified and discussed in support of the thesis. Crockett contends that Black Lives Matter and other nonviolent public protest movements point to a unique educational methodology warranting the support of religious educators in their endeavors.

In chapter 5, "Religious Education and Womanist Formation: Mothering and the Reinterpretation of Body Politics," Nancy Lynne Westfield cites the under-interrogated phenomenon of the role of African American Christian mothers who nurture the prophetic impulse in themselves, their children, and their churches. Black mothering, done by moms, aunties, big sisters, and neighbors, provides the epistemological lens through which liberation and justice are imagined and self-worth is known as sacred. This chapter looks at an exemplary mother, Nancy B. Westfield, who nurtured the prophetic impulse in her children and community. The author, daughter of Nancy, extrapolates from childhood experiences three key elements her mother employed to foster the prophetic impulse: (1) common sense, (2) truth-telling, and (3) authentic subversion as a routine way of living. Westfield suggests that an epistemology of resistance is not to create a counternarrative to the politics of inferiority and superiority—no counternarrative can shout louder than hate. Instead of a counternarrative, an epistemology of resistance maintains the metanarrative of *Ubuntu* as a guiding law of humanness, thus liberation and justice. The chapter seeks to unpack such questions as, What does it mean to nurture the prophetic impulse for the continuation of public ministry? What does it mean to foster public theologians in the communities of African American people? What can be learned from mothers who are exemplars as public theologians?

In chapter 6, "Religious Education and Prison Ministry: Where Public Theology and Public Pedagogy Meet," Sarah Farmer contends that mass incarceration not only affects the incarcerated individual but has drastic effects on the Black community. Religious education that centers on public ministry must remain in dialogue with issues of public concern. This chapter sits at the intersection of religious education approaches to criminal justice ministry and public theology. The question that drives the chapter is, In what ways does a pubic theological approach to religious education respond to the crisis of mass incarceration? Farmer argues that religious educators must reconceive criminal justice ministries as a continuum of experiences that people encounter before, during, and after incarceration. To this end, public ministry initiatives within religious education must encompass both prevention and intervention. The chapter draws on theological resources and the voices of ten formerly incarcerated women to explore meanings of nurture, prison education, prison programming, and ministry to children of incarcerated parents. It gives further attention to advocacy as a necessary action in criminal justice ministry that must take into account the various entry points along the incarceration continuum. Ultimately, the chapter calls for a vision of religious education that integrates principles of care, justice, and wholeness.

The role of women in public ministry-oriented religious education appears again in Richelle White's chapter 7, "Religious Education and the Public Role of the Sister's Keeper: A Historical Correlational Method." She brings into new focus the early-twentieth-century Christian educators and activists Nannie Helen Burroughs and Mary McLeod Bethune, who used the public sphere to bring quality Christian religious education to Black girls. Connecting with the pedagogical praxis of contemporary African American educators, the Historical Correlational Method proposed in the chapter offers innovative practices to publicly engage Black girls in responsible, affirming, enlightening, and transformative ways.

Finally, in chapter 8, "Religious Education for Making It Out of 'Da Hood': Spiritual Retreat Encounters for Youth and Young Adult Resilience and Spiritual Formation," Cynthia Stewart draws attention to effective means of responding to and nurturing youth who live in adverse environments pejoratively called "da hood." Specific attention is given to advocacy on behalf of youth who reside in the inner city of Chicago, where myriad life issues and difficulties exist. Here advocacy entails both the need and desire for opportunities to enhance life by promoting resilience, developing a sustaining spirituality, and envisioning a future vocation. The chapter explores how the Agape Scholars Program (ASP), a Catholic-sponsored nonprofit college readiness scholarship for low- to middle-income African American students, provided academic and spiritual development through annual retreats and teen masses. This program provided an opening to examine the role of spiritual development in forming resilience and spiritual anchoring in youth. Stewart describes a series of interventions that emphasize academic preparedness religious education endeavors held in conjunction with college readiness experiences. The chapter affirms the positive outcome of advocacy reflected in the youths' narrative disclosures of the impact of the program.

Annie Lockhart-Gilroy asserts in the epilogue that public spaces present their own curriculum by the problematic ways they represent Black bodies and Black lives. Drawing on the previous chapters in this book, she contends that religious education needs a countercurriculum to society's curriculum. Significant attention is given to younger generations, particularly millennials and Gen Z, and what can be gleaned from them about changing notions of advocacy-directed leadership and participation in justice efforts in public spaces as well as uses of the virtual world. At the same time, Lockhart-Gilroy suggests that envisioning the future of public ministry-centered religious education necessarily calls for a critique of activist leadership formation evolving in the virtual world.

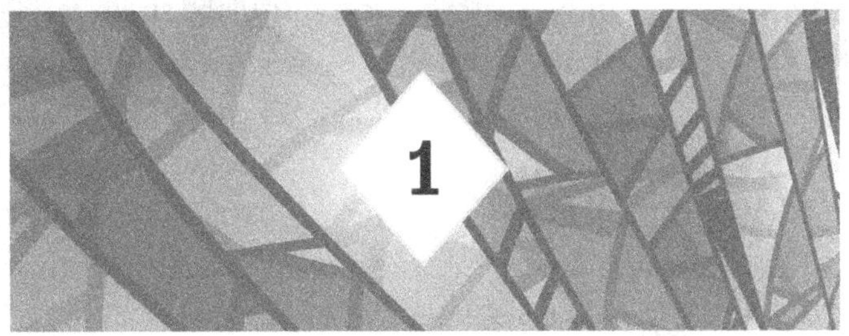

Religious Education and Lament

Inviting Cries from the Heart, Guiding the Way Forward

Anne E. Streaty Wimberly

> There must be room for rage and anger and despair. There must be room to ask about being forsaken and abandoned. There must be room to question if Black lives really matter to God.
>
> —Rev. Dr. Yolanda Pierce, "A Theology for a Grieving People"

A Time of Anguish and Urgency to Lament

Life is not without trials and tribulations. Dealing with this reality is not always easy and becomes even more difficult when it seems not to stop and is weighed down by deep jabs at the very essence of persons as valued creations of God and at the worth of their lives. This is the story of Black people whose history is replete with sit-ins, vigils, programs, strategies, and actions led by the Black Church, community residents, and civil rights organizations to confront egregious wrongs. But a new era is erupting with intensifying White supremacist ideology, steep rises in hate groups,[1] and racially motivated incidents,[2] bringing renewed anguish, silent vigils, loud protests, and forthright pleas to reverse encroachments on Black people's well-being and human flourishing. As a community, we grieve! In the depths of mourning, young people cry out, "I can't breathe!" and shout, "Black lives matter!" as expressions of pain and stimulus to move toward change and the untangling of threads of injustice and destructive conditions.

There is no promise that the movement forward will be without the need to confront the jab of racism and its consequences. Truthfully, for many children, youth, and adults, including those who engage in justice-seeking efforts, the journey ahead is met with deleterious consequences for health and well-being.[3] Grief, which is that

---

1 A 2018 Southern Poverty Law Center report showed 1,020 hate groups in 2018, a 30 percent increase in the United States from 2015, and a 7 percent increase in 2018 alone, sparked by changing demographics and the loss of absolute White hegemony. By 2044, the United States is expected to be majority minority; that is, the non-Hispanic Whites may no longer comprise more than 50 percent of the population. See *Projecting Majority-Minority: Non-Hispanic Whites May No Longer Comprise Over 50 Percent of the U.S. Population by 2044*, prepared by the United States Census Bureau in cooperation with the United States Department of Commerce, Economics and Statistics Administration (Washington, DC, March 3, 2015), www.census.gov/content/dam/Census/newsroom/releases/2015/cb15-tps16_graphic.pdf.

2 Hate crime incidents reported to the Federal Bureau of Investigation in 2017 showed an increase of 17 percent, including 7,175 hate crimes in 2017 compared to 6,121 in 2016, with race/ethnicity/ancestry as the most common bias incident category (59.6 percent), compared to religion (20.6 percent) and sexual orientation (15.8 percent). See Federal Bureau of Investigation, "2017 Hate Crime Statistics Released: Report Shows More Departments Reporting Hate Crime Statistics," November 13, 2018, www.fbi.gov/news/stories/2017-hate-crime-statistics-released-111318.

3 Kenneth V. Hardy, "Healing the Hidden Wounds of Racial Trauma," *Reclaiming Children and Youth* 22, no. 1 (Spring 2013): 24–28; Joanne M. Hall and Becky Fields, "'It's Killing Us!' Narratives of Black Adults about Microaggression Experiences and Related Health Stress," *Global*

experience taking place within ourselves and, empathically, with others in response to tough life happenings and loss, must be acknowledged as part of that journey. Spaces for lament must exist, which is about expressing the nature of our woundedness, questioning why, and seeking answers and responses from God. It may also be the case that permission needs to be given to weep and help given to form and express the language of lament. Religious education is an important locus and guide for these efforts, and for good reason.

The requirement of advocacy or action on behalf of justice and changes in society resulting in Black people's well-being and rightful participation in society depends on pathways of seeing and acting on possibilities to make it happen. An essential part of entering these pathways is stopping for a while and sitting with theodicy or experiences of suffering in ways that do not eventuate in meaningless suffering. There must be a coming to grips with woundedness, grief, and lament in ways that release and move us to declare *why* it is important to live, to engage in advocacy, and to demand change. Declaring the *why* that surely comes from tapping spiritual resources and from finding and relying on God's assistance become the crucial link to moving from despair to meaning and from meaning to action.[4]

Qualitative Nursing Research 2 (July 9, 2015): https://doi.org/10.1177/2333393615591569; Tara E. Galovski, Zoe D. Peterson, Marin C. Beagley, David R. Strasshofer, Philip Held, and Thomas D. Fletcher, "Exposure to Violence During Ferguson Protests: Mental Health Effects for Law Enforcement and Community Members," *Journal of Traumatic Stress* 29, no. 4 (August 2016): 283–92, https://doi.org/10.1002/jts.22105; Maria Trent, Danielle G. Dooley, Jacqueline Douge, "The Impact of Racism on Child and Adolescent Health," American Academy of Pediatrics Policy Statement, *Pediatrics* 144, no. 2 (August 2019): https://doi.org/10.1542/peds.2019-1765.

4 In her essay on suffering, Lucy Bregman cites the concentration camp experiences of Viktor Frankl and his arrival at the realization that "he who has a *why* to live for can bear with almost any *how*." Lucy Bregman, "Suffering," in *Dictionary of Pastoral Care and Counseling*, ed. Rodney J. Hunter (Nashville: Abingdon Press, 1990, 2005), 1231.

An important task of religious education as a practical theological endeavor is guiding persons from pain to possibility. This chapter responds to the question, What is needed to make this happen?

To begin, the church and religious education must pay attention to persons' woundedness, grieving, and the call for lamentation. Truthfully, we live in what is called a "mourning-avoidant culture."[5] Next, the following questions are addressed: Of what must we be aware? What difficult experiences and circumstances in the larger societal sphere evoke grief and the need to lament? This section highlights that an essential role of religious educators is being in touch with tough occurrences as well as inviting and hearing persons' stories that provide an opening for grief work and lamentation. We then move to differing manners in which Black people grieve and lament, with the understanding that religious education must offer spaces of presence where the woundedness of persons and ways in which they grieve and lament are seen and acknowledged. The chapter concludes with a way forward. As indicated in the introduction, I want to restate that the role of religious education is not simply to be the holding and listening space for persons who are devastated, hopeless, experiencing a sense of homelessness, and seeing God failing them. The nurturing practices of religious education must include openings for persons to discover where and how God may be found and what it means to continue in the walk of faith even amid life's ups and downs.

A Challenge in the Church

A problem exists that demands awareness. In the twenty-first-century church, apart from grieving and lamentation at funerals or

5 See Alan D. Wolfelt, "Grieving vs. Mourning," accessed January 8, 2020, https://www.taps.org/articles/24-3/grieving-vs-mourning. The article is excerpted from his book, *Eight Critical Questions for Mourners: And the Answers That Will Help You Heal* (Fort Collins, CO: Companion Press, 2010).

events addressing catastrophe, there is a tendency to override grief and lament with exuberant praise and worship along with the prophetic call for liberating action in response to oppressive realities.[6] The question may well be asked, Has the call for faithful living, a vital church, and action in the church and world denied the deep wounds and anxiety of the young and adults wrought by the toughness of their everyday lives and silenced their voices of pain and questions about God and faith and self? As religious educators, what might we consider about the sermons that are preached, the songs we sing, and the intentionally planned educational endeavors we offer?

Consider the Sermons

The urgency for actions directed toward change amid the mayhem of daily life is often felt in sermons such as one in which this critique was made: "I think that many of our brothers and sisters so bemoan our plight that they find it difficult to persevere and move on."[7] Yet, the manner of addressing this plight emphasizes the requirement to "cease your mourning! Stop your crying!"[8] Instead, the injunction is to focus on the menace of racism that is destroying Black people and come to a new social imagination that opens people to God's future.[9] Although action is absolutely necessary, it may indeed short-circuit the desired outcome by excluding grief and lament as an integral aspect in and even as part of a prerequisite to unfolding creative movements on behalf of justice.

6 Charles E. Booth cites the undue emphasis on worship and praise at the expense of being the historic conduits of encouragement and inspiration. However, his emphasis is not on praise and worship that exclude lament but rather on their hindrance to the challenging of congregants to liberative engagement. See Charles E. Booth, "The Loss of Our Liberation Quest and the Praise Craze," *The African American Pulpit* 4, no. 3 (Summer 2001): 18–20.

7 Charles E. Booth, "Stop Crying Over Spilled Milk!" Millennium issue, *The African American Pulpit* (Spring 2000): 143–49, esp. 147–48.

8 Booth, "Stop Crying Over Spilled Milk!," 149.

9 Booth, 149.

Of 114 sermons in eight volumes of sermons of Black preachers, only three sermons acknowledge the validity and need of mourning and lament.[10] In the sermon "Bringing Our Young People Back to Life," Ronald Stover affirms that there is nothing shameful about experiencing numbness and nothing wrong in raising the *why* question about difficulties and heartbreaking tragedies along life's journey. Building on the biblical text of 1 Kings 17:10-24, he emphasizes that being real about this aspect of people's storied lives is necessary in order to "do constructive things with the pieces left over after the tragedies."[11] The preacher does not say, but it is important to add that we are relational selves; thus, constructive acts are not simply about acting on behalf of self but being with and showing others that they too may be agents of justice construction. In her sermon "How to Handle the Silence of God," Jessica Kendall Ingram invites people's connection to Jesus's question on the cross, "My God, my God, why have you forsaken me?" found in Mark 27:46. She guides people through the spiritual deserts when God does not answer to an exploration of how God's speaking in silence invites people to sojourn *in the meantime* and seek God in new ways.[12] In the sermon "In This Moment, At This Dawn," Frederick Sampson II draws on

---

10 Randomly selected volumes include Walter B. Hoard, ed., *Outstanding Black Sermons*, vol. 2 (Valley Forge, PA: Judson, 1979); Ella Pearson Mitchell, ed., *Those Preaching Women: African American Preachers Tackle Tough Questions*, vol. 3 (Valley Forge, PA: Judson, 1996); Kirk Byron Jones and Martha Simmons, eds., *The African American Pulpit* 2, no. 4 (Fall 1999); Kirk Byron Jones and Martha Simmons, compilers and eds., *The African American Pulpit* 3, no. 1 (Winter 1999-2000); Kirk Byron Jones and Martha Simmons, eds., *The African American Pulpit* 3, no. 2 (Spring 2000); Martha Simmons, ed., *The African American Pulpit* 3, no. 3 (Summer 2000); Martha Simmons and Frank Thomas, eds., *The African American Pulpit* 4, no. 2 (Summer 2001); and Martha Simmons and Frank A. Thomas, eds., *The African American Pulpit* 6, no. 2 (Spring 2003).

11 Ronald A. Stover, "Bringing Our Young People Back to Life," *The African American Pulpit* 3, no. 1 (Winter 1999-2000): 45-46.

12 Jessica Kendall Ingram, "How to Handle the Silence of God," *The African American Pulpit* 6, no. 2 (Spring 2003): 47-50, esp. 49-50.

Jeremiah 24:6-7 to stress the point not to fear the pain and that in their suffering, people may well find themselves in company with the weeping prophet and the cries of the centuries on the way to a place of order out of disorder.[13]

Realities in the Music We Sing

Although the topics of healing and loneliness appear in the topical index of the *African American Heritage Hymnal*, published in 2001, there is no reference to lament in the index. Of 581 songs in the hymnal, only 35 appear in the two categories, with a fraction of this number reflecting complaint.[14] It is interesting to note that these findings differ from the earlier 1986 hymnbook, *Songs of Zion*, in which nearly 20 percent (15 of the 286 songs) speak to life's hardship, complaint, and appeal to God.[15] In our tech-savvy society, suffering is often a stranger, and the absence of the ability and intent to show genuine empathy causes a new need to sing the historical lament, "I was a way down yonder all by myself and I couldn't hear nobody pray!" In the current machinated ethos, we are, in fact, hard-pressed to hear and sing songs like those in previous times that narrate humiliation, suffering, and longing for a just world: "Nobody Knows the Trouble I See,"[16] "Sometimes I Feel Like a Motherless Child" or "Moanin' Dove,"[17] "I've Been Doing Some Hard Travelin',"[18] "Down on me Lord . . . Seem like everybody in this

13 Frederick G. Sampson II, "In This Moment, at This Dawn," *The African American Pulpit* 4, no. 3 (Summer 2001): 70–74, esp. 70, 72–73.

14 *African American Heritage Hymnal* (Chicago: GIA Publications, Inc., 2001), 693.

15 *Songs of Zion* (Nashville: Abingdon Press, 1981).

16 See "Nobody Knows the Trouble I See," *Songs of Zion* (Nashville: Abingdon Press, 1981), #170–71.

17 See "Sometimes I Feel Like a Motherless Child," *Songs of Zion*, #83; "Sometimes I Feel Like a Moanin' Dove," in *Songs of Zion*, #155.

18 See "Hard Travelin'," in *Sing for Freedom: The Story of the Civil Rights Movement Through Its Songs*, compilers and eds. Guy Carawan and Candie Carawan (Montgomery, AL: New South Books, 2007), 93.

whole wide world is down on me,"[19] "I've Been 'Buked and I've Been Scorned,"[20] "I Been in the Storm So Long,"[21] "I must tell Jesus all of my trials, I cannot bear these burdens alone."[22]

David Manner asks, "Have we been conditioned to believe that it is more spiritual to avoid expressing grief or despair in worship? Has our public questioning of God been considered irreverent or maybe even blasphemous? Have we conveyed that church must always be a happy place and that a positive appearance is less threatening? Has this attitude influenced our song selections and sermon topics?"[23] Nicholas Cooper-Lewter goes further by citing the historical Black Church's movement from a place of sharing to one of failing common grief.[24]

A Question about Religious Education

Similar questions may be asked about what we do in religious education. Over time, in intentionally planned religious educational experiences in church school, youth groups, and other study groups, for example, emphasis has been on nurturing children, youth, and adults in a spiritually vital faith that affirms the God-created humanness and somebodyness of Black people. People have received guidance in discerning God's liberating activity as well as the nature of their

19 See "Down on Me," in Carawan and Carawan, *Sing for Freedom*, 201.

20 See "I've Been 'Buked," in *Songs of Zion*, #143; and in *African American Heritage Hymnal*, #386.

21 See "I Been in the Storm So Long," in Carawan and Carawan, *Sing for Freedom*, 202.

22 See "I Must Tell Jesus," in *African American Heritage Hymnal*, #375.

23 David W. Manner, "Must Worship Always Be So Happy? The Language of Lament–Part 1," *Worship Evaluation* (blog), March 1, 2010, www.kncsb.org/blogs/dmanner/must-worship-always-be-so-happy-the-language-of-lament.

24 See Nicholas C. Cooper-Lewter, *Black Grief and Soul Therapy* (Los Angeles: Harriet Tubman Press, 1999), 7–8.

service in community after the pattern of Jesus Christ.[25] The truth is that models focused on this agenda often do not show intentional concern for grieving and lament. However, in recent years, the narrative orientation to religious education that engages Black people's everyday stories, particularly in formal religious educational contexts within churches, provides greater openness to mourning and lamentation.[26] But more is needed to forthrightly identify the need for, nature of, approaches to, and expected outcomes of engaging processes of grief and lament. The point is that lament is needed "not only to give spiritual expression to faith wrestling with pain, but also to re-energize communities of believers to name injustice, recognize political agency, envision possibility beyond or even amidst pain, grasp God's for-usness in the process, and sustain prophetic action."[27] What are the cries to which attention must be given?

An Outpouring of Cries That Evoke Grief and Lamentation

A seminal question in religious education in this current era of trials and tribulations is, Does anybody really see us and hear us? Greg Ellison makes plain: "Far too often, 'in the traffic of our daily round'

25 See Lora-Ellen McKinney, *Christian Education in the African American Church: A Guide for Teaching Truth* (Valley Forge, PA: Judson, 2003); Kenneth Hill, *Religious Education in the African American Tradition: A Comprehensive Introduction* (St. Louis: Chalice Press, 2007); Floyd-Thomas et al., "Christian Education in the Black Church Tradition," 151–78.

26 See Evelyn Parker, *Trouble Don't Last Always: Emancipatory Hope Among African American Adolescents* (Cleveland, OH: Pilgrim Press, 2003); Anne E. Streaty Wimberly, *Soul Stories: African American Christian Education*, rev. ed. (Nashville: Abingdon Press, 2005); N. Lynne Westfield, *A Womanist Practice of Hospitality* (Cleveland, OH: Pilgrim Press, 2007); and Yolanda Y. Smith, *Reclaiming the Spirituals: New Possibilities for African American Christian Education* (Eugene, OR: Wipf & Stock, 2010).

27 Andrew Williams, "Biblical Lament and Political Protest," Jubilee Centre, Biblical Thinking for Public Life, March 2014, www.jubilee-centre.org/biblical-lament-political-protest-andrew-williams/.

we render others invisible. We step over homeless persons, as if they are of no account. We talk on cellphones in checkout lines, giving little notice to the grocer bagging our food. We even discount hypervisible politicians, pastors and professional athletes by creating public personas that give them little room to express the fullness of their personalities."[28] But it is not simply the question of seeing. It is also one of hearing stories like mine.

Over the span of one month, I was jolted by four incidents. One was the shattering news that the Department of Justice refused to bring charges against the New York Police Department officer whose illegal chokehold resulted in the death of a Black male, Eric Garner, in 2014.[29] A second episode occurred as I turned on the evening news at the very moment of the broadcast of White police on horseback parading a Black male, Donald Neely, on foot through the streets of Galveston, Texas, with a rope tied to his handcuffs.[30] The third shock was hearing the words of a friend who approached me with an anguished look and quietly said, "My

---

28 Gregory C. Ellison, "When Pupils See," in *Let Your Light Shine: Mobilizing for Justice with Children and Youth*, ed. Reginald Blount and Virginia A. Les (Chester Heights, PA: Friendship Press, 2019), 105.

29 The report of the decision of the Department of Justice was broadcast widely, including in an article by Kevin Johnson and William Cummings, "'Today We Can't Breathe': DOJ Will Not Bring Civil Rights Charges against NYPD Officer in Death of Eric Garner," *USA Today*, July 16, 2019, www.usatoday.com/story/news/politics/2019/07/16/justice-department-not-bring-charges-death-eric-garner/1741169001/.

30 The incident, resulting in an apology by the Galveston Police Department, was also reported in numerous web articles, including one that connected this event to White patrols during the era of Black enslavement: P. R. Lockhart, "'This Is 2019 and Not 1819': Mounted Police Leading a Black Man by a Rope Sparks Outrage," *Vox*, August 19, 2019, www.vox.com/identities/2019/8/6/20757026/galveston-police-donald-neely-arrest-horses-texas-investigation. References to the White patrols during the era of Black enslavement as a predecessor of current-day policing appears in Victor E. Kappeler, "A Brief History of Slavery and the Origin of American Policing," Eastern Kentucky University (EKU) Police

nephew was murdered last night." A short period later, I received a plea for prayer from a mother whose son had died from gunshot wounds. These difficult happenings brought forth a cascade of unfathomable feelings and memories of seeming unrelenting heart-wrenching occurrences in the lives of Black people across the country. It is difficult to describe the full range of emotions that erupted inside me. But what screamed loudly in my heart and then from my mouth were the words of the psalmist that I have applied to our collective body of Black people: "How long, O LORD? How long? Will you forget [us] forever? How long will you hide your face from [us]?" (Ps. 13:1, NRSV).

From the situations I just described plus other personal experiences of pain, I confess to a deep anguish and impatience. I grieve! I also know that this personal experience is not unique to me alone. It is a collective happening. It is duplicated in the lives of Black individuals, families, and communities regardless of location, socioeconomic level, age or stage, gender, religious affiliation, or political orientation. I've heard the complaint on the one hand: "Life isn't easy. It isn't even fair!" From others, there comes the poignant theological view that "weeping may endure for a night, but joy comes with the morning (Ps. 30:5), or the old gospel song says, "This joy I have, the world didn't give it and the world can't take it away." They are common sentiments shared by Black people in conversations about tough realities of life that create, as it were, heavy weights on human shoulders that make of us a bowed-down, grieving people. In truth, these expressions of the heart, when probed, are the self's lament pointing to even deeper thoughts emerging from grieving persistent wounding and traumatic effects of discrimination, societal racism, and violence within and beyond the Black community.

Studies Online, January 7, 2014, https://plsonline.eku.edu/insidelook/brief-history-slavery-and-origins-american-policing.

A People's Reality Revealed

Reports and studies are replete with traumatic incidents including repeated brutality and loss of life of Black men, women, and young people at the hands of police;[31] mass incarceration,[32] racism in public schools, and the cradle-to-prison pipeline targeting children and youth, including those with disabling conditions and those who identify as LGBTQ;[33] the June 17, 2015, massacre of people in Bible study and prayer at Emanuel African Methodist Episcopal

---

31 Although much of the attention on police brutality and killing focuses on Black men, Black women also have a very real though often unnoticed history of violence perpetrated against them by law enforcement, including violence ending in death. Jacobs makes the point with numerous examples that "Black women are murdered by the police. They are assaulted by the police; and finally, they are tried, convicted and incarcerated for defending themselves against nonpolice violence." See Michelle S. Jacobs, "The Violent State: Black Women's Invisible Struggle Against Police Violence," *William and Mary Journal of Race, Gender, and Social Justice* 24, no. 1 (2017): 39–100, https://scholarship.law.wm.edu/wmjowl/vol24/iss1/4. Also see Beth E. Richie, *Arrested Justice: Black Women, Violence, and America's Prison Nation* (New York: New York University Press, 2012).

32 Alexander, *The New Jim Crow*; Wendy Sawyer and Peter Wagner, "Mass Incarceration: The Whole Pie 2019," Prison Policy Initiative, March 2019, www.prisonpolicy.org/reports/pie2019.htm.

33 Marian Wright Edelman, "The Cradle to Prison Pipeline Campaign: America's New Apartheid," Children's Defense Fund, February 6, 2009, www.chidrensdefense.org/child-watch-columns/health/2009/the-cradle-to-prison-pipeline-americas-new-apartheid/; National Education Association, "Discipline and the School-To-Prison Pipeline (2016) Action: Adopted," 2019 NEA Annual Meeting, accessed on January 10, 2020, https://ra.nea.org/business-item/2016-pol-e01-2/; Nicki Lisa Cole, "Understanding the School-to-Prison Pipeline," *ThoughtCo.*, modified May 30, 2019, www.thoughtco.com/school-to-prison-pipeline-4136170?; and Nadra Kareem Nittle, "How Racism Affects Minority Students in Public Schools," *ThoughtCo.*, modified August 8, 2019, www.thoughtco.com/how-racism-affects-public-school-minorities-4025361?.

Church in Charleston, South Carolina, and other attacks on Black places of worship;[34] disparities in health,[35] education,[36] employment, and wages;[37] and multiple types of micro-aggressions experienced as dehumanizing indignities from racial profiling on the highways, surveillance in places of business, and assumptions of

---

34 Emma Green, "Black Churches Are Burning Again in America," *The Atlantic,* June 25, 2015, https://theatlantic.com/national/archive/2015/06/arson-churches-north-carolina-georgia/396881; Elias Rodrigues, "Black Church Burning: Arson and the Long War on Black Progress," *n+1 Magazine*, February 2, 2017, https://nplusonemag.com/online-only/online-only/Black-church-burning.

35 "CDC Health Disparities and Inequalities Report–United States, 2013," *Centers for Disease Control and Prevention, Morbidity and Mortality Report* (MMWR), Supplement, 62(3), November 22, 2013:1–187; *2018 National Healthcare Quality and Disparities Report*, prepared by the Agency for Healthcare Research and Quality (AHRQ) (Rockville, MD, September 2019), www.ahrq.gov/research/findings/nhqrdr/nhqdr18/index.html; and Imari Z. Smith, Keisha L. Bentley-Edwards, Salimah E. Amin, and William Darity Jr., *Fighting at Birth: Eradicating the Black-White Infant Mortality Gap Report* (Durham, NC: Duke University Samuel DuBois Cook Center on Social Equity, Insight Center on Community Economic Development, March 28, 2018).

36 Liz Sablich, "7 Findings That Illustrate Racial Disparities in Education," Brown Center Chalkboard, Brookings Institution, June 6, 2016, www.brookings.edu/blog/brown-center-chalkboard/2016/06/06/7-findings-that-illustrate-racial-disparities-in-education/; Jonathan Rabinowitz, "Local Education Inequities across U.S. Revealed in New Stanford Data Set," *Stanford News*, April 29, 2016, https://news.stanford.edu/2016/04/29/local-education-inequities-across-u-s-revealed-new-stanford-data-set/.

37 Valerie Wilson and William M. Rodgers III, "Black-White Wage Gaps Expand with Rising Wage Inequality," Economic Policy Institute Report, September 20, 2016, www.epi.org/publication/black-white-wage-gaps-expand-with-rising-wage-inequality/; and Tomaz Cajner, Tyler Radler, David Ratner, and Ivan Vidangos, "Racial Gaps in Labor Market Outcomes in the Last Four Decades and Over the Business Cycle," Finance and Economics Discussion Series, 2017-071 (Washington, DC: Board of Governors of the Federal Reserve System), https://doi.org/10.17016/FEDS.2017.071.

criminality, to racial epithets voiced or written in public places.[38] Multiple levels of inequalities and racially motivated injustices are accompanied by trauma, stress, and health issues connected with loss of jobs, poverty, and difficult living conditions. These realities are juxtaposed with health crises and illness followed by the death of loved ones, natural disasters, transportation accidents, and incidents involving leaving or being left as in divorce or suicide. It is not surprising that the ongoing onslaught of trauma in the lives of individuals and the Black community as a whole prompted Carleen Brice to say, "With so many losses, it's difficult to resolve our collective grief."[39]

Scars from the Past

Pain that calls forth grieving and lament is further deepened by lingering scars from the legacy of Black people's enslavement through the civil rights movement.[40] Grief and lamentation emerge from "an ecology of memories" that connect past travesties of justice and

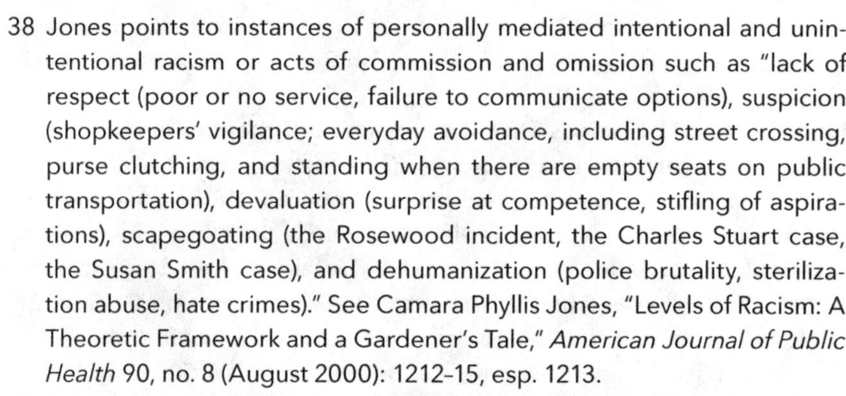

38 Jones points to instances of personally mediated intentional and unintentional racism or acts of commission and omission such as "lack of respect (poor or no service, failure to communicate options), suspicion (shopkeepers' vigilance; everyday avoidance, including street crossing, purse clutching, and standing when there are empty seats on public transportation), devaluation (surprise at competence, stifling of aspirations), scapegoating (the Rosewood incident, the Charles Stuart case, the Susan Smith case), and dehumanization (police brutality, sterilization abuse, hate crimes)." See Camara Phyllis Jones, "Levels of Racism: A Theoretic Framework and a Gardener's Tale," *American Journal of Public Health* 90, no. 8 (August 2000): 1212–15, esp. 1213.

39 Carleen Brice, *Lead Me Home: An African American's Guide through the Grief Journey* (New York: Avon Books, 1999), 4.

40 References to collective loss and grief connected to the legacy of the era of Black enslavement appear in Brice, *Lead Me Home*, 304; Allen E. Lipscomb and Wendy Ashley, "Black Male Grief through the Lens of Racialization and Oppression: Effective Instruction for Graduate Clinical Programs," *International Research in Higher Education* 3, no. 2 (2018): 51–60, esp. 53, https://doi.org/10.5430/irhe.v3n2p51.

continuing forms of unabating oppression.[41] This memory entered a conversation between friends following the murder of Black participants in Bible study at Emanuel Church in Charleston, South Carolina, in June 2015. A comment in the tearful exchange referenced enslaved forebears who were disdained as human beings by those claiming ownership of them, identified as "heathen," and relegated to the rear or balcony of places of worship as marks of their unfitness for equal seating. Yet, the long arm of scorn and hatred reached across history in Emanuel Church, a Black contextual ecclesial entity, where a White male was welcomed, sat as an equal in the study of scripture, and then killed the very souls who welcomed him. This tragedy happened in the childhood congregation of one of the conversation partners, who exclaimed: "I grew up in that church. I know people in that church. Oooh! I am hurting!"

Another case in point is the memory of the 1955 Mississippi Delta kidnapping, torture, and brutal murder of fourteen-year-old Emmett Till based on the later recanted testimony of a White woman who accused him of inappropriate advances.[42] The disposal of his maimed body in a watery grave and disregard for his remains refuels anger and grief when recalling the lifeless body of unarmed eighteen-year-old Michael Brown, left uncovered on the street after being killed by police in Ferguson, Missouri, in 2014.[43]

Historical memories also surfaced in the aftermath of Hurricane Katrina in 2005 from accounts that numbers of African Americans remained stranded without basic resources and were left out in evacuations that favored White Americans. This claim of racism was

---

41 Outcomes of interviews that point to an ecology of memory are reported in Paul C. Rosenblatt and Beverly R. Wallace, *African American Grief*, Series on Death, Dying, and Bereavement (New York: Routledge, 2005), xx.

42 The story of Emmett Till is recovered and examined in Dave Tell, *Remembering Emmett Till* (Chicago: University of Chicago Press, 2019).

43 A response to the treatment of Michael Brown appears in: Rev. Dr. Yolanda Pierce, "A Theology for a Grieving People," *Sojourners*, August 10, 2015, 1, https://sojo.net/articles/how-Blacklivesmatter-changed-my-theology/theology-grieving-people.

likened to the occurrence during the 1927 Mississippi flood when "rich New Orleanians sought to relieve pressure on levees that protected the city by dynamiting levees and intentionally flooding other areas, including poor Black communities in St. Bernard Parish. During and after the flood, African Americans . . . were not only denied Red Cross supplies and forced to live in deplorable conditions at displacement camps but also were compelled at gunpoint to repair the compromised levees."[44] Added connections between the past and the present, also called "genetic memory," are cited by Jacobs, who likens the wanton violent inhumane treatment of Black women during the era of enslavement with the maltreatment, violence, and death of Black women today by law enforcement and the judicial system.[45]

Movements of Grief and Lamentation

As we contemplate attention to grieving and lament in religious education, it is well to remember that grieving is a human reaction. It is universal. It is defined as a process or movement from the point where it began to a place of readiness to reframe, reorganize, or become proactive agents on behalf of a positive direction in life.[46] However, for Black people, grieving takes on a complex nuanced quality as the result of the particular multilayered realities of Black life. It bears repeating that an essential step in and beyond the process of grieving is telling the grief-producing story or sharing thoughts and feelings the story evokes. This is lament that may also include considering a way forward meant to right existing wrongs or,

---

44 Reference to the comparison appears in Laurie T. O'Brien and Jessica C. Nelson, "Perceptions of Racism in Hurricane Katrina: A Liberation Psychology Analysis," *Analysis of Social Issues and Public Policy* 6, no. 1 (2006): 213–35.

45 See Jacobs, "The Violent State," 97.

46 Robert A. Neimeyer and Joanne Cacciatore, "Toward a Developmental Theory of Grief," in *Techniques of Grief Therapy: Assessment and Intervention*, ed. Robert A. Neimeyer (New York: Routledge, 2016), 3.

in essence, pressing for "justice [to] roll down like waters, and righteousness like an ever-flowing stream" (Amos 5:24, NRSV). As such, for Black people, lament is *narrative release* that may encompass a theological and political struggle to make sense of the future. Ugandan theologian Emmanuel Katongole describes it as "a complex set of sentiments and responses, ways of crying out, seeing, standing, hoping, and groping for restoration in the midst of ruins."[47]

In an important sense, lament does not neatly happen apart from the grieving process. Grieving and lament are interactive movements. Here, the use of the term *movements* of grief and lamentations is intentional. The interactive involvement of grieving and lament are not, therefore, understood as stages. They are dynamic behaviors. Informal conversations, observations, reports, and analyses provide a window into seven movements in which grieving and lament interact. They are included here as important informative realities of people's lives that deserve attention in religious education.

Silence: In the throes of multiple levels of trauma, grieving is noted in three kinds of silence. One is numbing silence. This movement of grieving is a feeling that takes the breath and speech away. The earlier-mentioned friend whose nephew was murdered told of receiving the news by phone. He said that upon hearing it, the phone fell to the floor. No words would come. For a time, it was impossible to move. Even at the point of sharing the news, he told of a remaining feeling of numbness. Another individual, a Black man who had noted White people's micro-aggressive stance of clutching their belongings around him, experienced this numbing silence during a painful incident. He lamented by retelling a time when, at seventeen years old, he "was chasing a ball on the street, and a White toddler yelled 'nigger, nigger!' A baby stopped me in my tracks! . . . Literally I mean. . . . I froze . . ."[48]

---

47 Emmanuel Katongole, *Born from Lament: The Theology and Politics of Hope in Africa* (Grand Rapids, MI: Eerdmans, 2017), 94.

48 The story is told in Joanne M. Hall and Becky Fields, "'It's Killing Us!' Narratives of Black Adults about Microaggression Experiences and Related

A second form of speechless grieving is called "silence in motion," in which persons sit restlessly or rock, pace the floor, wring their hands, or connect with others in a silent vigil as ways of struggling to take in and wrestle with the shock or senselessness of a personal experience or that of someone they either know or identify with because of their Blackness. A particular historical example of silence in motion that has been repeated in various forms is that of the Negro Silent Protest Parade on July 28, 1917. In that instance, 10,000 Black people walked in silence down Fifth Avenue in New York City to confront the racial atrocity of lynching, Jim Crow segregation, discrimination, disenfranchisement, and a host of other evils foisted on Black people. According to one description, "children led the parade, followed by women dressed in white and men in suits, bringing up the rear . . . [and] walked to the sound of muffled drums."[49] This example of silent grieving may be said to be a form of speech—a covert communication or lamenting by "telling" a story of trauma on foot while at the same time advocating or drawing attention to it by way of silent protest.

A third form of silence is appropriately called "coerced silence," which is silence imposed on people by systems of oppression that literally take away the voice of the oppressed. It is further rightly understood as a silent lamentation reflecting people's forced voicelessness. An example of this kind of silent lamentation is that of Black women who are left without words by repeatedly being ignored and unheard following experiences of brutality and unjust

---

Health Stress," *Global Qualitative Nursing Research* 2 (January-December 2015): 18, https://doi:10.1177/2333393615591569.

49 W. E. B. Du Bois, an NAACP founder, was one of the protesters, as well as James Weldon Johnson, NAACP field secretary and writer of the Negro National Anthem, "Lift Every Voice and Sing." This report of the event appears in DeNeen L. Brown, "Google Memorializes the Silent Parade When 10,000 Black People Protested Lynchings," *The Washington Post*, July 28, 2017, www.washingtonpost.com/news/retropolis/wp/2017/07/28/google-memorializes-the-silent-parade-when-10000-Black-people-protested-lynchings/.

treatment by law enforcement,[50] and that of Black youth who dare not speak when they are racially profiled for fear of brutal attack or of being killed.

The holler: Wailing and hollering are emotive expressions of grief or lamentation. It is not a deliberate response but rather a spontaneous, involuntary giving way to overwhelming, irrepressible pain. Womanist theologian A. Elaine Crawford writes that in the Black community, the "holler is the primal cry of pain, abuse, violence, separation. It is a soul-piercing shrill . . . the renunciation of racialized and genderized violence perpetrated against them generation after generation."[51] As such, it is both the body's grief response to trauma and the voice's announcement of lament. From Crawford's perspective, "The Holler is also a cry to God to 'come see about me,' one of your children."[52] I confess to this expression of soul-deep uncontrollable lament at the loss of my husband's and my first child in the 1960s, having been left unattended in my own vomit on a stretcher in the hospital hallway because there was no room in the "colored wing" and being sent to the "White wing" was prohibited.

Fear: Many years ago, Howard Thurman described fear as "one of the persistent hounds of hell that dog the footsteps of the poor, the dispossessed, the disinherited."[53] Here, attention is given to fear as a deeply felt or emotional part of grieving evoked by recalling hellish events and situations and by the uncertainty of what is yet to come. It takes shape in the middle of people's sense of loss of control

---

50 Jacobs makes the point that situations of violence against Black women by law enforcement rarely make the news or that the coverage is scant or slanted. In fact, there is a sense in which it is ignored by society. See Jacobs, "The Violent State," 53, 97–98.

51 A. Elaine Crawford, *Hope in the Holler: A Womanist Theology* (Louisville, KY: Westminster John Knox, 2002), xii.

52 Crawford, *Hope in the Holler*, xii.

53 Howard Thurman, *Jesus and the Disinherited* (Nashville: Abingdon, 1949; Richmond, IN: Friends United Press, 1981), 36. Citations refer to the Friends United edition.

and un-safety amid oppressive and violent circumstances. Fear is concretized as a nagging, foreboding, perhaps terrifying, even paralyzing sense or threat of recurring violence. Inherent in fear is grieving not only feelings of helplessness or of being out of control but also the absence of peace so deeply needed. Fear becomes an expressed lamentation in the words I have heard from Black people, for example, that police cannot be counted on for protection. In one case, a young adult man told that upon seeing the flashing lights of a police car in the distance behind the car he is driving, his heart begins to pump harder and "goose bumps pop up," even though he knows he has done nothing wrong.

Rage: As a form of grieving, Bowen adroitly describes Black rage as a "visceral reaction to a severe victimization when all else seems hopeless."[54] When this inner reaction emerges in voiced anger or outward action, it becomes an intensely expressed lamentation. Two forms of rage-infused lamentations are presented here. The first is called "constructive rage." It is Black people's anger or "explosive lashing out" when Black people's backs are against the wall. As purposeful grieving, it contains a radical critique of injustice, calls out the necessity of change, and evokes the will to change reality. It sets forth a vivid picture of Black rage such that it functions both as a lament and a forceful corrective to injustice. Mychal Denzel Smith says that it "announces itself at the Women's Convention in Akron, Ohio, and says: 'Ain't I a woman?' Black rage stands before hundreds of thousands at the Lincoln Memorial and says, 'America has given the Negro people a bad check, a check which has come back marked insufficient funds.' Black rage says to the Democratic National Convention, 'I'm sick and tired of being sick and tired.'"[55] In another depiction of it, bell hooks told of a meeting with Thich Nhat Hanh and of feeling that she "was encountering some kind of racism

---

54 M. D. C. Bowen, "Black Rage: What Is It?, April 1999, www.mdcbowen.org/cz/parables/rage.htm.

55 Mychal Denzel Smith, "The Rebirth of Black Rage," *The Nation*, August 13, 2015, 7, www.thenation.com/article/the-rebirith-of-Black-rage/.

or sexism" on her way to the encounter. She said: "When I got to him, the first thing out of my mouth was, 'I am *so angry*!' And he, of course, Mr. Calm himself, Mr. Peace, said, 'Well, you know, hold on to your anger, and use it as compost for your garden.' And I thought, 'Yes, yes, I can do that!' "

The second kind of rage-infused lamentation may be referred to a "destructive rage." When words fail to create possibility for life opportunities and positive change or when assaults to dignity result in clearly racially motivated reprehensible, merciless acts of maiming or death from violence, the lament takes a more forceful or assertive manner through destructive, aggressive behavior. In their absence of voice, in being silenced and having no control over the affairs of life that affect them, Black people's grieving emerges as a sense of deep hurt and anger that does not allow them to sit still. For a substantial number of Black males, the resulting lament takes the form of self- or other-directed violent behavior as noted by Lipscomb and Ashley's description of Black male violence. It is a way of drawing attention to the story of their marginalization, societal oppression, and economic exploitation in American society.[56] This way of lamenting erupts, for example, in rioting inclusive of looting, destruction of property, and violence directed at those deemed to be oppressors or at those within the Black community.

This second form of lamentation also affects Black females. The story of teenaged Gakirah Barnes told by Rod McCullom is an example. Gakirah was a recognized "hitta," or killer, who became involved in "internet banging or cyberbanging." Her archived Twitter timeline, discovered after her violent death, revealed random thoughts and preoccupation with violent imagery that also included the picture of a friend who had been killed. She had been deeply hurt by this friend's death and apparently grieved deeply that loss as noted by her words, "My pain ain't never been told." What emerged was clear evidence of violence and grief as common themes. In fact,

---

56 Lipscomb and Ashley, "Black Male Grief through the Lens of Racialization and Oppression," 53.

according to McCullom, "She adopted Facebook and Twitter names that paid homage to slain friends, and she vowed vengeance on their killers."[57]

Questioning: Grieving resulting from experiences of dehumanization, oppression, and violence is often accompanied by lamentation in the form of questioning. In these instances, people interrogate the self: "What can I do? What could I have done?" Children may ask, "Is it my fault?" or simply ask, "Why?" Youth and adults may raise any number of questions: Why are these things continuing to happen to us as a people? When will things ever change? What do we have to do to avert wounding situations or demand change? Lamentation may also extend to interrogating God: "Why? How long?" Young people in ministries I lead often ask, "Why does God allow all of this bad stuff to happen to us?" Or to use the words of Mychal Denzel Smith, "How long are we supposed to remain calm when the laws we are called to respect exist in an open assault on our humanity?"[58] Katongole goes further by saying that questions to God are laments that challenge God's silence. They "proclaim boldly that not everything is all right. God has not delivered . . . has hidden."[59] The questions are pleas for an answer to whether God is uncaring and unmovable.

It may also be said that lamentation through questions to God frame a struggle that, on the one hand, risks loss of confidence or belief in God. On the other hand, it holds the possibility of grasping God, who gives human beings free will, which they misuse by hurting others. Through these acts, God laments and shows this

57 Rod McCullom, "A Murdered Teen, Two Million Tweets and an Experiment to Fight Gun Violence," *Nature*, September 4, 2018, www.nature.com/articles/d41586-018-06169-8.

58 This question was raised in response to the report of the "not guilty" verdict in the case of George Zimmerman, who used a "stand your ground" defense in the murder of seventeen-year-old Trayvon Martin in Florida on February 26, 2012. See Mychal Denzel Smith, "Trayvon Martin: From Lament to Rallying Cry," *The Nation*, July 15, 2013, 1.

59 Katongole, *Born from Lament*, 111.

lament through Jesus Christ, who, even though he lived God's perfect example of loving and caring relationships, was nailed to a cross and raised the question, "My God, why have you forsaken me?"

Repression: Grieving turned inward may be called "repressed grief." When repressed or bottled up inside, grief becomes felt as death while still alive, a kind of nagging or immovable hurt to selfhood.[60] On the other hand, this intense form of grieving can press people to the point of either gasping or stridently lamenting, "I can't breathe," as the marchers did in remembrance of these same words of Eric Garner in 2014 as he was dying from the illegal chokehold of a police officer in New York City. Grieving takes an even more forceful or assertive manner through aggressive behavior. For some, even an approach to God and the question of "How long?" is not tenable. In this situation, a person's statement becomes, "God isn't listening. Nobody's listening." For some, it is considered improper or even blasphemous to summon God's wakefulness with questions and appeals for answers. And since there seems to be no answer to the mayhem of life and no light appearing at the end of the tunnel, the thought turns to life's uselessness. The unresolvable grief that follows is cause for great concern. It is noted, for example, that "suicide deaths among Black females aged 13 to 19 rose 182% between 2001 and 2017, while the rate among Black teen males rose 60% during that same period."[61]

Faith-infused struggle: For some, the struggle to continue on in life amid harsh difficulties becomes possible through an unyielding

---

60 Harold W. Neighbors and David R. Williams highlight the effect of racism and discrimination on the ego identity of its victims. They make the point that "for some African Americans the normative cultural characterization of the superiority of Whiteness and the devaluation of Blackness, combined with the economic marginality of Blacks, can lead to self-perceptions of worthlessness and powerlessness." See Lipscomb and Ashley, "Black Male Grief Through the Lens of Racialization and Oppression."

61 Robert Preidt, "Suicide Rates Soaring among Black Teens," *US News*, June 26, 2019, www.usnews.com/news/health-news/articles/2019-06-26/suicide-rates-soaring-among-Black-teens.

faith perspective. Sorrow is diminished by belief in life-sustaining spiritual resources. The lament comes forth in the words of songs such as "I must tell Jesus all of my trials. . . . In my distress He kindly will help me."[62] Or it is shared in narrative form as in the story of my grandmother, who told of harrowing struggles throughout her life and new ones now and yet to come. But her lament came in the form of a commentary on life as a mountain railway that includes passing through verdant valleys, rounding treacherous curves, and going through blinding rains and storms. But she firmly said the only option is to stay on the train and, through the difficult parts of the journey, know who the engineer is–God. For others, lament.

Meaning-making: All of the aforementioned movements of grieving and lamentation are about making sense of profoundly hurtful, life-altering, and life-taking experiences of societal racism, oppression, and acts of injustice. Sense-making is also called *meaning-making*, which, as a concretely experienced movement, centers on next steps. It is movement toward a vision for justice in the middle of injustice. Mychal Denzel Smith tells a meaning-making story in which he followed the question of "How long?" by recounting the grievous injustices occurring both in the killing of Trayvon Martin and the "not guilty" verdict of the perpetrator, George Zimmerman. He recalls reports of how Zimmerman profiled and killed Trayvon because of the perception that the seventeen-year-old youth was "up to no good" and out of place in a gated community. Smith continued by telling of "crying rage-filled tears as 'ZIMMERMAN NOT GUILTY' appeared on television" and went on to cite Trayvon's lifeless body as being placed on trial "for having the audacity to exist and be Black."[63] But meaning-making proceeded to yet another step. A new question came forth: So, what's next?[64] It was followed with the answer: "What's next is that each of us takes whatever gift

---

62 "I Must Tell Jesus," *African American Heritage Hymnal* (Chicago: GIA Publications, 2001), #375.

63 Smith, "Trayvon Martin: From Lament to Rallying Cry," 2–3.

64 Smith, "Trayvon Martin: From Lament to Rallying Cry," 6.

we have and use it in a way that honors and values Black life. That is the legacy Trayvon Martin can leave to this world."[65]

The Call for a Revisionist Role of Religious Education

Building on the foregoing sections, I propose a pedagogical course of action. One that centers on movement from the travesties of injustice to answering the question "What next?" in responding to the prophetic command to "let justice roll down" (Amos 5:24) and God's summons to "bring good news to the oppressed, to bind up the brokenhearted, to proclaim liberty to the captives" (Isa. 61:1, NRSV). Here, I am saying that Christian religious education is about pointing persons through grief and lamentation, so that they can claim God's call to confront actions and change structures that hinder persons' wellness, rightful place, and equal participation in community, as well as equal access to opportunities to both survive and thrive. I strongly agree with Reginald Blount, who makes clear, in fact, that Christian religious education "is about helping persons embrace an ontological vocational understanding that their lives have meaning and purpose. It is helping persons embrace an understanding that they are called by God to serve as God's agent, steward, and partner in caring for and re-creating God's creation."[66] I propose here three pivotal phases of pedagogical action to be followed by religious educators to enable this outcome.

A pedagogical process of assessment: This action consists of looking, observing, critically reviewing, and calling for change in those ways in which worship, preaching, music, and attitudes toward grief and lament reflect the prevailing mourning-avoidant culture. Change means engaging in cross-generational dialogues and decision-making based on the question, Is it all right to weep?

---

65 Smith, 7.

66 Reginald Blount, "From Sabbath Schools to Freedom Schools: Christian Vocation and the Power of Voice," in Blount and Lee, eds., *Let Your Light Shine*, 79.

Inviting responses to this question is necessary when there is reluctance to affirm the need to tend to grief and lament borne of what Wright calls "an implicit pressure to stifle real feelings based on the view that one ought to have 'faith.'"[67] The foreword to Card's book *Sacred Sorrow* helpfully reminds the reader that "Jesus wept. Job wept. David wept. Jeremiah wept. They did it openly. Their weeping became a matter of public record. Their weeping, sanctioned by inclusion in our Holy Scriptures, [is] a continuing and reliable witness that weeping has an honored place in the life of faith."

A pedagogical process of awareness: In this era of increasing numbers of disengaged individuals from congregational life, this process necessarily takes religious education outside the cloistered church and classroom environment. Instead, it places religious educational activities in the community in order to recognize and respond, as Soon-Chan Rah says, to "the unfettered suffering . . . that leaves a community in disarray and in deep pain without any recourse."[68] It is to answer the question, What are the tough realities evoking grief and lamentation in the community that demand attention? This action means relating to the community "out there" that includes people who are connected and involved in church but whose lives take shape outside church while also seeking people who are disconnected from the church. As part of the Connecting with Hope Innovation Hub Young Adult Initiative at Interdenominational Theological Center (ITC),[69] being in the community has been activated by meetings organized by leaders in restaurants, homes, parks, movies, and on the web through Zoom meetings and other interactive means. The purpose is to learn what is going on in

---

67 Christopher J. H. Wright, *The God I Don't Understand: Reflections on Tough Questions of Faith* (Grand Rapids, MI: Zondervan, 2008), 52.

68 Soon-Chan Rah, *Prophetic Lament: A Call for Justice in Troubled Times* (Downers Grove, IL: Intervarsity Press, 2015), 115.

69 The Connecting with Hope Innovation Hub is a Black young adult ministry initiative involving twenty-three congregations led by a team of ministry leaders including a millennial. The initiative is supported by the Lilly Endowment.

persons' lives that raise personal and community concern, feelings, grief, and questions that open the way to exploring "What next?"

A pedagogical process of engaging grief, lament, and the question of what's next: Religious educational endeavors respond best to wounded people when they have knowledge of the grieving process. This includes understandings of the ways persons grieve and enter into lament that are presented in a foregoing section. An added essential step involves engaging participants in recalling their stories of hurt and injustice and sharing how they have typically dealt with these instances using the earlier-mentioned movements of grief and lament. They may be invited to use songs, including previously mentioned ones, to get in touch with their feelings and to give them words to express lament. I am reminded, too, that songs may become the center of reflection as in the case of an individual who raised the question with me about why the song "Amazing grace, how sweet the sound, that saved a wretch like me" is sung at rallies and vigils in response to violence perpetrated against Black people. The individual commented, "That's not what I feel! Justice has not been found. I and my faith in the systems of justice have not been found. I do not see justice!" When asked to name a more appropriate song, the answer simply was, "No song! Let silence speak!" The point here is that there must be readiness to engage the questions and struggles of persons in dealing with their grief, their critique of the content of lamentations, and their chosen expression of lament.

Importantly, pedagogical processes in Christian religious education rightly bring the resources of the faith to bear in its emphasis on grief and lament. It is necessary to explore answers to these questions: What does it mean to turn to God, and how may turning to God happen? Who and where is God in the toughness of life, and what does the silence of God mean? The religious educator becomes an important agent by drawing on biblical stories that point to God's participation in grieving and lamentation; the ones Stover, Ingram, and Sampson cited earlier may be used as reflection materials. Moreover, an important pedagogical task in religious education is to draw on biblical texts such as the first-person narrative in Lamentations 3, which moves from complaint to views of God's presence and activity in the ups and downs of the walk of faith. Additionally, the Psalms of Lament are means of guiding persons in forming a language of lament and discovering responses. Particular attention may be given to psalms that ask the *why* question (Psalms 10 and 22); psalms of yearning for help (Psalms 13 and 42); psalms that are prayers in distress (Psalms 28 and 55); and psalms that are prayers for deliverance (Psalms 56, 57, 69, 70, 140, and 142). Pedagogical approaches may include reading the psalms silently and aloud, or discovering the language forms by asking the following questions: What language is used to cry out, complain, or pray? What language is used to seek help? What responses appear? What is the meaning for you? The encounter is to move finally to reflections on the questions: What next? To what justice-making actions is God calling each individual and the group?[70]

For more than a decade of meeting with teens in a summer residential program, intentional sessions on grief elicited stories of negative and wounding encounters in schools, on the roads, and in public places. When asked if they told anyone about their experiences, they often responded that they had remained silent about it. These teens' need to grieve became magnified as deep emotions erupted through sharing stories. What also became clear was that the leaders' self-disclosures as part of the communal ritual of mourning and lament confirmed that they, too, needed opportunities to engage the process of grieving and lament. But what became powerfully evident in many cases was the sense of release as the result of engaged, guided processes. At the same time, however, it was noted that for some, the depth of grief required added occasions for

70 The questions are akin to ones raised by Katongole: How is it possible to turn to God amid the mayhem of existence? What does turning to God look like? How is it possible to express the unspeakable? What directions for justice-making action and seeds of promise planted by God can come from the crucible of lament? See Katongole, *Born to Lament*, 19.

dialogue with a caring other or recommendations for more intense and formal help.

It is important to state that in follow-up sessions, when the questions "How may you go on with life beyond your grief? To what is God calling you to be and do?" were posed, references to what may be called advocacy on behalf of justice emerged in a variety of ways. Young people spoke of being propelled toward vocations in law, teaching, social work, and medicine where they could make a direct difference. Others spoke of school clubs of which they were either already part or ones they intended to form with a central intent to address inequalities observed and experienced in community organizations, work opportunities, and healthcare. Still others mentioned church-related service endeavors to fill the gaps in assisting those experiencing homelessness, as well as organizing meetings with law enforcement regarding negative treatment and fostering improved community relations. These follow-up sessions made clear that when invited and guided, persons are able to see a way forward in ways that make concrete Christ's message of love, justice, and liberation in their own lives and in the lives of others.[71]

Still another aspect of engaging movements of grieving and lamentation has to do with what occurs in contexts beyond the church. An example is the Black Lives Matter movement. The question is, What can be learned from this organization's involvement with grief and lament? From its inception, for example, the movement began with grief and then, from that process, moved from outrage to resilience centered on optimism and action toward change. In an interview, Patrisse Cullors, one of the movement's founders, references this action toward change in terms of the formation of Black Lives Matters chapters and affiliated groups that tend to grief and trauma

71 This example reflects efforts carried out in a summer residential program by the Youth Hope-Builders Academy (YHBA), a Lilly Endowment–funded theological program for high school youth and outreach program of Interdenominational Theological Center in Atlanta beginning in 2002 and continuing through 2014.

to build health, wholeness, and meaning; combat burnout; and foster organizational efficiency and activism.[72]

Reflections

In her book *The Louder Song: Listening for Hope in the Midst of Lament,* Aubrey Sampson makes the audacious claim that "grief won't be contained. Grief won't stay hidden. Grief explodes."[73] From her perspective there is a louder song to be sung, a summons from God to accept the invitation to "create a pathway from pain to possibility."[74] Lament is that pathway. It is the soul's cry or an active way of being and becoming. Through it, people enter a journey of creating "a pathway between the Already and the Not Yet. . . . [It] anticipates new creation but *also* acknowledges the painful reality of now. Lament helps us hold on to God's goodness while battling evil's evil at the same time."[75] This is a helpful way to view the nature and process of Black people's grieving and lamentation in the throes of confronting multiple layers of challenges in everyday life. It is also a useful guiding view for the efforts of religious education on behalf of answering the question, What next? The following chapters present answers to this question from the perspective of religious education as an advocacy-promoting ministry in the public lives of Black people.

---

72 See Hebah H. Farrag, "The Role of Spirit in the #BlackLivesMatter Movement: A Conversation with Activist and Artist Patrisse Cullors," *Religion Dispatches,* June 24, 2015, http://religiondispatches.org/the-role-of=spirit=in-the=Blacklivesmatter-movement-a-conversation-with-activist-and-artist-patrisse-cullors/.

73 Aubrey Sampson, *The Louder Song: Listening for Hope in the Midst of Lament* (Colorado Springs, CO: NavPress, 2019), 5.

74 Sampson, *The Louder Song,* 161.

75 Sampson, 12–13.

Religious Educators as Public Ministry Leaders

Nathaniel D. West

> Our dreams and commitment to justice cannot depend on a single leader or be destroyed if one, a few, or many are lost to acts of hate and violence. . . . We must always refill and ensure there is a critical mass of leaders and activists committed to nonviolence and racial and economic justice who will keep seeding and building transforming movements.
>
> —Marian Wright Edelman, "Ask What You Can Do for Your Country"

Examining the Established Approach

Movements for change require leaders. This has been continually demonstrated in Black life to the degree that it is said that "leadership is a vital concept in the African American community and has shaped its history."[1] The veracity of this view is seen in the lives of

1 Lisa Respers France, "Emerging Leaders Energized in the Black Community," Black in America 2, CNN Report, July 20, 2009, www.cnn.com/2009/LIVING/06/02/bia.emerging.black.leaders/index.html.

exemplars such as Harriet Tubman, abolitionist and identified Moses of the Underground Railroad to Freedom during the era of slavery; Mary McLeod Bethune, early-twentieth-century educator and civil rights activist; and Martin Luther King Jr., pastor and mid-twentieth-century civil rights leader and public theologian. In actuality, across the history of Black people's sojourn in America, people have relied upon and followed nationally prominent Black leaders in order to confront egregious injustices and achieve urgent civil rights goals. Religious leaders in particular have been politically active and applied faith in confronting social issues. They have served essential roles as frontline activists and spokespersons on behalf of identified causes while at the same time functioning as "inspirational guides, spiritual resources, and ideological advisors to grassroots movements."[2]

It must not be forgotten that grassroots leaders and groups have also been important "boots on the ground" in mobilization efforts directed toward justice and the fulfillment of democratic ideals.[3] As in the civil rights era, third-millennium young people are important leaders in social activism and mass demonstrations from which the Black Lives Matter movement emerged. Yet unlike the earlier social political engagement of young people that tended to connect with or evolve from within the church, newer forms of organizing are occurring outside the Church with grassroots authority rather

---

2 Clayborne Carson, "African-American Leadership and Mass Mobilization," *The Black Scholar* 24 (Fall 1994): 1, https://web.stanford.edu/~ccarson/articles/Black_scholar.htm.

3 Carson reviews the history of mass mobilization by grassroots leaders and groups such as Rosa Parks, an officer of the local National Association for the Advancement of Colored People (NAACP); the Southern Christian Leadership Conference (SCLC); Congress on Racial Equality (CORE); Mississippi Freedom Democratic Party (MFDP); Lowndes County, Alabama Freedom Organization (LCFO); Malcolm X and other leaders in the Black Power Movement; and the Student Nonviolent Coordinating Committee (SNCC). See Carson, "African-American Leadership and Mass Mobilization," 1-7.

than ecclesial.[4] Moreover, one report on young Black activism indicates that some activists clearly say, to use the words of one of them, that "emulating Jesus is central to their work. 'Jesus was a freedom fighter. The cops came to arrest Jesus and dragged him off and executed him. I don't know how much more in tune with today's time we can get.'" Others say that neither the Church nor Christianity form the foundation for their youth-led activism.[5]

The evolving multiple sources, ages or stages, and contexts of leadership are pivotal in dispelling the notion that exceptional, nationally acclaimed Black leaders, senior pastors in congregations, and adults are the primary actors in improving Black life. In fact, Carson states that "the revival of African-American mass militancy is vital for future Black progress and for realizing democratic ideals."[6] This reality must be taken seriously by religious educators who are in the role of pastor, religious education director, church school teacher, youth and young adult ministry leader, discipleship guide, religious educator in seminary or higher education institutions, or community organizer who prepares leaders. Whether clergy, lay, or volunteer, the direction is toward a participatory orientation to religious educational leadership. This emphasis is not singularly top-down, linear subject-matter transmission or information-giving. Rather, it also functions from a bottom-up, story-sharing, inspiration-giving position in which leaders recognize they cannot be fully aware of the full range of needs and actions in the continuing demand for justice-seeking and social activism. This chapter is about exploring in more

4 Trends in Black young people's activism are described in Jon C. Rogowski and Cathy J. Cohen, "Black Millennials in America: Documenting the Experiences, Voices, and Political Future of Young Black Americans," Black Youth Project, October 27, 2015, 49–53. Emma Green, "Black Activism, Unchurched," *The Atlantic*, March 22, 2016, 1–18, www.theatlantic.com/politics/archive/2016/03/black-activism-baltimore-black-church/474822/; and Joshua L. Mitchell, *Black Millennials and the Church: Meet Me Where I Am* (Valley Forge, PA: Judson, 2018), 79–80.

5 Green, "Black Activism, Unchurched," 18.

6 Green, 6.

detail the nature of this challenge; the role of the religious educator as a public theologian; and essential views, practices, and primary strategies that are needed to activate this role.

A Very Present Challenge

The challenge in the journey ahead is for what may be called "crescive leadership,"[7] which counters a tendency toward a loner orientation and silo church stance.[8] It points to the Church's and religious educators' connecting with, learning from, and engaging with young activists who are not necessarily in the church.[9] It further recognizes that people in and outside the church are "waiting to be anointed . . . waiting for somebody to empower them."[10]

Activists, civil rights groups, nonprofit organizations, and others are attempting to address the concerns for participation. This was noted in the Black Leadership Forum, a civil rights and service group begun in 1977, which functions as

> an umbrella organization for national African American Civil Rights, Civic, and Professional organizations . . . to promote creative and coordinated Black leadership, diverse in

---

7 The crescive leadership orientation is applied here as an important communication strategy and is drawn from business management found in David R. Brodwin and L. J. Bourgeois III, "Five Steps to Strategic Action," *California Management Review* 26, no. 3 (Spring 1984): 176-90, https://doi.org/10.2307/41165088; and Travis L. Russ, "Communication Strategies for Implementing Organizational Change," EC Beez: Working Knowledge for the Business Minded, May 8, 2010, https://ecbeez.blogspot.com/2010/05/communication-strategies-for_08.html.

8 Robert Franklin, *Crisis in the Village: Restoring Hope in African American Communities* (Minneapolis: Fortress Press, 2007), 230–32.

9 Green, "Black Activism, Unchurched," 15.

10 This statement was made by Richard Lewis, leader of the Colorado Black Chamber of Commerce Foundation's Chamber Connect Program, and appears in France, "Emerging Leaders Energized in the Black Community."

> membership but clear on its priority to empower African Americans to improve their own lives and to expand their opportunities to fully participate in American social, economic, and political life.[11]

Another example exists in the Concerned Black Clergy (CBC) of Metropolitan Atlanta, an organization comprising mostly African American ministers and laity in Atlanta, begun in 1983 in response to the need to care for the families of numbers of missing and murdered Black children. Although commencing with this crisis, CBC has continued with a mission of learning critical community issues and needs and of listening to responses from members and from community and governmental entities, as well as providing "leadership, advocacy, and service to the homeless, helpless and hopeless in the community."[12]

The pivotal point is that churches are needed to affect the religious, social, economic, educational, and political concerns of the communities in which they exist, and church leaders, in particular, are generally expected to play a critical role. Crescive leadership means that strategic leaders are needed. The responsibility of the pastor as primary educational minister remains for engaging congregations in biblically informed ritual practices of the church in ways that contribute to "the fundamental transformation of persons

---

11 Franklin lists the initial participants, including "leaders of the National Urban League, National Urban Coalition, NAACP, Southern Christian Leadership Conference, Joint Center for Political and Economic Studies, National Council of Negro Women, NAACP Legal Defense and Educational Fund, Martin Luther King Center for Nonviolent Social Change, Congressional Black Caucus, National Conference of Black Mayors and the National Business League." Franklin, *Crisis in the Village*, 231.

12 "Our Vision," Concerned Black Clergy, accessed January 14, 2020, https://concernedBlackclergy.com/. The history and functions of the organization appears in Edward P. Wimberly, *The Gathering of the Village for Justice and Participatory Democracy: The Concerned Black Clergy of Atlanta* (Atlanta: ITC Press, 2017).

and institutions of society."[13] This is equally true for others who are in a place of responsibility in the Church's educational ministry. However, crescive leadership pushes the Church and religious educators to rethink, as a millennial church member did, what church and spirituality are. In this young person's words: "When I think about what the Bible calls us to do, it is very much in my mind tied to the work we do as activists and organizers. . . . The church space is not always in the four walls of Pleasant Hope Baptist Church."[14] For young people, there must be recognition that they may not come to or have interest in the church, but the church and its leaders must be interested in them. As Green so adroitly remarks, "That's how young, unchurched activists may inadvertently end up leading not only political change, but also change within the Church itself."[15]

Awareness means taking seriously that churches are living organisms that have the propensity to change over time, as evidenced on the one hand by a number of vital, growing congregations engaged in or positioned for transformative ministry. On the other hand, increasingly, churches' memberships consist of aging members with little influx of young people and decreasing resources for public action. Still others embrace inward-focused ideologies and are directed toward a routinized ecclesiology focused more on personal salvation than on community empowerment and social justice.[16] Franklin makes plain the importance of critiquing the church

---

13 Gayraud S. Willmore, ed., *Black Religion and Black Radicalism: An Interpretation of the Religious History of Afro-American People* (Maryknoll, NY: Orbis Books, 1994), 357.

14 Green, "Black Activism, Unchurched," 11.

15 Green, 11.

16 See discussions on the differing and changing organizational dynamics of churches in Sandra L. Barnes and Anne E. Streaty Wimberly, *Empowering Black Youth of Promise: Education and Socialization in the Village-Minded Black Church* (New York: Routledge, 2016), 3-4, 151-55; Franklin, *Crisis in the Village*, 132-34; Earl Ofari Hutchinson, *The Disappearance of Black Leadership* (Los Angeles: Middle Passage Press, Inc.), 20-21; Dale Andrews, *Practical Theology for Black Churches: Bridging Black Theology*

and its leaders and admitting that something is wrong, but he continues by highlighting the necessary call for a new level of leader accountability that takes them out into the community.[17]

Applying the Challenge to Religious Education

Kenneth Hill documents six models of Christian religious education that have been most operative in Black Churches over time, including kerygmatic, holiness, Afrocentric, contemplative, confessional, and liberation.[18] Briefly, *kerygmatic* education tells the gospel story in preaching and teaching; *holiness* education emphasizes the indwelling of the Holy Spirit; *Afrocentric* education affirms Black unity, cultural pride, and self-determination; *contemplative* education stresses prayer life; *confessional* education passes on denominational or church beliefs, wisdom, values, and practices; and *liberation* education centers on people's reflection on action directed toward social transformation.[19]

As part of a research project to compare the level of emphasis of each model, Hill discovered that the least emphasis was placed on the liberation and holiness models. Only 7 percent of the respondents cited liberation- and holiness-oriented religious education as important compared to the models emphasizing the kerygmatic (88 percent), confessional (88 percent), contemplative (37 percent), and Afrocentric (25 percent).[20] However, a third of the respondents desired greater emphasis on liberation and holiness. This suggests that religious educators are interested in connecting faith and action based on the biblical demand for justice, analysis, and reflection on social issues, and intentional practices of advocacy, social action,

---

and African American Folk Religion (Louisville, KY: Westminster John Knox, 2002), 91–105.

17 Franklin, *Crisis in the Village*, 133.

18 Kenneth H. Hill, *Religious Education in the African American Tradition: A Comprehensive Introduction* (St. Louis: Chalice Press, 2007), 120–35.

19 Hill, *Religious Education in the African American Tradition*, 121.

20 Hill, 134.

and mobilization for needed social and political transformation.[21] Hill draws the emphatic conclusion that "Christian religious education in Black churches has a social mandate."[22] And, with regard to young people, Joshua Mitchell makes clear their "sense of activism and a desire to be a part of social change in the sphere of justice and quality of life for people of color. The congregations who will remain relevant among Black millennials are the congregations who win souls while engaging in community activism and organizing, policy reform, and social justice initiatives that increase the vitality of Black and brown life."[23]

The Religious Educator as Public Theologian

Public theology invites and even demands that churches and other religious institutions employ their faith to address numerous injustices faced in their communities. The religious educator and the practice of participatory, crescive leadership are key in this regard. But a prerequisite of entering into authentic connection with others is the religious educator having an intrapersonal knowledge of self. The religious educator's self-understanding sets the tone. Calvin Mackie's statement is a profoundly applicable one: "Leadership is a mindset that is not always easy to achieve. . . . First and foremost, you have to believe that about yourself. You have to dream, you have to be a scholar, you have to be a doer, and you have to want to become more."[24] Then, to answer the question "How do you know you're a leader?," Mackie states, "If your actions inspire others to dream more, learn more, do more and become more, you are a leader."[25] This is a guiding principle. But the deeper question about the self is about

---

21 Hill, *Religious Education in the African American Tradition*, 131.

22 Hill, 131.

23 Mitchell, *Black Millennials and the Church*, 79–80.

24 Calvin Mackie's statement appears in France, "Emerging Leaders Energized in the Black Community."

25 France, "Emerging Leaders Energized in the Black Community."

calling. Individuals must know that they are summoned by God to create space to struggle with how to engage in life-changing, life-affirming action so desperately needed in a hostile world.

What actually underlies the religious educator's affirmation of self is an ongoing willingness to reflect on the self as leader. During intentional revelatory occasions, leaders examine what is taking place in educational ministry and what must yet be done to address very real issues confronting individuals and communities. This aspect of reflection is also to bring leaders back to consideration of who they are and what they bring to the leadership role such as the level of motivation, their attitudes toward what the ministry requires, their capacity to engage fully in what is required, and the nature and depth of their faith or spirituality.[26]

In addition, the religious educator serves as a public theologian based on a view of the self as a participant in God's empowering and redemptive history for the sake of human justice and wholeness of God's people. In this view, God is present and acting in the world now. This view repudiates the assertion in this post-Christian, post-church, and racially charged era that somehow both the Church and God have deserted or forsaken the oppressed as noted in one millennial's statement: "If the Black Church couldn't take a basic stance on my life, maybe God is incapable of it too."[27] The challenge and need is for the religious educator to be present with people in community, thereby showing God's presence. The intent is to demonstrate through everything that is said and done "that God is passionately, eternally, vigorously concerned about the flourishing of Black people. God as the 'God of the oppressed' is concerned

---

26 These aspects of self-reflection or engagement in revelatory occasions are described in Anne E. Streaty Wimberly and Sarah Frances Farmer, *Raising Hope: 4 Paths to Courageous Living for Black Youth* (Nashville: Wesley's Foundery Books, 2017), 81.

27 The statement appears in Tyree Boyd-Pates, "Why Black Millennials Are Hopping from Church-to-Church," Huffington Post, December 6, 2017, www.huffpost.com/entry/this-is-why-Black-millen_b_9640358.

about souls, but of equal importance, God is concerned about the personal well-being of Black bodies and minds."[28]

The religious educator as public theologian then places the self in solidarity with the community with responsibility for those within and beyond the church's physical location. This task centers on valuing people as God's creations, the "somebodyness" of Black people, having or coming to evolving "disruptive awareness" of the realities of people's lives that disturbs and propels the self to act both by guiding and acting with or on behalf of others.[29] The educator is therefore a relational self–in relationship with God and others that becomes activated in "a prophetic, practical task of Christian ministry."[30] At the same time, the view of public theology that centers on community is not based on the leader's or the church's decision to take action in the community to the exclusion of knowledge about the community and insights and desires of community members or partnerships that either exist or are waiting to be developed. There is a pivotal need for awareness of the self's residential proximity to the church and the community around it as well as who is or is not presently associated with the church.

Historically, individuals who lived, worshiped, and even worked in the same community benefited from the organic development of bonds and relationships. As a result of these relationships, persons were privy to the struggles and injustices in their community, held common concerns and interests needing response, and sought responses from the church. But because of changing residential patterns, numbers of church members no longer live in the same

---

28 Stacey Floyd-Thomas, Juan Floyd-Thomas, Carol B. Duncan, Stephen C. Ray Jr., and Nancy Lynne Westfield, "Christian Education in the Black Church Tradition," in *Black Church Studies: An Introduction* (Nashville: Abingdon Press, 2007), 151–75.

29 The term *disruptive awareness* is described as a way that leaders "come face-to-face with the situation of young people and of having our thinking–our very souls–disturbed enough that we cannot sit still." Wimberly and Farmer, *Raising Hope*, 87.

30 Wimberly and Farmer, *Raising Hope*, 104.

geographical location of the church, and those around the church are not necessarily actively involved. Moreover, churches may not focus on fostering relationships with the community around them. Alessandra Ram reminds us that "changing demographics are a daunting challenge for an institution that used to occupy an integral role in the community. . . . To understand this struggle is to understand the changing role of the Black Church in the American narrative, and what vulnerable communities stand to lose if it disappears."[31]

Disconnections between leaders and community and between the church and the community prevent the church and its religious education leaders from having a pulse on the realities the communities around them are facing. Ram makes the point that Black churches "are realizing that alliances must be formed if they want to retain their presence in the community."[32] Participatory, crescive leadership means that there is recognition of and desire to learn from those who are in the community, are part of the daily struggle, and have been marginalized and experience the repercussions of policies and politics. This kind of leadership acknowledges that community residents are better suited to define what is going on in their lives. In short, it is with them that partnerships are needed for mutual learning, responsibility-taking, and action. Simply put, religious educators, community members, and concerned others have to be part of an advocacy and social justice team that addresses their issues and concerns.

---

31 Alessandra Ram, "In Changing Neighborhoods, Black Churches Face an Identity Crisis," *The Atlantic*, October 12, 2012, www.theatlantic.com/national/archive/2012/10/in-changing-neighborhoods-Black-churches-face-an-identity-crisis/263305/.

32 Ram, "In Changing Neighborhoods, Black Churches Face an Identity Crisis," 8.

Activating the Role of the Black Religious Educator

The Black Church's and the religious educator's embrace of public ministry and an understanding of crescive leadership requires a productive approach or a set of implementation practices. The goal of these practices is to make concrete a justice agenda. Brad Braxton noted the impact of Pentecost among the early Christians, who opponents saw as "turning the world upside down" (Acts 17:6), and states that "we, like our ancestors in the faith, are called to shake the foundations of demonic injustice and in so doing turn the world right side up."[33] Historically, Black religious institutions, and churches in particular, have done just that by providing numerous services not available in the wider society and by initiating and engaging in activism on behalf of opportunities for a better life for Black people. However, this current millennium requires more.

This section continues to build on the requirement of crescive leadership and practices that do not engage the community as a problem to be fixed but that partner with community members to deal with community concerns. Neither do these practices fail to recognize the giftedness within the people in these communities. The mandate is for practices that invite and even demand that churches and leaders employ their faith but also meet people where they are. This orientation extends to the use of Afrocentric and other race-oriented strategies and supports that acknowledge and celebrate the African heritage of African Americans.[34] Moreover, it recognizes that in the Black community, Afrocentricity takes

---

33 Brad R. Braxton, "The Holy Spirit, Jesus and Social Justice in Black Churches: Making Noise or Making a Difference?" Huffington Post, May 25, 2011, 2, www.huffpost.com/entry/the-spirit-jesus-and-soci_b_829665.

34 Barnes and Wimberly's report of a cross-denominational study of Black churches shows that 65 percent of them "sponsor events related to Kwanzaa and/or Black History. Moreover, a sizable number, 146 or 23.0% of congregations, specifically discuss how they incorporate Afrocentric and other race-related curricula and programs in their youth initiatives." See Barnes and Wimberly, *Empowering Black Youth of Promise*, 71.

the form of consciously negating White supremacist notions of Black identity by adopting African styles of dress and hairstyles. In a real sense, these emphases represent an intentionally changed "political consciousness."[35] Based on these cultural and political understandings, attention will be given to the practices of *Ubuntu* and *Ujima*.

Ubuntu

The religious educator's practice of crescive leadership entails connecting with, being present with, and engaging persons in community within and beyond the physical location of the church to receive their stories, ideas, feelings, and suggested actions. This demand on the part of the religious educator is one of establishing, maintaining, and promoting meanings of interdependent relationships. In practice, it exhibits the African understanding of *Ubuntu. Ubuntu* comes from the sub-Saharan language of Bantu and is a form of spirituality centered on human relationships and the relationships between human beings and God's being.[36] South African Archbishop Desmond Tutu indicates that the term itself is not easily translated into a Western language. But "it speaks of the very essence of being human. It is to say, 'My humanity is caught up, is inextricably bound up, in yours.' We say: 'A person is a person through other persons.' "[37] He goes on to say: "We are made for community, for togetherness, for family, to exist in a delicate network of interdependence."[38]

Ubuntu also reveals that individuals are not separated from the community–it is within the community that individuals evolve into their personal and particular giftedness (personality, spiritual

---

35 Shawn Ginwright, "Toward a Politics of Relevance: Race, Resistance and African American Youth Activism," SSRC Web Forum on Youth Activism, June 7, 2006, http://ya.ssrc.org/african/Ginwright/printable.html.

36 A comprehensive exploration of the nature of *Ubuntu* appears in Michael Battle, *Ubuntu: I in You and You in Me* (New York: Seabury Books, 2009), 3.

37 Desmond Mpilo Tutu, *No Future Without Forgiveness* (New York: Doubleday, 1999), 31.

38 Tutu, *No Future Without Forgiveness*, 197.

gifts, skills, talents, purpose, and passion). The community, which includes immediate and extended family, friends, neighbors, and church members, nurtures individuals who in turn use their giftedness for the benefit of the community. This aspect of *Ubuntu* means that persons in the community contribute to the evolving humanity of every community member.

As a principle, then, *Ubuntu* joins people via their humanity. A person's being is the point of connection. People are to be treated with dignity and respect for no other reason except they are a person. Persons are not defined by or reduced to their socioeconomic status, their titles or positions, their race or ethnicity, or their present condition of existence. Because of the centrality of relationships, justice-seeking efforts and social activism are not reduced to a set of tasks. Rather, they embody a collective attitude and action motivated by a quality of generosity and affirmation of life that inspires standing in opposition to marginalization and discrimination, contesting destructive values, and seeking transforming alternatives that promote life.[39]

In practice, this understanding of *Ubuntu* happens in instances such as the new Poor People's Campaign out of which a series of Moral Mondays was developed around social justice under the guidance of Rev. Dr. William Barber II, North Carolina minister and political activist. This movement set out to hear the voices of poor and hurting people and, in fact, to engage them as the featured speakers. Their testimonies were followed by public policy experts, lawyers, and economists who presented an agenda for change. The Moral Mondays offered a space for people to join together across denominations and faiths in the practice of democracy.[40] The under-

39 This view of *Ubuntu* rephrases one set forth by Rev. Dr. Suzanne Membe-Matale, "Ubuntu Theology," The Free Library, accessed January 15, 2020, www.thefreelibrary.com/Ubuntu+theology.-a0426765939.

40 A description of the Moral Mondays movement appears in Rev. Dr. William J. Barber II, "The Battle for the Soul of America Is Being Fought in the States," Moyers, May 5, 2017, https://billmoyers.com/story/the-third

standing of *Ubuntu* is further demonstrated in the pedagogical practices appearing in the monthly program generated by Rev. Barber and Jonathan Wilson-Hartgrove called "The Gathering: A Time for Reflection, Revival and Resistance," which includes a community-based education program. The monthly program, which began June 4, 2017, brings people together around "Movement music, interviews with impacted people in the Poor People's Campaign, a timely sermon for the public square, and an 'altar call'" designed to inspire commitment to the movement for social transformation and justice.[41] The community-based education program appearing on livestream and podcasts "equips communities with resources for faithful reflection and public action on moral issues through storytelling, music, interviews with community organizers and people, and a call to join the Poor People's Campaign: A National Call for Moral Revival."[42]

Ujima

Another central principle in constructing a framework for the practice of crescive leadership in African American communities is *Ujima*. *Ujima* is a Swahili word that stands for collective work and responsibility. It is one of seven basic values of African culture highlighted during the celebration of Kwanzaa, an African American holiday period from December 26 to January 1.[43] As a practice, *Ujima* is to

---

-reconstruction/#. The description is excerpted from William J. Barber II with Jonathan Wilson-Hartgrove, *The Third Reconstruction: How a Moral Movement Is Overcoming the Politics and Division of Fear* (New York: Beacon Press, 2016).

41 A brief summary of the program appears in "Rev. Barber: America Needs a New Poor People's Campaign," Think Progress, May 15, 2017, https://thinkprogress.org/rev-barber-why-america-needs-a-new-poor-peoples-campaign-dd406d515193/.

42 The program is described on the website www.schoolforconversion.org/the-gathering/.

43 The celebration of Kwanzaa was established by Maulana Karenga in 1966 to honor African heritage. One of the goals of this holiday period is to

"contribute to building and reinforcing family, community and culture among African American people as well as Africans throughout the world."[44] Through it, people form and maintain a collective existence in which the problems of one are considered the problems of all and are solved by all. Within this framework, persons cannot be viewed as an isolated individual but as a *person in community.*[45]

Gyeke notes that the value of the communitarian order is that it offers an "intricate web of social relationships," which "tend to ensure the individual's social worth" and "affords the individual the opportunity to make a meaningful life through his or her contribution to the general welfare."[46] Thus, embracing community as an aspect of the normative framework of *Ujima* does not diminish individuals. On the contrary, individuals become whole in relationship with others in community. In its emphasis on community, *Ujima* bears kinship with *Ubuntu* by virtue of its emphasis on communal relationships. However, it goes on to emphasize an obligatory responsibility of one for another or a sense of communal accountability. Kevin Onuma describes this dimension: "If anyone is oppressed, exploited, enslaved or wounded in any way, all are, and insofar as persons are in this state, it is the responsibility of persons to struggle to create a context in which all can be free."[47]

---

utilize African culture as an aid to building community. It is described in Maulana Karenga, *The African American Holiday of Kwanzaa: A Celebration of Family, Community and Culture* (Los Angeles: University of Sankore Press, 1988, 2008).

44 This description appears on the official Kwanzaa website, www.officialkwanzaawebsite.org/7principles.shtml.

45 See Maulana Karenga, *Kwanzaa: A Celebration of Family, Community and Culture* (Los Angeles: University of Sankore Press, 1998).

46 Kwame Gyeke, *An Essay on African Philosophical Thought–The Akan Conceptual Scheme* (New York: Cambridge University Press, 1987).

47 Kevin Onuma, "Kwanzaa Day 3: 'Ujima': Collective Work & Responsibility," Inform Africa, December 28, 2013, https://elev8.hellobeautiful.com/655478/day-3-celebration-of-kwanzaa-ujima-collective-work-and-responsibility/.

In short, the practice of *Ujima* speaks to shared responsibility to build the good families, communities, society, and world we want and deserve to live and flourish in—places of freedom, justice, caring, sharing, security, well-being, and peace.[48] It is central to crescive leadership that espouses a public theology that does not speak solely to the benefit of an individual or a few individuals but rather speaks to the transformation of the masses. Consequently, its manifestation in leadership that is set in the direction of transformation cannot rely on one person or a few persons. Leadership requires shared communal responsibility, including churches sharing with other faith bodies and institutions in advocacy and public action.

Although *Ujima* reflects an African spirituality, there is no mistaking its kinship with Christian values found notably in Galatians 6:1–5 (NRSV), which notes how Christians should treat one another and makes pointed reference in verse 2 to the responsibility of believers to "bear one another's burdens." An added revolutionary requirement of responsibility-taking is posed in Matthew 25:31–46, which emphasizes the necessity of giving food to the hungry, clothing the naked, caring for the sick, and visiting those in prison.

An example of crescive leadership that models *Ujima* while also living out the Matthean passage is reflected in the Huffington Post story of the Black Church Security Network.[49] As part of it, one pastor, Rev. Dr. Heber Brown, and his staff and members joined other churches, farmers, and community leaders in Baltimore to tackle and take forthright responsibility for reversing the reality of

---

48 Maulana Karenga, "Annual Founder's Kwanzaa Message 'Reimagining and Remaking the World: A Kwanzaa Commitment to an Inclusive Good,'" *Los Angeles Sentinel*, December 20, 2018, https://lasentinel.net/annual-founders-kwanzaa-message-reimagining-and-remaking-the-world-a-kwanzaa-commitment-to-an-inclusive-good.html.

49 Antonio Blumberg, "How Black Churches Are Helping Their Communities Get Access to Healthy Food," Huffington Post, July 7, 2015, https://www.huffpost.com/entry/black-churches-baltimore-food-justice_n_559c5622e4b04e28f1e52ec1.

food deserts and food security injustice. The issue has to do with inaccessibility to fresh, healthy, and affordable food, particularly by Black and Hispanic residents in lower-income neighborhoods, which results in poor diets and health issues of obesity, diabetes, and heart disease.[50] The church, Pleasant Hope Baptist Church, became involved because of the lived stories of members' hospitalizations resulting from diet-related issues. The church's yard was transformed into an urban garden with food made available after Sunday services and taken to pick-up spots around the city. The members tend the gardens.

In addition, the Black Church Security Network developed a Soil to Sanctuary Program that includes "Bible studies, small group sessions, and presentations at churches on food justice and care."[51] The message the Network wants to convey is that "faith communities teach us how to live. With healthy food being such an integral part of a vibrant, full life, it is only natural for faith communities to take on the issue of food security, and healthy eating."[52] Advocacy also extended beyond the faith community. Church efforts were appended by Baltimore city policy-making and development of strategies in partnership with the Johns Hopkins Center for a Livable

---

50 The article by Blumberg references a Johns Hopkins study that affirms the prevalence of food deserts in lower-income areas, primarily affecting Blacks and Hispanics. The report of the study appears in Kelly M. Bower, Roland J. Thorpe Jr., Charles Rohde, and Darrell Gaskin, "Neighborhood Racial Segregation, Poverty, and Urbanicity and Its Impact on Food Store Availability in the United States," *Preventive Medicine* 58 (January 2014): 33-39. In addition, the article reveals that "in Baltimore, 34 percent of the city's African American population lives without access to fresh, healthy foods, compared to just 8 percent of White residents." See Blumberg, "How Black Churches Are Helping Their Communities Get Access to Healthy Food."

51 Information on the Black Church Security Network and the Soil to Sanctuary Program is found on https://blackchurchfoodsecurity.net/home.html.

52 Blumberg, "How Black Churches Are Helping Their Communities Get Access to Healthy Food."

Future to promote equitable access to healthy, affordable food for all residents.[53]

The Interplay of Ubuntu and Ujima

Black Churches in the past have typically been regarded as being at the forefront of public advocacy and social action. Moreover, it is assumed that the accountability and responsibility of the Church on behalf of justice and human wholeness of Black people must continue to be forthright, active, and, in many cases, rekindled and not forsaken. But the Church is not alone in the urgent response to current-day struggles. Both *Ubuntu* and *Ujima* call attention to a wider understanding of peoplehood and communal being and acting that goes beyond a one-dimensional view of activism carried out by religious leaders and church members.[54] Too many times religious institutions act as if God is only with them and that they have the responsibility and privilege of taking God to "other" communities. This divisive approach creates an "us versus them" mentality that prevents "us Christians" from seeing and acknowledging God in places they claim they want to serve. In fact, young people, particularly in the Black Lives Matter movement, are clearly demonstrating that there are others directly, passionately committed to and involved in confronting racial injustice and pushing for change. Their locus of activity is also a reminder that the church or religious building is not the only habitation where the manifestation of God's activity appears. From them comes the challenge to the

53 See Thomas J. Stosur, Dr. Leana S. Wen, and William H. Cole IV, *Mapping Baltimore City's Food Environment*, Johns Hopkins Center for a Livable Future, June 1, 2015, https://clf.jhsph.edu/publications/mapping-baltimore-citys-food-environment.

54 Attention is drawn to the problematic view of protest from a one-dimensional view "of the twentieth-century Civil Rights Movement as the brainchild of Black churches, orchestrated by religious leaders, and populated by church members," in Anthony Pinn, "How Black Lives Matter Challenges Twentieth-Century Models of Protest," Berkley Forum, October 24, 2016, https://berkleycenter.georgetown.edu/responses/how-Black-lives-matter-challenges-twentieth-century-models-of-protest.

church to reconsider meanings of God's omnipresence and to reflect on God's presence in God's creation—all of God's creation. *Ubuntu* and *Ujima* function as foundational reminders of interconnected relationships, partnership, and a whole community's responsibility in the push for fundamental change.

It is also well to consider that youth and young adult activists may not and often do not use God-language, yet they are concrete evidence of what constitutes community and make clear that the presence and activity of God is not reserved for religious institutions. God's presence already exists in the community because God's creation is the community. The church's role is to acknowledge, see, be aware of what they do, learn from them, and join them. Doing so is to simultaneously acknowledge the presence of God because their presence in community is a sign of God's presence. To dismiss, denigrate, or define them otherwise is to be anti-God. One should also take seriously Anthony Pinn's suggestion that in the Black Lives Matter movement, there is "a Christian dimension marked by the involvement of individual Christians and Christian leaders, while also reflecting the righteous outrage of other theistic traditions."[55] But more than this, the young people tend not to espouse a hierarchical arrangement of leadership. They are more egalitarian and press for accountability and responsibility without emphasis on distinctive preparation, skills, or calling as prerequisites for involvement.[56] Even though the movement has spokespersons and organizers who gather people together and cite a way forward, others join in and share their ideas and opinions. The actual push forward is not top-down. It is a community together in action.

An example is a story in *The Nation* of a group called the Dream Defenders.[57] It was not a Sunday school class that met in a church on

---

55 Pinn, "How Black Lives Matter Challenges Twentieth-Century Models of Protest," 1.

56 Pinn, "How Black Lives Matter Challenges Twentieth-Century Models of Protest."

57 The story appears in Mychal Denzel Smith, "How Trayvon Martin's Death Launched a New Generation of Black Activism," *The Nation*, August 27,

Sunday morning. Rather, it was a group that, on a Sunday morning after the acquittal of George Zimmerman of his murder of Trayvon Martin, met in Tallahassee and occupied the state capitol building. Phillip Agnew, aged twenty-nine, called forth a group of college students and recent graduates across Florida to carry out a forty-mile march from Daytona Beach to Sanford, Florida, to demand justice for Trayvon. He confessed that they weren't sure of their demands. They simply needed to be there and make a statement by their presence. Yet out of the group's action of "going on the fly" amid grief and anguish came the Dream Defenders and a month-long protest that included what they called "Trayvon's Law." It was an ambitious package of bills calling for an end to the school-to-prison pipeline, racial profiling, and the repeal of the self-defense law called "Stand Your Ground." Even though the bills they proposed were not introduced, the Dream Defenders met with several supportive legislators to discuss them.[58]

The Religious Educator's Guidance of Prophetic Inquiry

This final section presents a pedagogical approach called Prophetic Inquiry (PI) that builds on the Appreciative Inquiry (AI) model that emerged from research on organizations and management. The adaptation of some key aspects are helpful to the strategic responsibilities of religious educators involved in political action and advocacy.[59] The presentation of PI here emphasizes the formation of a

---

2014, www.thenation.com/article/how-trayvon-martins-death-launched-new-generation-Black-activism/.

58 Smith, "How Trayvon Martin's Death Launched a New Generation of Black Activism."

59 Appreciative Inquiry (AI) emerged in the 1980s out of research undertaken by David L. Cooperrider and his associates. A complete description of AI appears in David L. Cooperrider and Diana Whitney, *Appreciative Inquiry: A Positive Revolution in Change* (San Francisco: Berrett-Koehler Publishers, 2005). Summaries of the nature and process of AI appear in David Cooperrider and Associates, "What Is Appreciative Inquiry?,"

prophetic consciousness through self-inquiry that heightens awareness of urgent advocacy and people's activist roles, which then leads to revocation of continuing racial disparities and injustice. It emphasizes religious practices and incisive social responses based on a faith stance of God's intent for human wholeness and, as such, connects the social with spiritual dimensions. PI encompasses a process for use in Sunday schools, discipleship classes, other church meeting groups, and church-based public advocacy or action groups where the pastor, volunteer, or other group leaders become strategic prophetic agents. Recall that crescive leadership hinges on intentional collective involvement rather than on a top-down approach. Therefore, the expectation of the religious educator's strategic role is to assure the presence of collaborative participation in which individual leadership unfolds.

The Tenets of Prophetic Inquiry (PI)

PI is a collaborative process that engages people in story-sharing around the nature of prevailing circumstances, past and present approaches to needed change, and the strengths people have to envision and effect change. As a pedagogical tool in religious education, PI invites people's inquiry into their personally experienced, observed, or newly discovered stories of what is occurring in the public sphere that demands attention; why it is urgent to respond; what constitutes the possible ways of responding; and what is sought as the result of the response. Its kinship to AI lies in its stress on positivity and a leader's guidance of people to imagine what is needed to move toward the goal of creating a preferred future. Moreover, like AI, PI captures what Harder notes as building meaning-full

---

accessed January 15, 2020, www.davidcooperrider.com/ai-process; and Robyn Stratton-Berkessel, "Appreciative Inquiry-Overview of Method, Principles and Applications," *Positivity Strategist*, June 10, 2019, https://positivitystrategist.com/appreciative-inquiry-overview/.

communities,[60] which is understood here to mean communities in which the holistic well-being of people and justice prevail.

As a collective effort, the role of the religious educator in PI processes also includes receiving and utilizing creative resources from outside the group in decision-making and action. This was the case, for example, in the previously shared story of the New Poor People's Campaign in North Carolina in which public policy experts, lawyers, and economists were invited to forums to provide pertinent information. In this way, the leader sought to help the group see themselves as connected to other organizations, teams, and community groups and to move collectively and passionately toward the goal.[61]

PI draws further on the tenets that undergird inquiry processes set forth in AI. First, the leader's guidance of groups in inquiry is seen as a constructionist process that "is to stimulate new ideas, stories and images that generate new possibilities for action."[62] Recall the earlier-mentioned community-based program generated by Rev. Dr. William Barber II and Jonathan Wilson-Hartgrove, who used music, storytelling, livestream, and podcasts to engage people and equip and move them toward organizing for change. This example further accents the essential responsibility of religious educators in utilizing technology and social media in social action and advocacy education efforts. Second, inquiry is a simultaneous process wherein the seeds of change are planted as people think, talk, discover, and learn.[63] It was this process of sitting together on a Sunday morning that resulted in the formation of the Dream Defenders, discussed earlier. Third, inquiry-directed processes have a deeply expressive quality in which words and topics evoke varieties of meanings,

---

60 Cameron Harder, *Discovering the Other: Asset-Based Approaches for Building Community Together* (Herndon, VA: Alban Institute, 2013).

61 This idea in AI is based on the collective orientation and goal for corporate entities and management described in Gervase Busche, "The Appreciative Inquiry Model," in *Encyclopedia of Management Theory*, ed. E.H. Kessler (Thousand Oaks, CA: Sage Publications, 2013), 1–4.

62 Busche, "The Appreciative Inquiry Model," 2.

63 Busche, 2.

sentiments, and imagination that "enliven and inspire the best in people."[64] Especially in leader-guided PI, difficult stories may arouse great sadness and grief. However, the intent is for the inquiry process to move people to a point of seeing a necessary way forward toward change and how to be one's best self so as to contribute to that direction. Again, in the case of the Dream Defenders, sharing uncovered the young people's deep grief about the senseless death of Trayvon Martin. But their grief inspired their intentional journey, which inspired the development of Trayvon's Law.

Fourth, leader-guided inquiry processes have an anticipatory dimension that inevitably helps people to project "ahead of themselves a horizon of expectation that brings the future powerfully into the present as a mobilizing agent."[65] An example of this is the previously mentioned efforts of Rev. Dr. Heber Brown, the church staff, and members who envisioned and created gardens with the expectation of reversing the injustice of food deserts and food insecurity and of bringing about healthy eating and policy change. Finally, inquiry processes in all of the examples presented on the functions of *Ubuntu* and *Ujima* highlight the leader's coalescence with groups in creating a sense of connectedness and readiness to receive one another's ideas and points of view, which are requirements of collective inquiry and moving toward desired change.[66]

Methods of Prophetic Inquiry

The religious educator's guidance of PI involves particular methods, which bear kinship to but go beyond the discovery, dream, design, and delivery or destiny approaches appearing in the AI model. In brief, in PI the religious educator engages groups in five pedagogical approaches.

1. Discovery is a process of inviting individuals' stories of problems, bad situations, crises, and injustices, as well as getting at real

64 Busche, 2.
65 Busche, 2.
66 Busche, 2.

facts of the story. This initial phase of PI invites those involved into the practice of *Ubuntu*, of recognizing humanity, through engaging one another under the guidance of the religious educator, who acts as a strategic leader. The approach is not one of simply moving toward fixing a problem but rather becoming involved in problem-solving that affects people who are "seen" and "known" by God and us. When individuals have an opportunity to both convey their stories and listen to the narratives of others, the opportunity to honor people and discovery arises. Pertinent questions are, What has happened? What is the issue, and how did you become aware of it? What are your feelings and interpretations? What are the various sides to the occurrence or issue and the sources of data?

2. Determination centers on what may be called cold calculating, *evolving from responses to pertinent questions.* These include, What choice(s) are to be made regarding the issue(s) to be tackled? Who will a response to the issue affect and how? Who will be helped or hurt? Is the issue worth tackling and why? What is the group's will to enter the fray? Through inquiry, participants aspire beyond what is currently happening and beyond past limitations or obstructions to change. Yet there must be awareness of any tendency toward self-sabotage that surfaces in statements such as, "We don't have the money," or "That's not the way we have done it in the past," or "It sounds too time intensive." The determination aspect is reserved for imagining and proclaiming an intent to move forward.

3. Discernment invites people to explore the religious beliefs and teachings they hold that guide their views about, interest in, and decisions to address an identified issue. The kinds of questions that frame discernment include, What is God calling us to do? What have we learned or need to learn about the faith of forebears that informs ways of confronting tough circumstances and issues? How do God's Word and the teachings of Jesus Christ inform and promote our views on and involvement in advocacy and activism? How may prayer, worship, and other liturgical practices help us grapple with social-political issues, and what guidance and support may they offer us in deciding our role or actual advocacy or activist function? How may we now engage in them as informative and encouraging spiritual resources?

4. Decision entails a participatory process of readiness to step out on behalf of change. It involves what AI proponents describe as making a plan to act or concrete proposals "often called possibility statements or design statements."[67] In PI, the assumption underlying decision-making draws from the position of Grant Shockley, noted religious educator and proponent of liberation-centered pedagogy, that religious education is "for change. . . . It must be proactive in relation to change, shaping it for responsible engagement with 'open' and 'possible' futures. . . . Whatever the need and/or circumstance of the Black community might be—survival, protest, consciousness-raising, reform, or revolution—the Black Church and its resources have been (and will be) an ever-present foundation."[68] Decision also gives attention to the role of the religious educator as strategic leader. Specifically, this role is one of monitoring and supporting group decisions and creating opportunities and processes to energize the group's direction toward change. Importantly, the religious educator should not seek to be a controlling presence but instead a support giver.

Decision-making questions in PI are, What institutions, associations, or groups needing change will be the target, or what responses are needed to call attention to injustice? What are our goals, and what are the specific steps we need to take to reach them? What specific actions will be agreed upon (e.g., lawful demonstration or protest; picket; boycott; petition; list of demands; public meeting; meeting with identified representatives of institutions, associations, or groups; press conference)?

---

67 Busche, "The Appreciative Inquiry Model," 3.

68 Grant S. Shockley, "Black Theology and Religious Education," in *Theologies of Religious Education*, ed. Randolph Crump Miller (Birmingham, AL: Religious Education Press, 1995), 323–24.

5. *Demonstration entails acting on agreed-upon decisions.* From a Black faith and ecclesial perspective, action proceeds from the absolute need to act and the theological assertion that is shared by the religious educator as theologian that the "Black Church should be mission-oriented rather than 'institution' oriented."[69] Moreover, action should be devoid of any notion of institutional prestige and image but rather proceed on as did the prophet Amos in challenging a disreputable society to "let justice roll down like waters, and righteousness like an ever-flowing stream" (Amos 5:24, NRSV). Questions such as the following may be raised: What is our timeline? What is our point of departure and connection before, during, and after our actions? What happens if we confront resistance? What resources for information and guidance are available for our use?[70]

In summary, PI continues the biblical tradition of Black religion and ecclesiology that centers on an agenda of social justice, action, and religious piety based on God's will for liberation from oppression to wholeness of marginalized people. It also places religious educators at the forefront of engaging people in religious education for change.

Reflections

The role of religious educators as public theologians is an obligatory one amid Black people's continuing experiences of racial

69 Shockley, "Black Theology and Religious Education," 324.

70 The following resources may provide assistance: Dave Beckwith, "Community Organizing: People Power Form the Grassroots," Center for Community Change, accessed January 16, 2020, https://comm-org.wisc.edu/papers97/beckwith.htm; Prue Breitrose, "Overview: Getting an Advocacy Campaign Off the Ground," Community Tool Box, accessed January 16, 2020, http://ww2.nasbhc.org/roadmap/Advocacy/Getting%20Advocay%20Off%20the%20Ground.pdf; and Anthony S. Mangeri Sr., "Preparing for Protests, Civil Unrest Requires Coordination Among Agencies," InPublicSafety, July 25, 2016, https://inpublicsafety.com/2016/07/preparing-for-protests-civil-unrest-requires-coordination-among-agencies/.

oppression. At its core, this role is one of insisting on an educational agenda whereby people develop a prophetic consciousness and acumen for public action needed to bring forth human rights, dignity, and justice in the lives of Black people amid continuing oppressive circumstances. As public theologians, religious educators are called to be crescive leaders who empower, connect with, engage, learn from, and stand and act with participants for the sake of a more promising future. Religious educators must commit to a communal activism pedagogy that connects the Afrocentric practices inherent in *Ubuntu* and *Ujima* with PI, which invites attention to the historic Black Church's emphasis on both social justice and religious piety.

Religious Education and Communities of Learning and Practice

Inspiring Advocacy in Public Ministry

Mary H. Young

> Living together as a community of faith is the way the entire congregation learns and matures in its faith journey. It is in community that strategies of survival and hope are passed from generation to generation.
>
> –Stacey Floyd-Thomas, Juan Floyd-Thomas, et al., "Christian Education in the Black Church Tradition"

Speaking of Community

The public sphere is commonly regarded as a comprehensive arena shaped by open and accessible conversation and comprising the political participation of differing communities. As a democratic entity, the public sphere depends on the constituents' opinions and arrival at consensus to bring about the common good reflected in social justice and political equality. Clearly, a unitary public sphere does not exist but is a complex network of communities, making it necessary to give our initial attention here to the nature of community.

When we talk about community, often our immediate thoughts turn to geographical communities, the local neighborhoods we live in, or different sides of a metropolitan area in which we may reside. However, it is possible to conceptualize community beyond this basic view such that it includes what can be called "identificational communities." Stephanie Zazgi and her associates describe identificational communities on the basis of gender, race or ethnicity, religion, cultural affiliation, or other identifying interests such as politics, health, and educational status.[1] Gripsrud and his colleagues refer to collectivities of the public sphere "(occupational, political, ethnic, religious, sexual) and geographic areas (local, national, regional, global), with different thematic foci (science, politics, economy, arts, sports, fashion), and modes and genres of communication," as in the case of online, face-to-face, public media.[2] All persons belong to an identificational community and to more than one of the described collectivities.

Identification with a certain community is not a monolithic connection but rather tends to be intersecting and fluid. Because one belongs to a given community does not mean that one is affiliated with a homogeneous group of others who all model the same actions and ascribe to the same beliefs. The type of community one belongs to also affords him or her certain power and privilege, or lack thereof. For example, one who is male, White, and middle class is most often afforded the conveniences of White privilege, whereas a Black, female, single mother must employ a different set of survival tactics. Communities where male or class privilege are operative

1 Stephanie Zazgi, Terry Mizrahi, Elizabeth Rossi, and Jozi Zwerdling, "Community Change and Social Activism: A Curriculum Module for the CUNY Workforce Development Initiative," The City University of New York, September 2015, https://sssw.hunter.cuny.edu/pdf/cnr/wdi_community_change_and_social_activism.pdf.

2 Jospein Gripsrud, Hallward Moe, Anders Molander, and Graham Murdock, eds., *The Idea of the Public Sphere* (Lanham, MD: Lexington Books, 2010), xv.

also create dynamics with which many persons struggle. The nature of these privileged realities affects the ways people relate to other communities and what they might need to do to negotiate such differences. In fact, communities in the public sphere have continued to reflect a hierarchical ordering of social relations where expressions of power dynamics and social, political, and structural inequalities exist. This reality occasions the formation of "subaltern counter-publics,"[3] or what Black leaders call oppositional or communal resistance movements that confront exclusionary tactics, unjust policies, and dehumanizing, life-threatening behaviors.[4]

The Faith Community

The faith community is the primary context in which religious education takes place, so it is helpful to comment on this entity in the public sphere. Charles Foster defines a community of faith as "a people whose corporate as well as personal identities are to be found in their relationship to some significant past event."[5] With persons who

3 The description of subaltern counter-publics, their causes, and actions related to them are presented in Nancy Fraser, "Rethinking the Public Sphere: Existing Democracy," in *Habermas and the Public Sphere*, ed. Craig J. Calhoun (Boston: MIT Press, 1992), 109–42.

4 Historical and contemporary descriptions of these movements appear in Stephanie M. H. Camp, *Closer to Freedom: Enslaved Women and Everyday Resistance in the Plantation South* (Chapel Hill: University of North Carolina Press, 2004); Mary Frances Berry, *Black Resistance, White Law: A History of Constitutional Racism in America* (New York: Penguin Books, 1995); Patricia Hill Collins, *Black Feminist Thought: Knowledge, Consciousness, and the Politics of Empowerment* (New York: Routledge, 1990), 91-114; Kumea Shorter-Gooden, "Multiple Resistance Strategies: How African American Women Cope with Racism and Sexism," *Journal of Black Psychology* 30, no. 3 (August 1, 2004): 406–25; and Akiba Solomon and Kenrya Rankin, *How We Fight White Supremacy: A Field Guide to Resistance* (New York: Bold Type Books, 2019).

5 Charles R. Foster, "The Faith Community as a Guiding Image for Christian Education," in *Contemporary Approaches to Christian Education*,

call themselves Christians, this community is defined and guided by the creative work of God in the biblical text and in the redeeming sacrifice of Jesus Christ. This corporate identity is solidified through rituals and traditions, institutions, and the use of ancient creeds, as well as retelling faith stories in ways that keep the faith alive as it is reinterpreted in each new era. In this way, the community of faith becomes a community of learning where persons are constantly called to respond with practices that reflect its values, beliefs, truths, and convictions.

From its inception in this country, the Black faith community evolved with a "people's identity and religion" that paralleled rather than replicated the religious culture of those who held them captive.[6] A distinctive communal character, learned by new generations, formed and included an intimate connection with God; God's involvement in history; and core values of freedom, justice, and equality. These values undergirded "a community of faith, a community of oppressed people seeking liberation, a community of persons dedicated to the discipleship of Jesus Christ."[7] For Black Christians, that has meant tangibly living into practices that exemplify the work and ministry of Jesus, which is to serve for justice, embrace the disposed and despised of society, care for the lonely and the lost, and advocate for those who have no voice.

As in the past, the faith community is called to teach the nature of speaking truth to power and actually speak it! It is to embolden the cry of the eighth-century-BCE prophet Amos to "let justice roll down like waters, and righteousness like an ever-flowing stream" (Amos 5:24, NRSV). The power and life of the Christian community is to be

---

ed. Jack L. Seymour and Donald E. Miller (Nashville: Abingdon Press, 1987), 54.

6 C. Eric Lincoln and Lawrence H. Mamiya, *The Black Church in the African American Experience* (Durham, NC: Duke University Press, 1990), 2.

7 Stacey Floyd-Thomas, Juan Floyd-Thomas, Carol B. Duncan, Stephen C. Ray Jr., Nancy Lynne Westfield, "Christian Education in the Black Church Tradition," *Black Church Studies: An Introduction* (Nashville: Abingdon Press, 2007), 151.

linked to the work of God in Christ and, as such, to acknowledge and "link the social, theological, and emotional with the cultural, economic, and political aspects of Back life."[8] According to Raphael Warnock, it can be said that the Black Christian faith community has lived into this mission while navigating a "double consciousness" that on the one hand is shaped by a focus on individual salvation (piety) and on the other hand is motivated by the impact of slavery and therefore drawn to seek freedom (protest).[9] From this tension, a Black theology developed, with influences from the academy and the church, that seeks to answer the perennial question of whether the mission of the faith community is to "save souls or transform the social order."[10] So there is a heterogeneous nature of Black Christian faith traditions and communions in North America. These traditions vary in how they have responded to the call of this community to be a countercultural, sociopolitical, public voice seeking justice and freedom. Robert Franklin summarizes it in the following way: "The Black church tradition emphasizes that personal conviction, moral renewal, and sanctification should manifest themselves in acts of justice, charity, and service in the wider world."[11]

Foster identifies three ways the Christian community expresses its corporate identity.[12] The first is a historical connection to ancestors of the faith that forms a spiritual embodiment connected by rituals and symbols pointing to a shared human experience. Though evolving in differing ways, denominational entities, locations, and times, Black Christian faith community life reflects a tradition of cultural forms of worship, music, preaching, and generations learning

---

8 Floyd-Thomas et al., "Christian Education in the Black Church Tradition," 152.

9 Raphael G. Warnock, *The Divided Mind of the Black Church: Theology, Piety, and Public Witness* (New York: New York University Press, 2014), 3.

10 Warnock, *The Divided Mind of the Black Church*, 3.

11 Robert M. Franklin, *Another Day's Journey: Black Churches Confronting the American Crisis* (Minneapolis: Fortress Press, 1997), 34.

12 Foster, "The Faith Community as a Guiding Image for Christian Education," 56.

to be faithful and seeking to maintain the tradition of enlivening hope and survival.[13]

The second aspect of identification is that of a corporate identity experienced relationally through structures and customs, which allow persons to be connected across time and space. This type of connection allows those in the Christian faith community to know God more clearly in interactions with one another. Critical for a community's identity is the way in which it shares not only structures and customs but also symbols of what it believes and treasures in ways that connect it to a broader community or the public. In this regard, Dale Andrews affirms that the Black Christian community has historically functioned according to a covenantal model with heavy emphasis on the biblical semblance of Black Churches as "a people of God. . . . [This] faith identity shaped personhood and people-hood into a covenantal understanding of their relationship to God that reclaimed and redefined their humanity."[14] Building on the activity of God appearing in scripture, this covenantal identity has continued to have implications for relationships beyond the faith community that include social reform and justice-seeking efforts.

Finally, the corporate community spontaneously experiences its identity as new life and energy are breathed into it through the action of a transcendent God who draws near. The Pentecost event is an example of a spontaneous happening that marked a new beginning for the community of faith by forging the church.

It is appropriate to highlight the current necessity of God's revelation that occasions the radical reformation of the corporate identity of the Black Church as the result of tendencies to capitulate to those who would impose silence and invisibility amid ongoing

13 Lincoln and Mamiya, *The Black Church in the African American Experience*, 7; and Floyd-Thomas et al., "Christian Education in the Black Church Tradition," 153.

14 Dale P. Andrews, *Practical Theology for Black Churches: Bridging Black Theology and African American Folk Religion* (Louisville, KY: Westminster John Knox, 2002), 90.

difficult issues of daily life. As Andrews insists, there is a current call for renewed "divine relationality that insists upon human relationality" that creates a covenant community centered on the transformation of humanity and the wholeness of God's people.[15]

A revelatory experience is needed through which the Black Christian faith community comes to know anew that it is known and sustained by God and is called to critically discern how best to confront dehumanizing forces in daily life. This requires new considerations of what it means to act on God's desire for social justice in the midst of the continuing realities of racism, poverty, violence, and generational separation fueled by tensions between adults and youth and by young people's disconnection from church.[16] What is really called for is the faith community's experience of divine inspiration and the formation of an intergenerational community of learning that inspires religious, social, and political activism. The following sections of this chapter will turn to the formation and functions of a viable community of learning and practice, the role of religious education, and uses of pedagogical models within it.

Formation and Functions of Communities of Learning and Practice

The discipline of education often discusses the topics of both *communities of learning* and *communities of practice*, terms that are often used interchangeably. Some scholars agree that the goal of the learning community is to create an environment in which learning and deepening understanding can occur, and they emphasize

15 Andrews, *Practical Theology for Black Churches*, 104.

16 Ginwright makes the point that "African American adults from the civil rights generation often cannot fully understand Black youth culture, and many are disconnected from the political issues that are most important to African American youth." Shawn Ginwright, "Toward a Politics of Relevance: Race, Resistance and African American Youth Activism," SSRC, June 7, 2006. Accessed on http://ya.ssrc.org/African/Ginwright.

four characteristics of such communities: "Diversity of expertise among its members, who are valued for their contributions and are given support to develop; a shared objective of continually advancing collective knowledge and skills; an emphasis on learning how to learn; and mechanisms for sharing what is learned."[17] Other scholars have written more broadly about "communities of practice," defined by characteristics that reflect joint enterprise, mutual engagement, and shared repertoire, as well as participants learning through their engagement with each other and sharing of experiences.[18] However, practice is further defined here as intentional and defined action that responds to what is learned. Therefore, communities of practice are also called communities of action.

The philosophy of a learning community is based on instructional models of learning, and that of a community of practice is on production or increased performance; however, the two phrases are indeed used interchangeably and in association with other configurations of groups in which people and learning activities can be classified.[19] When one considers the historical role and current challenges of the Black Church to be a community of the faithful whose belief is put into action, it is appropriate for the purposes of this discussion to use the two phrases *community of learning* and *community of practice* interchangeably. How do these two aspects come together in ways that result in faith communities living out their faith in the public square and giving their faith a public voice?

---

17 Katerine Bielaczyc and Allan Collins, "Learning Communities in Classrooms: A Reconceptualization of Educational Practice," in *Instructional Design Theories and Models*, vol. 2, ed. C. M. Reigeluth (Mahwah, NJ: Erlbaum Associates, 1999), 269.

18 E. Wenger, *Communities of Practice: Learning and Identity* (Cambridge: Cambridge University Press, 1998).

19 Christopher Hoadley, "What Is a Community of Practice and How Can We Support It?," in *Theoretical Foundations of Learning Environments*, 2nd ed. (Abingdon, UK: Routledge, 2012), 287–300.

The Black Church, Religious Education, and Communities of Learning and Practice

Much attention is given to Black Churches as communities of learning and practice in the public sphere. In fact, Lawrence Jones reminds us that since their inception in the 1790s, Black Churches have been identified as central gathering points and communities of practice in literally every movement directed toward change for Black people.[20] This role evolves from the view that faithfulness to the Christian gospel they proclaim requires gathered communities of faith to be involved in the changing panorama of political, economic, social, demographic, educational, and cultural realities in which persons live out their lives.[21] The function of religious education has been and continues to be pivotal because it invites people's disclosure and acknowledgment of sociopolitical circumstances that require advocacy, engagement, and critical reflection. Further religious education explores methods and offers guidance about action. This also means that religious education guides communities of learning in the formation and demonstration of effective practices.

The role of the church as communities of learning and practice has typically occurred both within and beyond churches. Goal-directed action is typically seen as the outcome of learning. However, the actual engagement of communities in sociopolitical action becomes itself an educational endeavor of immense significance. While there is learning in the process of educational preparedness for action, learning also occurs in and as the result of action.

Religious Educational Activities in Churches

Prior to and through the civil rights movement, Black Churches were in the community and served as centers of community life. The people

20 Lawrence N. Jones, "Foreword," in *Mighty Like a River: The Black Church and Social Reform*, ed. Andrew Billingsley (New York: Oxford University Press, 1999), xiii.

21 Jones, "Foreword," xiv.

in the community were the church, and because of this interrelated functioning, the stories of individual and communal experiences of disrespect, violence, and injustice became personally and intimately known by the entire church body. Black Churches became communities of learning as they consciously noticed and critically reflected on biblically based social teachings and discerned responses to the impact of negative attitudes; gaps in social services; economic, health, and public educational insufficiencies; and breaches in political efficacy in the lives of members who resided in the community.[22]

The availability of integrated housing in city and suburban areas following the civil rights era resulted in some individuals' and families' movement to various locations beyond the vicinity of their church membership. Yet regardless of community locale, Black residents held in common continuing stories of racial bias, denigration, injustice, and the need for persistent attention to these issues. Churches needed to become communities of learning with an intentional focus on advocacy and sociopolitical ministry on behalf of a scattered community and those who became disconnected from the church. During and beyond the civil rights era, religious educational activity was carried out within many churches in the form of reflexive and discernment activity, or what may be described as *conscientization*, to use Paulo Freire's term. This activity signaled that when people became alive or conscious of how they have been dehumanized and misnamed or mislabeled by others, educational conscientization provided the power to create a new perspective on their predicament.[23] Moreover, through education, an oppressed community can be mobilized to participate in its own liberation.[24]

---

22 Reference to Black churches' and clergy's interpretations of Old and New Testament scriptures, prophetic material, and social teachings that gave rise to a broad range of political activities appears in Lincoln and Mamiya, *The Black Church in the African American Experience*, 202.

23 Paulo Freire, *Pedagogy of the Oppressed*, trans. Myra Bergman Ramos (New York: Continuum Publishing, 1992), 69.

24 Freire, *Pedagogy of the Oppressed*, 12.

This kind of learning from actual experiences became the basis for efforts of communities of practice or action and was undergirded by what Wilmore referred to as the "determination to survive"; it also moves not simply to "make do" but to a stance of "must do more."[25] The 1999 report of the study undertaken by Andrew Billingsley documents the engagement of Black Christian faith communities in action over time directed toward change so as to benefit Black life. The study recounts that the community's efforts in the 1950s and 1960s took the form of "social action and protests against the oppression from forces external to the Black community" resulting in civil rights legislation.[26] However, before and into the twenty-first century, church community actions centered more on internal strategies in the form of "social service or community development, addressing problems within the Black community."[27]

Churches have moved toward functioning as communities of learning and practice through educational pursuits such as health awareness programs, parenting classes, drug-abuse prevention forums, youth rites-of-passage programs, tutoring, AIDS support efforts, senior adult information resource centers, and the formation of Christian academies.[28] In another important way, religious education, then, has continued as a practice of "the Black Sacred Cosmos" in which both spiritual and public realms operate. This "public" role of Black religion and religious education is mandatory in confronting critical urgencies pervading Black life.[29] The emergence of this internal orientation to learning and action is also connected to an

---

25 Gayraud Wilmore, *Black Religion and Black Radicalism: An Interpretation of the Religious History of Afro-American People*, 2nd ed. (Maryknoll, NY: Orbis Books, 1982), 121.

26 Billingsley, *Mighty Like a River*, 89.

27 Billingsley, 89.

28 A range of educational endeavors appears in Billingsley, *Mighty Like a River*, 85–131.

29 References to the "Black Sacred Cosmos" appear in Lincoln and Mamiya, *The Black Church in the African American Experience*, 17; and C. Eric Lincoln, "Introduction," in Billingsley, *Mighty Like a River*, xix–xx.

in-church focus on contextually consistent religious education literature and study agenda.

Franklin summarizes a "politically empowering religious education" that was designed to meet "the cultural and political needs of a new generation . . . [and] facilitate the nurture of both Christian and Black identity."[30] These endeavors were often undergirded by materials published by Black religious educators that extended to educational forums and other practices carried out within churches. Moreover, these practices have tended to incorporate an instructional approach of the leader as "coach" and dialogical partner, particularly with youth, as a means of building self-esteem and agency by acknowledging and honoring their often-silenced voices.[31] Franklin draws on Dr. Kawanza Kunjufu, who emphasizes this necessary movement away from "instructors [who] specialize in dispensing information to the coach to a dialogical orientation."[32]

The dialogical methodology bears kinship to Freire's notion of creating a learning space where oppressed people can gather as a community, speak words that name their reality, and together seek to transform it.[33] It is "revolutionary praxis" that moves beyond a process where leaders among the oppressed realize that the group does not simply follow their guidance but is intricately involved in the discerning and decision-making processes.[34] For the leader to do otherwise is to model the oppressive action of the dominant culture. The oppressive culture maintains control and power by antidialogical processes, but the praxis of the oppressed group opens the door for transformative breakthroughs not only for the oppressed but also for the oppressor. The prerequisites for dialogue include a love for the people, humility, an intense faith in humankind, hope, and critical thinking.

30 Franklin, *Another Day's Journey*, 35.

31 Franklin, 35–36.

32 Franklin, 36.

33 Franklin, 69.

34 Franklin, *Another Day's Journey*, 107.

Prominent Black educator bell hooks also emphasizes the notion of engaged pedagogy as praxis that involves both reflection and action.[35] As an educator, she posits that in order to create a learning community within the classroom, the classroom itself should be a place that is life-sustaining and mind-expanding, enabling teachers and students to work together in partnership.[36] Seeing education as the practice of freedom, she believes that the classroom should be a place where teachers and students alike can become empowered and transformed as they dialogue in intimate, educational settings. In this way, she envisions dialogue as a pedagogical process that leads to liberation of the mind and results in transforming action.[37]

The views of Kunjufu reported by Franklin, Freire, and bell hooks have further roots in the early educational theory of John Dewey, who focused on the importance of the learner's experience in determining the degree to which education finds its relevancy. For Dewey, education cannot be effective unless it is based on the actual lived experience of the learner.[38] These perspectives give shape to the character of communities of learning and action that have begun and must continue to occur in Black Churches. The point here is that a clear pedagogy of action must exist that grows out of predefined rules of relationship and engagement in the community of learners. In these communities, leaders and learners share a common cause, value the contributions of every voice, and construct a plan of action that reflects unified wisdom. This pedagogical process is in fact constitutive of a community of learners *being* the community of practice while at the same time preparing for further action in the public sphere.

35 Barry Burke, "bell hooks on education," *The Encyclopedia of Informal Education*, last modified September 12, 2019, www.infed.org/mobi/bell-hooks-on-education.

36 Burke, "bell hooks on education."

37 Burke, "bell hooks on education."

38 John Dewey, *Experience and Education* (New York: Macmillan Publishing, 1938), 89.

Religious Education Activities Extending beyond Churches

Communities of learning and practice are needed beyond local congregations. The call for these communities is set forth in the 2006 document *The Covenant with Black America.* Beginning with an introduction by Tavis Smiley, followed by Marian Wright Edelman's purpose statement, the document lays out a national action plan to address critical concerns of Black Americans.[39] It was written as a roadmap to remind the Black community of its responsibility to create a sustainable and just world for successive generations. In the document, professionals from varied fields address issues of healthcare, public education, the justice system, community policing, affordable neighborhoods, democratic processes, immigrant roots, jobs, wealth and economic prosperity, environmental justice, and the racial divide.

Marian Wright Edelman emphasizes the imperative call to all leaders to act decisively in securing a bright future for our children.[40] The church was not excluded but rather deemed part of a coalition of preachers, parents, educators, social service providers, community leaders, and policy makers who must create a community of learning and acting to change troubling conditions in the lives of people of African descent in America. The wisdom contained in the document is a comprehensive guide for Black America in navigating key issues and concerns affecting Black communities. As a whole, it presents an educational curriculum that informs the learning and acting community about the agenda for Black America and facts about agenda topics; community, individuals, leaders, and elected official responsibilities; and examples of activists who are making a difference. Real-life examples consist of currently existing community programs with concrete actions directed toward transforming unjust realities.

The community-based initiatives reported in the volume were founded because people were tired of systemically imposed

---

39 The Tavis Smiley Group, Inc., *The Covenant with Black America* (Chicago: Third World Press, 2006).

40 Tavis Smiley Group, *The Covenant with Black America*, xiv.

injustices that wreaked havoc in the community and consequently rose up to do something about it. They formed learning communities that engaged in a process of reflection on their reality and became empowered to move into decisive action. For example, Maya Harris, in her essay about community-centered policing, said that if we "familiarize ourselves and our children with our rights and with local police personnel, and if we hold our elected officials responsible for adequate recruiting, hiring, and training community-conscious personnel and creating efficient police oversight mechanisms, then we can foster community-centered policing."[41] According to Cornel West, the *Covenant for Black America* is an "act of full-fledged Black self-determination as well as a call for each one of us to act and do something in order to be an organized force for good in our struggle for justice and freedom."[42]

Evidence shows that the Black Church and other community organizations have become collaborative communities of learning and action in response to specifically named challenges of Black people and urban life. Here are some examples.

The Kellogg Foundation Initiative

Evidence-based data on troubling circumstances of Black men and boys resulted in a task force founded in the early 1990s by the Kellogg Foundation. The initiative brought together a community of learning and action comprising ministers, scholars, and community leaders to respond to the crisis facing African American men and boys.[43] The foundation offered leadership grants that would allow community and grassroots organizers to collaboratively propose strategies for mediating positive life circumstances for young Black

41 Tavis Smiley Group, 92.

42 Tavis Smiley Group, 240.

43 Bobby William Austin, ed., *Repairing the Breach: Key Ways to Support Family Life, Reclaim Our Streets, and Rebuild Civil Society in America's Communities: An Executive Summary* (Dillon, CO: Alpine Guild, Inc., 1996), 16.

males and their families as well as creating intervention structures for boys in trouble.[44] The Black Church, through its leaders, was an invited part of the initiative since it is deemed a pivotal community organization with potential influence in promoting the social, economic, and political well-being of Black men and boys.

The efforts of the identified local community of learning and action were guided by a value-orientation of promoting self-respect for others and communal concern for neighbor. The goal of the work was to empower civic leadership among grassroots constituencies and foster civic and economic transformation.[45] Curriculum-building efforts were to be carried out by cultural and spiritual leaders.[46] Cultural leadership was designed to help Black men and boys see their contribution to society as necessary. Spiritual leadership was deemed pivotal in inspiring Black men's and boys' courage and hope to remake their personal existence and community life.

One Church One School

In 1992 the visionary Bishop Henry M. Williamson Sr., pastor of Carter Temple CME Church in Chicago and National President of Operation PUSH (Rainbow/Push Coalition), founded One Church One School (OCOS) in response to cries for attention to the mounting issue of school failures of Black children combined with issues of violence and other social ills. Beginning with the church's partnership with Ruggles Elementary School, situated a few blocks from the church, efforts expanded to include tutoring in reading and math, approaches to student behavioral modification, and parental supports.[47] Workshops for parents, children, and community leaders followed and have continued over the years with an emphasis on approaches to school, teacher, and student support;

44 Austin, *Repairing the Breach*, 9.

45 Austin, 11.

46 Austin, 39.

47 "OCOS History," One Church One School, accessed January 20, 2020, www.onechurchoneschool.org/history/.

skills-building for students in various academic areas; and immersion in creative arts.[48]

In 1994 the effort was "endorsed as an outreach ministry of the national church," following the presentation of it to the General Conference of the CME Church.[49] Subsequently, a network of communities of learning and action formed that included churches across the denominational spectrum and other organizations with the goal of partnering with schools.[50]

The Community's Journey to Black Lives Matter: Two Instigating Events

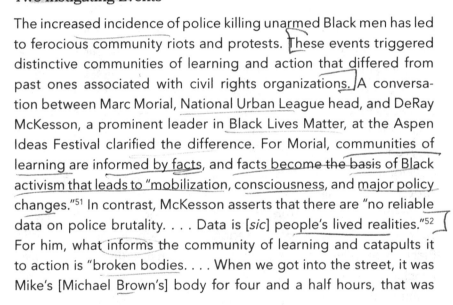

The increased incidence of police killing unarmed Black men has led to ferocious community riots and protests. These events triggered distinctive communities of learning and action that differed from past ones associated with civil rights organizations. A conversation between Marc Morial, National Urban League head, and DeRay McKesson, a prominent leader in Black Lives Matter, at the Aspen Ideas Festival clarified the difference. For Morial, communities of learning are informed by facts, and facts become the basis of Black activism that leads to "mobilization, consciousness, and major policy changes."[51] In contrast, McKesson asserts that there are "no reliable data on police brutality. . . . Data is [*sic*] people's lived realities."[52] For him, what informs the community of learning and catapults it to action is "broken bodies. . . . When we got into the street, it was Mike's [Michael Brown's] body for four and a half hours, that was

48 Examples of these events appear at www.onechurchoneschool.org/events/.

49 "OCOS History," One Church One School, www.onechurchoneschool.org/history/.

50 "OCOS History," One Church One School, www.onechurchoneschool.org/history/.

51 Conor Friedersdorf, "Generational Differences in Black Activism," *The Atlantic*, June 30, 2016, 3, www.theatlantic.com/politics/archive/2016/06/generational-differences-in-Black-activism.

52 Friedersdorf, "Generational Differences in Black Activism," 3.

real."[53] He stated that it isn't a tape of an incident that gets played on the news that prompts community action; rather, "I can tweet right now and I have 400,000 followers. . . . The space is different."[54] Importantly, McKesson does not denounce adult cooperation but calls for real partnership between generations.[55] These contrasting views of communities of learning and action provide important opening thoughts to the following two incidents leading up to the formation of the Black Lives Matter movement.

One incident, the tragic 2012 shooting of teenager Trayvon Martin, was one of many that set in motion the Black community's journey toward the Black Lives Matter movement. This event reminded Black mothers everywhere about the dangers of the world for their sons and the urgent need, insists Kelly Brown Douglas, for soul searching in our nation as the numbers of Black lives lost mount up.[56] In her examination of the "stand your ground" culture, she locates the seeds for the law in a myth of racial superiority and a narrative of exceptional identity.[57] In the Black community, the assassination of Trayvon and the acquittal of his killer was another notch in an ever-developing pattern in this country of disregard for Black lives and a subconscious belief in White superiority.

In the continuing struggles for freedom and justice in the "stand your ground" culture, Black people have risen up, and prophetic Black voices have emerged to hold the nation accountable to its own proclamation of exceptionalism.[58] They have inspired learning communities of people within and beyond the church whose refusal to let wrong reign is buttressed by a Black theology that insists God is a God of justice and freedom and that this God equips the

53 Friedersdorf, 4.

54 Friedersdorf, 4.

55 Friedersdorf, 5.

56 Kelly Brown Douglas, *Stand Your Ground: Black Bodies and the Justice of God* (Maryknoll, NY: Orbis Books, 2015), xiii.

57 Douglas, *Stand Your Ground*, 4.

58 Douglas, 207.

Black community with tools to survive and resist oppressing power. Douglas uses the term *signifyin'* to describe the Black community's capacity for survival. It further exemplifies the Black community's empowerment to speak truth to power and birth empowering and liberating educational strategies.[59]

The second incident was the assassination of Michael Brown in Ferguson, Missouri, which gave rise to a protest movement, led by a group of young activists with community clergy, that awakened an entire community of religious and other leaders.[60] Just as community involvement around this event was layered, there were also layers of learning. In Ferguson the law enforcement community stood under grave blame for a fellow officer's mishandling of the incident. Oppositional forces included the community of young activists, the clergy community who stood with them, the community of persons who tracked the incident through social media or came to the scene to stand in solidarity with the protestors, and other varied communities who were too afraid to say or do anything. The community of young activists refused to let the injustice go unnoticed. For months after Brown's death they gathered in front of the police station and chanted for justice, often marching into the early morning hours. Young people had already engaged in protests before the clergy joined them. When word spread that more of them were being arrested, the clergy also came and knelt outside of the police station, using their bodies to speak of their faith in justice but also using their bodies to shield the young activists from arrest.[61] This collaborative process on behalf of activists by clergy points to helpful cross-generational action from which activist groups, churches, and the larger community can benefit.

The learning and acting community of the protestors was organized around their desire to name an injustice, effect change, and

---

59 Douglas, 208.

60 Leah Gunning Francis, *Ferguson and Faith: Sparking Leadership and Awakening Community* (St. Louis: Chalice Press, 2015), 8.

61 Francis, *Ferguson and Faith*, 9.

have the Ferguson Police Department own the wrong that had been done. Interviews with some of the young people also suggested that their community was necessary because they were unclear about the role the church would play in speaking out against this grave injustice.[62] The clergy's standing with them, resisting taking over their cause, showing up on their behalf, and working with them in gaining platforms where the issues could be discussed and strategies developed gave some activists a very different perspective of the church than they previously held.[63] They learned that the clergy who stood with them embodied their faith and gave feet and hands to the words of scripture that guided their lives. The young protestors also learned that the clergy enabled them to lead and supported them in their work of liberation. The clergy's goal was not to take over the movement but rather to help spark it. One activist noted the clergy's involvement in this way: "They didn't try to take over or commandeer our protest. They gave us the space and the ability we needed, as young people, to shift the narrative in the direction we felt it should go. . . . I guess, bipartisanship between young and old people or people with different views is part of the movement."[64]

The group of clergy also became a learning community of sort who gained priceless insights from the group of young activists. Clergy, male and female, from varied denominational communions came together on Moral Monday to march against the injustice in Ferguson.[65] They learned (or perhaps relearned) from the young

activists that faith in action is risky. They also learned that God speaks sometimes in mysterious ways and through unexpected sources. The young activists sparked in the clergy a willingness to walk the walk as well as talk the talk. The practices of the clergy were seen in ways that were different and creatively relevant to the cause. Altars got moved out of the churches and onto the streets,

62 Francis, 61.
63 Francis, 63.
64 Francis, 65.
65 Francis, 94.

risk-taking behavior took the form of bodies in the street standing in solidarity with the activists, safe sanctuary became a practice of providing meeting and kitchen space for the movement, and the clergy practice of "letting go" was best expressed by stepping aside so that the young leaders could step up front.[66]

An even greater impact this movement had on the sparking of learning communities took place among educational church-based institutions and local congregations. Seminary leaders and pastors alike joined in the cause against racial injustice. Congregational leaders began to teach and preach a gospel that ignited members to become involved in the movement and to see the gospel's mandate to love in a different way. One pastor, reflecting on the impact of what happened in Ferguson, stated that the effectiveness of the church in the world requires that we are "willing to be where the people are and understand that the church is not just the place to bring the sinners to get saved. The church is the place to bring the saved to be empowered to go out into the world and be love."[67] This example reaffirms the understanding of a community of learning as a habitus within which data and other matters provide information needed to determine action while at the same time, action itself exists as a learning event.

Signs of Hope in the City: Ministries of Community Renewal

A final example of communities of learning and action that extend beyond the church is seen in outreach ministries of urban congregations. In *Signs of Hope in the City: Ministries of Community Renewal*, Robert D. Carle and Louis A. DeCaro highlight several of New York's most effective ministries that are reversing urban decay and revitalizing depressed communities. The power of these stories is seen in their practical theologies of urban ministry that equip people of faith to do creative and sustainable ministries in challenging city contexts. While stories of urban blight are pervasive, there is another side to

66 Francis, 157.
67 Francis, 151.

what is happening in the city, particularly in New York, where some of the most effective ministries are changing the landscape of hopelessness and despair.[68] Churches play a major role in urban renewal and community development in large cities. One community leader, in speaking about the power of the church, wrote, "If it weren't for the churches, nothing would be happening. This is the only really hopeful group in terms of development. The rest are fragmented, kept quiet, co-opted."[69]

Effective ministries in Black urban areas have traditionally given priority to the needs of the community. Pastor Gary V. Simpson described the ministry at Concord Baptist Church in New York as "a social outreach church where ministry opportunities are themselves worship stations."[70] The church has become a mission-minded community of learning where persons understand their work in the community as an extension of their worship. Following in the outreach legacy of the renowned Dr. Gardner C. Taylor, Simpson continues the tradition of public ministry established over a forty-year period that expanded its imprint in the community by forming nine not-for-profit corporations. Among them are a credit union, a nursing home, an elementary school, and a community development corporation.[71] The ministries spawned by this congregation make it one of the largest employers in the Brooklyn area and have brought hundreds of jobs to people in the community. Concord Baptist Church is only one example of a community of faith that, through visionary leadership, understands its role as a learning community whose faith must be put into action in the public space of the community.

---

68 Robert D. Carle and Louis A. DeCaro Jr., eds., *Signs of Hope in the City: Ministries of Community Renewal* (Valley Forge, PA: Judson Press, 1997), 2.

69 John Mollenkopf and Manuel Catells, eds., *Dual City* (New York: Russell Sage Foundation, 1991), 323.

70 Carle and DeCaro, *Signs of Hope in the City*, 42.

71 Carle and DeCaro, 43.

Assuring the Voices of the Young in Communities of Learning and Action

In the earlier focus on the journey to the Black Lives Matter movement, attention was given to generational differences and the collaborative cross-generational involvement occurring in Ferguson, Missouri. Added consideration is given here on assuring the voice of the young in communities of learning and action. These communities must be spaces where younger voices are heard and young leadership emerges. Dori Baker labels what is happening in some congregations that are connecting with and allowing the younger generation to lead as "greenhouses of hope." She states, "Churches with deep roots and ancient ways are catching glimpses of the future reflected in the eyes of their young. Teens and twentysomethings are seeing visions. When adults who love them embrace this glimmer, when they nurture these young leaders, churches engage in God's good work of making green a desert place."[72]

Baker points to communities of learning and action that intentionally give attention to the emerging vocations of young people. In the cases she describes, a learning community was formed around a common goal of allowing the callings and visions of young people to shape the life of the gathered faith community. In her report of a study of congregations, Baker indicates that researchers working with congregations had the aim of observing specific practices that foster particular ways of being open to and welcoming younger voices in the work of God.[73] The researchers discovered four core

72 Dori Grinenko Baker, ed., *Greenhouses of Hope: Congregations Growing Young Leaders Who Will Change the World* (Herndon, VA: The Alban Institute, 2010), 8.

73 Dorothy Bass makes the point that practices are "clusters of activities within which meaning and doing are inextricably woven, practices shape behavior while also fostering a practice-specific knowledge, capacities, dispositions, and virtues. Those who participate in practices are formed in particular ways of thinking about and living into the world." See Dorothy C. Bass, "Ways of Life Abundant," in *For Life Abundant: Practical*

practices in what is described as Vocation-CARE, including the following.

C–Create hospitable space to explore Christian vocation.
A–Ask self-awakening questions.
R–Reflect theologically on self and community.
E–Explore, enact, and establish ministry opportunities.[74]

These practices form a curriculum model for a learning and acting community whose aim is to call younger people to a vocation of ministry within and outside the church. The first practice is a way for the community to listen to youth, whether creating physical spaces for story-sharing to occur or embodying a welcoming spirit that assures young people that they belong. Opportunities must also exist in faith communities where persons can ask self-awakening questions. The second practice might occur in a small-group Bible study session, in one-on-one conversations, and at other times when persons are listening for God's voice and leading. As persons are able to ask questions about who God is and how God acts in life's experiences, they engage in the third practice of theological reflection, which puts their understanding of God in conversation with what is going on. In the final practice in the Vocation-CARE process, young people are included in all of the aspects of the church's life and public witness. This allows them to shadow and learn from adults and for adults to value the young people's unique leadership skills, gifts, and callings. When congregations' participatory space includes young people, they are teaching that "young people are a vital, necessary, life-giving part of the body of Christ."[75]

Regarding Black faith communities, Anne Wimberly uses the concept of the village (taken from the African Akan proverb, "It takes a village to raise a child") to describe the nature of the learning

Theology, Theological Education, and Christian Ministry, ed. Dorothy C. Bass and Craig Dykstra (Grand Rapids, MI: Eerdmans, 2008), 29.

74 Baker, *Greenhouses of Hope*, 30.

75 Baker, 31.

community. Village connotes a place where patterns of guidance, support, and community solidarity exist, and where values enable members of the community to gain a positive and hopeful identity amid challenges of being Black.[76] The needed role of the Black Church is to create a new paradigm of relationship with Black youth. Black youth must know that the church welcomes them and has created a space for their gifts and callings to incubate. Wimberly argues that different from what may be the world's perspective on their value and worth, Black youth need the church to affirm what is "real"—what God intends for their lives. As leaders in today's and tomorrow's world, "our youth have a role to play; and one of the village functions of local congregations is to help youth to discern and prepare to take their place in God's plan for transforming the world to what is real in God's eyes."[77]

Wimberly proposes a curriculum for the church to follow in becoming a learning community. In order for Black youth to see the church as vital for their present and future lives, the church must (1) embrace adolescence as God's gift of the youth among us; (2) make room to hear the youth and provide a space for their stories and experiences; (3) encourage adults to show gratitude for constructive criticism from the youth; (4) mentor the youth, becoming positive role models for them to emulate; and (5) stand as partners alongside youth as they grow into and discern God's will for their lives.[78]

Reflections: A Tool Kit for Forming a Community of Learning and Public Action

Cultural theory promotes a framework for talking about how learning and action communities are formed in the Black Church in order to exercise a public witness. It posits that "social groups possess a cultural repertoire or tool kit that reflects beliefs, ritual practices,

76 Baker, xviii.

77 Baker, xix.

78 Baker, xx.

stories and symbols that provide meaning and impetus for resource mobilization."[79] Cultural theorists indicate that the Black Church, as a community of learning, has cultural rituals such as songs, prayers, and other Christian symbols that are useful in framing social issues such that persons are moved to community action.[80] Building on the tenets of cultural theory and a large national cross-denominational sampling of Black congregations, Sandra L. Barnes discovered the direct and consistent relationship between prayer groups and gospel music in sparking community action.[81] Moreover, prayer, singing, preaching, scripture, and collection of funds in worship are used to garner support of and involvement in programs that ultimately bring about change in the community.[82] While these elements have different levels of impact for motivation toward community action, they all have some bearing on the process. Of particular interest is the consistent, positive influence of prayer groups in effecting community action. This clear message about the power and impact of prayer in the Black Church tradition is worthy of consideration for leaders who want to organize persons for community action.

How might religious education practices shape the church's public witness? Religious education is in the business of helping persons to wrestle with deep and important questions of faith that ultimately lead to change-directed practices or action. This wrestling also results in a theology that guides values and actions. The examples of community-based organizations and church-based groups mentioned in this chapter provide an array of curricular matters to be considered for the public witness of the Black Church.

The historical *role and purpose* of the Black Church as a bulwark in the community must not wane for the sake of functioning as a community of learning and acting that embodies a public theology.

79 Sandra L. Barnes, "Black Church Culture and Community Action," *Social Forces* 84, no. 2 (December 2005): 967.

80 Barnes, "Black Church Culture and Community Action," 969.

81 Barnes, 967.

82 Barnes, 972.

In such a community, people necessarily function as public theologians who reinvigorate in the present the skills of the past of grassroots organizing, being fluent in the religious idioms of the Black community, and speaking before a broader public.[83] One guiding strategy for communities of learning engaging in public theology is that the community must be formed around a cause rather than a group of people. The cause becomes the educational purpose for the community that drives its reflection and action. This was the case with the deaths of Michael Brown and Trayvon Martin at the hands of police. People were propelled to action by the cause. The expansive social outreach ministries of Concord Baptist Church in New York also speak to how members are driven by a theology where faith finds expression in action. Community ministry opportunities are causes synonymous with worship.

A second strategy for communities of learning engaging in public theology is to be open to shifts in the roles of *teachers and learners*. These roles will change as new wisdom bearers and young activists emerge who refuse to be silent in the face of injustice and are unafraid in standing on the front lines of opposition and speaking truth to power. In Ferguson, youth and young adults became teachers, and clergy discovered themselves as learners. Openness is needed in traditional churches to partner with voices and visionaries who may not be among their own ranks but whose virtues and values are consistent with the truth of the gospel message. From within its ranks, the church can honor young wisdom bearers and permit them to help give birth to what Dori Baker calls "greenhouses of hope." As these congregations give way to the arsenal of gifts from within, they become communities of learning and acting that make space for emerging leaders who will change the church, community, and world.

---

83 Vincent Lloyd, "Why We Need a Public Black Theology for the 21st Century," Religion Dispatches, September 20, 2016, https://religiondispatches.org/why-we-need-a-public-black-theology-for-the-21st-century/.

Communities of learning engaging in public theology recognize that the *context* for the practice of religious education is shifting out of the four walls of the church and into the streets. This guiding strategy suggests that a public faith should witness for a widening community of learning and action that takes seriously not simply hearing the word but doing the word. The witness of the Concord Baptist Church is a good example of faith in action as priority is given to the needs of the Brooklyn area. The mission-mindedness of that congregation allows them to see work in the community as an extension of their worship. The pastors who participated with the young activists in Ferguson reflected on that experience and were themselves transformed to preach in new ways—ways that would empower the believers to go out into the world and *be* love.

A final strategy for communities of learning engaged in public theology is to realize that the *content* of Christian education must focus on the quality of existence in this present world rather than on the hope that is in the world to come. Charles Foster identifies the sense of community as the greatest gift that the Christian heritage offers to the world because of its ability to confront the messages of fragmentation and violence.[84] This gift is lived out as we share a common ancestry, common heritage, and common experience, and as we listen for God's intent through scripture, stories, prayers, or creeds. Listening requires a turnaround and transformation in our relationship to God, others, and the world around us. It is this ability to listen for God's voice that makes a community responsive to God and the people around them.[85] Black Church faith certainly includes a theology of hope that "soon we will be done with the troubles of this world and we'll go home to live with God." But that faith is also grounded in the prophetic preaching and teaching tradition of Old Testament prophets like Amos, who cried, "Let justice roll on like a river, righteousness like a never-failing stream!" (Amos 5:25, NIV).

84 Charles R. Foster, *Educating Congregations: The Future of Christian Education* (Nashville: Abingdon Press, 1994), 57.

85 Foster, *Educating Congregations*, 60.

It is captured in the instructive mandate from the prophet Micah, who declared, "He has shown you, O mortal, what is good. And what does the LORD require of you? To act justly and to love mercy and to walk humbly with your God" (Micah 6:8, NIV). With passion, purpose, and promise, Christians in the Black Church faith tradition live into Raphael Warnock's "double consciousness" of individual salvation (piety) and enslavement (protest)—a tension that has given rise to a theology that understands the purpose of the church is both to save souls and transform the social order.

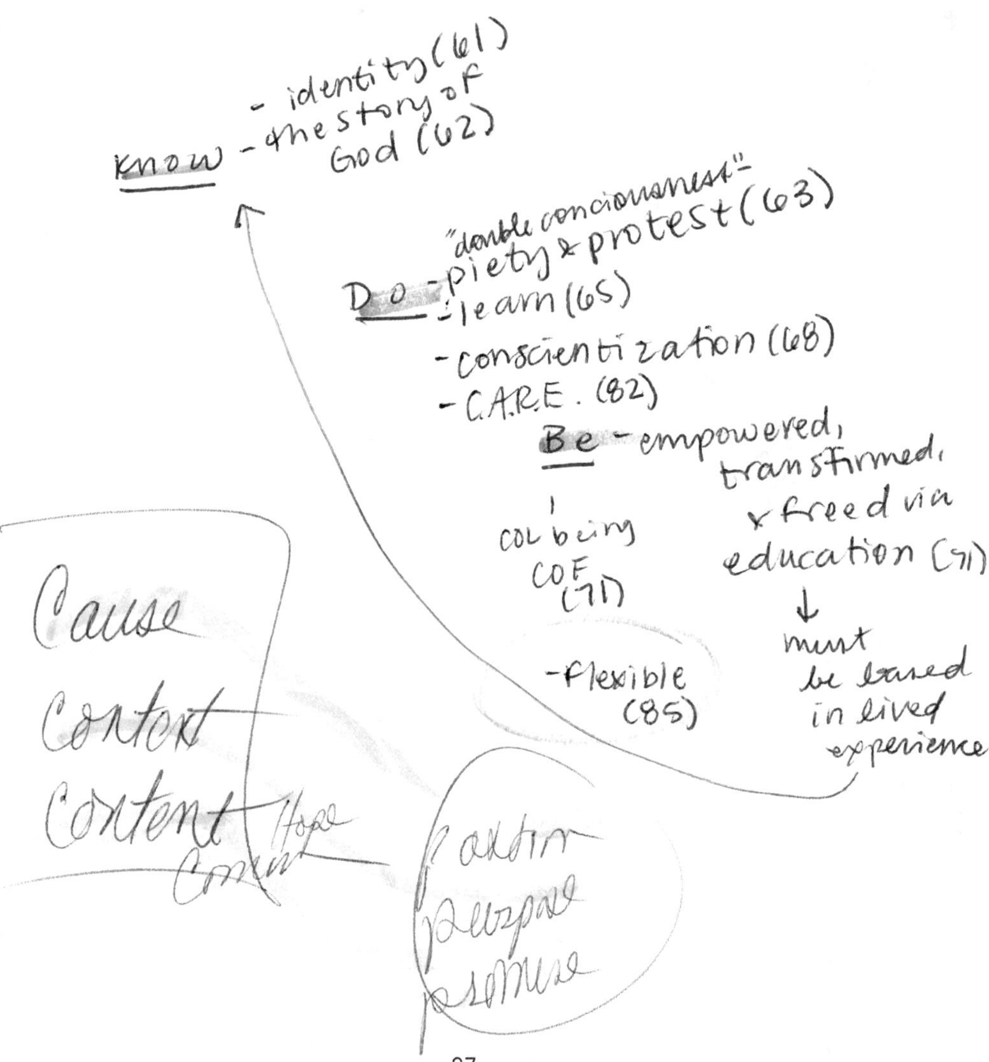

Religious Education in Response to Black Lives Matter

A Case for Critical Pedagogy

Joseph V. Crockett

> Please try to remember that what they believe, as well as what they do and cause you to endure, does not testify to your inferiority but to their inhumanity and fear.
>
> —James Baldwin, "A Letter to My Nephew"

Opening Views on Black Lives Matter and Religious Education

Black Lives Matter (BLM) has become a dominant statement of Black consciousness and mode of public advocacy and action prompted by alarming and increasing incidences of brutal treatment and killing of Black people by police. The following anonymous quotes, taken from the Pew Research Center website, express varied views and sentiments about the statement, the BLM movement evolving from it, and race in America.[1]

- Black lives matter, especially in Chicago!–Bernard Davis
- Just wondering about the slogans such as "Black Lives Matter" and "Blue Lives Matter," etc. It seems to me that these slogans aren't very good. . . . They tend to imply that the "intended" statement is "ONLY (insert color) lives matter." Of course, for most people that isn't what they want to say. What they want to say (and should say) is "(insert color) lives matter too!" In reality, ALL lives matter, but just saying that is [*sic*] response to "Black Lives Matter" is a bit dismissive. Just an opinion.
- BTW–Pew surveys should include Asian-Americans (part of ALL Americans).

According to the Pew Research Center study "How Americans View the BLM Movement" in summer 2016, support for and opposition to the BLM movement varies by race and political affiliation. Forty-three percent of Americans support the BLM movement. Among Blacks and Hispanics, almost two-thirds (65 percent) and one-third (33 percent), respectively, "strongly support" or "somewhat support" the BLM movement. Among Whites, 64 percent of Democrats "support strongly" or "support somewhat" the movement, while 52 percent of Republicans "oppose somewhat" or "oppose strongly" the movement. This makes clear the political divide.

Some opponents to the movement say, "White lives matter" or "Blue lives matter." Others argue, "All lives matter." The BLM movement presents a clear and forceful articulation of the power and importance of language and action. Educator Henry A. Giroux states, "If language is inseparable from lived experiences and

---

1 The responses are reactions appending Kim Parker, Juliana Horowitz, and Brian Mahl, "On Views of Race and Inequality, Blacks and Whites Are Worlds Apart," Pew Research Center, Social and Demographic Trends, June 27, 2016, www.pewsocialtrends.org/2016/06/27/on-views-of-race-and-inequality-Blacks-and-whiute-are-worlds-apart/.

from how people create a distinctive voice, it is also connected to an intense struggle among different groups over what will count as meaningful and whose cultural capital will prevail in legitimating particular ways of life."[2]

What is involved in the statement "Black lives matter" and the protest-centered BLM movement? What can religious educators learn from public protest and BLM? How might religious educators draw on insights of BLM and other public protest movements for engagement in teaching and learning? I argue that the BLM movement–and other nonviolent public protest movements–first present religious educators with a salient reminder that words matter. Words grounded in experience and animated by actions have the capacity–power–to reconstruct significations of difference, or "otherness," for use in framing and refreshing prophetic visions of teaching and learning. Public theology provides content to frame the meanings of those experiences and actions.

Nonviolent public protests are actions that incarnate the words, text, and context that can initiate and support learners' religious education and spiritual development. Both "words" and "text" refer to the tools used to enact action.[3] Key features of critical pedagogy–context, power, praxis, "otherness," and critical literacy–provide tools to examine the BLM movement and to appropriate those insights in formal education settings and beyond.

An analysis of the BLM movement provides public theologians and religious educators occasion for perceiving and resisting the domesticating assertions and practices they have come to accept as normative. Like public theology, at its best, the BLM movement critiques social and political self-interests that devalue significations of "otherness," intentionally and unintentionally. Both are concerned with challenging the unequal forms of stratification that are

---

2 Henry A. Giroux, *Pedagogy and the Politics of Hope: Theory, Culture, and Schooling–A Critical Reader* (Boulder, CO: Westview, 1997), 121.

3 Kenneth Burke, *A Grammar of Motives* (New York: Prentice Hall, 1945), xv, 6–7.

manifested in racism, sexism, classism, and the fears of difference—xenophobia. Indeed, the audacious use of the phrase "Black lives matter," even amid criticism and the courageous, unapologetic engagement in the BLM movement, moves beyond a claimed Black consciousness to a self-assertion of power to define and act on behalf of justice and human possibility. What comes through is an emancipatory mind-set and anticipated outcome, both of which invite reflection on religious education.

Religious educators often frame religious education from one of three perspectives: positive empiricism,[4] hermeneutic interpretation,[5] or conflict.[6] Like the principles of the BLM movement, critical pedagogy educators value ideas and actions for their emancipatory importance. Carter Godwin Woodson, though not labeled as such, was an early critical pedagogy pioneer. He critiqued the education of his day by saying forthrightly that it "does others so much more good than it does the Negro, because it has been worked out in conformity to the needs of those who have enslaved and oppressed weaker peoples."[7] He goes on to describe it as controlling rather than liberating:

---

4 For examples of positive empiricist approaches to education, see Mortimer J. Adler, *The Paideia Proposal: An Educational Manifesto* (New York: Macmillan, 1982); or James Michael Lee's educational trilogy found in *The Shape of Religious Instruction* (Birmingham, AL: Religious Education Press, 1971); *The Flow of Religious Instruction* (Birmingham, AL: Religious Education Press, 1975); and *The Content of Religious Instruction* (Birmingham, AL: Religious Education Press, 1985).

5 For works illustrating the hermeneutic approach to religious education, see Jack Seymour, *Educating Christians: The Intersection of Meaning, Learning, and Vocation* (Nashville: Abingdon Press, 1993); Gloria Durka, *Modeling God: Religious Education for Tomorrow* (Mahwah, NJ: Paulist, 1976); and Craig Dykstra, "The Formative Power of the Congregation," *Religious Education* 82, no. 4 (1987): 530–46.

6 See Jack L. Seymour and Donald Miller, eds., *Theological Approaches to Christian Education* (Nashville: Abingdon Press, 1990).

7 Carter G. Woodson, *The Mis-Education of the Negro* (Nashville: Winston-Derek Publishers, Inc., 1933), x–xi.

> When you control a man's thinking you do not have to worry about his actions. You do not have to tell him not to stand here or go yonder. He will find his "proper place" and will stay in it. You do not need to send him to the back door. He will go without being told. In fact, if there is no back door, he will cut one for his special benefit.[8]

Paulo Freire, Brazilian educator and a leader of critical pedagogy, wrote a seminal work, *Pedagogy of the Oppressed*, in which he addressed both public and religious contexts.[9] Freire articulated and promoted a problem-posing approach to learning that was constructively distinct from "banking" models of education and their domestication results. Banking models of education perceive learners as empty vessels into which knowledge is to be poured. Problem-posing pedagogies start with learners' current knowledge base and connect content to be learned to their daily experiences. This makes learning relevant. From their lived experiences, learners receive information that they describe, question, analyze, and use to construct creative solutions to matters affecting their existence.

One thread that joins together these secular and religious educators is that their pedagogies are grounded in works of emancipatory teaching and learning for justice. Or, to use Joe L. Kincheloe's words, it is necessary that "educators deal not only with questions of schooling, curriculum, and educational policy, but also with social justice and human possibility."[10] Religious educators and teachers who ascribe to critical pedagogies desire that learners gain the power to control their own lives in solidarity with a justice-oriented community.[11] Public theologians and religious educators who take up a critical pedagogical approach to learning and teaching also

---

8 Woodson, *The Mis-Education of the Negro*, xi.

9 Paulo Freire, *Pedagogy of the Oppressed*, trans. Myra Bergman Ramos (New York: Continuum Publishing, 1992), 69.

10 Joe L. Kincheloe, *Critical Constructivism Primer* (New York: Peter Lang, 2005), 7.

11 Kincheloe, *Critical Constructivism Primer*, 6-7.

do so as a prophetic vocation. Or, to state it another way using bell hooks's words, as teachers "educate as a practice of freedom,"[12] they are sharing in a prophetic vocation. Words grounded in experience and animated in actions possess the capacity to transform constrained individuals and domesticated educational systems into prophetic visions of justice for teaching and learning.

In the following sections, expanded attention will be given to the Black Lives Matter movement, including situating it in a historical framework and connecting it in a more specific way first to critical pedagogy and then directly to religious education. Brief comments will follow on what religious educators can offer the BLM movement.

BLM Movement Historically Situated

The BLM movement may be seen within a broader background of public protest actions as a means of pursuing human freedom and a more just world.

Public Protests

Public protests and nonviolent actions can be legitimate, responsible, and just forms of critical pedagogy and praxis. In his 1849 essay "Civil Disobedience," Henry David Thoreau, impassioned abolitionist, points to the efficacy of protest in response to slavery in Massachusetts. For him, "action from principle, the perception and the performance of right, changes things and relations; it is essentially revolutionary, and does not consist wholly with anything which was."[13]

---

12 bell hooks, *Teaching Critical Thinking: Practical Wisdom* (New York: Routledge, 2010), 182.

13 It is instructive that earlier in the essay, Thoreau disavows the political organization of the government that is "the slave's government also." He goes on to state that "all men recognize the right of revolution; that is, the right to refuse allegiance to, and to resist, the government, when its tyranny or its inefficiency are great and unendurable." Thoreau's views of

Thoreau's writings were echoed in the nonviolent direct actions of Martin Luther King Jr. as the civil rights movement struggled against the evils of inequality in pursuit of civil and human rights for all. Martin Luther King Jr., in his "Letter from a Birmingham Jail," writes of nonviolent direct action as a form of protest and means of dramatizing what must not be ignored. For King, an unjust law was any law that denigrated human personality; that led a person or group to feel or perceive themselves as superior, leaving others captured in a sense of inferiority; and that substituted the "I-thou" relationship established by the Creator for an "I-it" relationship that permitted some individual or group to treat another individual or group as a thing.[14]

Years before King took to the national stage to protest racial discrimination and economic inequalities, Ida B. Wells-Barnett, in the 1880s, filed a lawsuit against a railroad company in response to her ejection from a Whites-only "ladies'" car. But it was Rosa Parks's defiant act of refusing to move from her seat demanded by a White man in the 1950s that sparked a bus boycott, a citywide economic protest against segregated bus policies in Montgomery, Alabama. From December 5, 1955, to December 20, 1956, and more than a month after the US Supreme Court ruled the Montgomery bus system unconstitutional, protestors refused to support Montgomery's segregated transportation policy.[15]

---

civil disobedience appear in Henry David Thoreau, "Civil Disobedience," in *The Major Essays of Henry David Thoreau*, ed. Richard Dillman (Albany, NY: Whitson, 2001), 53.

14 King's views on civil disobedience penned in a Birmingham jail appear in Martin Luther King Jr., "Letter from a Birmingham Jail," in *Why We Can't Wait*, Martin Luther King Jr. (Boston: Beacon, 1963), 85–109.

15 The social activism of Ida B. Wells-Barnett and Rosa Parks appears in Christina Greene, "Women in the Civil Rights and Black Power Movements," American History, *Oxford Research Encyclopedias*, November 2016, https://oxfordre.com/americanhistory/view/10.1093/acrefore/9780199329175.001.0001/acrefore-9780199329175-e-212; and Darlene Clark

In the 1960s Fannie Lou Hamer engaged in civil rights protests, informed, if not directly motivated, by a hysterectomy performed on her by a White doctor without her knowledge or consent in order to satisfy Mississippi's plan to reduce the state's population of impoverished Blacks. Hamer became a principal organizer of the Student Nonviolent Coordinating Committee (SNCC) to help register Black Mississippians to vote. She gained insights from working with SNCC about connections between registering Black voters and other aspects of US political structures. Her leadership in a protest movement for racial equality prepared her to become a cofounder of the Mississippi Freedom Democratic Party. Through her tombstone epitaph, "I'm sick and tired of being sick and tired," Hamer continues to cry out from the grave to protesters yet unborn.[16]

Public protest movements are not an exclusive province of Western society, nor are public protests limited to the work of a group. Enslaved fugitive, novelist, playwright, and historian William Wells Brown protested the Jim Crow laws after his return to the United States from Europe, where he had experienced an integrated society.[17] The Archbishop of San Salvador, Oscar Romero, protested by becoming a voice for the voiceless in his documentation and publication of thousands of murders, tortures, and kidnappings taking place in El Salvador in the 1970s. Nelson Mandela, in his 1964 speech "I Am Prepared to Die," forcefully articulated that his engagement in protest and dissent against the South African system of apartheid was influenced not by foreigners or communists but by the stories of his elders.[18]

Hine, ed., *Facts on File Encyclopedia of Black Women in America: Social Activism* (New York: Facts on File, 1997).

16 The journey of Hamer toward and into civil rights activism is chronicled in Kay Mills, *This Little Light of Mine: The Life of Fannie Lou Hamer* (New York: Dutton, 1993).

17 William Wells Brown, *Narrative of William W. Brown, A Fugitive Slave, Written by Himself* (Boston: The Anti-Slavery Office, 1847).

18 Nelson Mandela, "I Am Prepared to Die," April 20, 1964, Statement at the Rivonia Trial, African National Congress, www.sbs.com.au/news/transcript-nelson-mandela-speech-i-am-prepared-to-die.

When public theologies are connected to critical pedagogies and interrogate routine ideas and normative practices associated with social and political issues, they often take the form of protest. Religious educators have opportunities to draw upon public theologies, protest movements, and critical pedagogical practices to promote a prophetic vision that is grounded in experience, is animated by reflective actions, and has the capacity to reconstruct significations of difference–"otherness."

At their best, these factors–public theology and critical pedagogy–are rooted in emancipated practices in efforts to pursue human freedoms in a more just and equitable world. As religious educators mutually engage with learners in struggles against oppressive policies and dominating practices, their joint actions have the possibility of dissolving the teacher/learner dichotomy. The relationship between teacher and learner is changed. Such relational experiences provide a basis for extending alternative patterns of living with others. As educators and students unite to petition for justice and equity, they support the well-being of all, while moving beyond the dichotomous we/they, insider/outsider social arrangements and ways of understanding.

Exemplars such as Henry David Thoreau and Fannie Lou Hamer have taught, and people have witnessed important insights and parallels among, the three key aspects of public theology, public protest, and critical pedagogy. All three aim to challenge and contest inequities and injustices. Past nonviolent public protest movements prepared the path for understanding and supporting new forms of dissent, like the BLM movement, toward the fulfilment of a prophetic vision of freedom and justice for all.

Black Lives Matter

BLM was conceived and organized in the spirit of prior public protest movements. Alicia Garza, Patrisse Cullors, and Opal Tometi began what became the BLM movement in 2014 in response to the killing of seventeen-year-old African American Trayvon Martin in

Sanford, Florida, and the fatal shootings of other Blacks. It is important to remember the unfolding events. In the case of Trayvon Martin, George Zimmerman, a White man, fatally shot Trayvon Martin on February 26, 2012. Zimmerman was a neighborhood watch coordinator in the gated community where he lived. Trayvon Martin was living in the same community with relatives. Zimmerman claimed that he shot Martin in self-defense even though Martin did not possess a weapon. During the trial, the defense lawyers turned the case from a trial about Zimmerman's use of deadly force to an attack on Trayvon Martin under a Florida statute, "stand your ground." The prosecutor's tactics, in principle, put Martin on trial posthumously for his own death. Martin's killer was found not guilty and set free. The BLM movement sought redress not simply for the outrageous miscarriage of justice in this case but for the daily incidents in the world where "Black lives are systematically and intentionally targeted for demise."[19]

The BLM movement is a public protest effort informed by belief in Black self-determination. It promotes the human dignity and rights of Blacks against the pernicious persistence of state-sanctioned acts of violence, as well as the goal of a "world free of anti-Blackness, where every Black person has the social, economic, and political power to thrive."[20] The BLM movement is a chapter-based organization across five regions of the United States (North Coast, East Coast, West Coast, Midwest, South) and Canada.[21] Thirteen guiding principles inform the activities and practices of the BLM movement. Those principles include affirmations that BLM is unapologetically

19 Alicia Garza, "A Herstory of the #BlackLivesMatter Movement," The Feministwire, October 7, 2014, https://thefeministwire.com/2014/10/Blacklivesmatter-2/.

20 "What We Believe," Black Lives Matter, accessed January 21, 2020, https://Blacklivesmatter.com/about/what-we-believe/.

21 For a current listing of chapters, go to https://blacklivesmatter.com/chapters/.

Black, queer, and transgender affirming, is intergenerational, stands for diversity, and works for restorative justice.[22]

These and other principles lead them to engage in dialogue, action, and reflection to uphold human worth and dignity of Blacks everywhere. Through loosely coupled networks, the BLM movement makes use of collective action to dramatize unjust increases of surveillance and other social controls in communities of color. It organizes rallies to protest mass incarceration and other state-sanctioned systems of control that disproportionately strip away the rights and dignity of Black and brown individuals. Central to its activity is presenting a sociopolitical critique of ideologies and operations that sanction and enforce the militarization of American police forces as the state's remedy to social, political, and economic inequalities in urban communities across the United States. The BLM movement gives voice to a prophetic vision of unity in diversity through loving engagement–the embodiment and practice of justice, liberation, and peace with others.[23]

Black Lives Matter and Critical Pedagogy

What can religious educators learn from the BLM movement? What might religious educators contribute to the BLM movement? Critical pedagogy is an educational philosophy that allows for an examination of the BLM movement on terms consistent with its aims of human liberation and practices of justice. Promoters of critical pedagogies, like members of the BLM movement, work to correct unequal stratifications in society, particularly those social arrangements related to race, gender, and class. On the one hand, critical pedagogy seeks to identify educational processes, mechanisms, and challenges that perpetuate and promote social domination, injustices,

---

22 The principles appear in "What We Believe," Black Lives Matter, https://Blacklivesmatter.com/about/what-we-believe/.

23 "What We Believe," Black Lives Matter, https://Blacklivesmatter.com/about/what-we-believe/.

and inequalities. On the other hand, critical pedagogy strives to empower teachers and learners to transform unjust societal relationships and structures for emancipatory learning and teaching so that learners may realize and embody their full humanity.[24]

The BLM movement demonstrates that words matter. The movement grounds words in experiences and animates actions through public protest to reconstruct ideologies, policies, and practices that devalue differences through significations of "otherness." Five features of critical pedagogy help explore the activities and efforts of the movement to pursue a prophetic vision of justice: context, power, praxis, otherness, and critical literacy. In fact, these qualities are valued aspects of both progressive religious educators and the BLM movement. Here, brief descriptions of these key elements of critical pedagogy are presented as each factor bears upon the issues that public theologians frame. How religious educators might employ these features in teaching as public theology is also discussed.

Context

Critical theory educators comprehend context in terms of micro- and macroenvironments and the interactions between them. Microenvironments refer to elements of the classroom setting such as personnel, material resources, tasks, challenges, and opportunities within that physical setting. Macroenvironments, the social, cultural, and historical situation of persons enacting activities and events,[25]

---

24 Aspects of the nature and goals of critical pedagogy are explored in Paulo Freire, *Pedagogy of the Oppressed*; Michael W. Apple, *Ideology and Curriculum*, 2nd ed. (New York: Routledge, 1990); and Michael W. Apple, *Power, Knowledge, Pedagogy: The Meaning of Democratic Education in Unsettling Times* (Boulder, CO: Westview, 1998); Peter McLaren, *Critical Pedagogy and Predatory Culture: Oppositional Politics in a Postmodern Era* (New York: Routledge, 1995); Giroux, *Pedagogy and the Politics of Hope*; and Kincheloe, *Critical Constructivism Primer.*

25 See James V. Wertsch, *Mind in Action* (New York: Oxford University Press, 1998), 24.

determine and regulate the resources of the community or state. The focus for critical pedagogic educators is the interactions between these entities as they advance or inhibit teaching and learning as public theology. Learners' lived experiences—their actions and interactions in interpersonal, communal, and societal settings—provide important content for public theologies.

The BLM movement understands the context in which Blacks exist and the importance of this context in the struggle for human liberation. To summarize Garza, Blacks exist in a state of violence. Their situation robs them of "basic human rights and dignity. They are surrounded by poverty and genocide. . . . One million Black people are segregated, isolated, and caged. . . . Black women continue to bear the burden of a relentless assault on their children and families. It is a place where Black queer and transgender folk bear a unique burden in a hetero-patriarchal society."[26] Members of the BLM movement investigate the dynamics of classrooms and communities to identify and alter dead-end, life-suffocating trajectories. Teachers and learners, from this theoretical approach, interrogate learners' experiences that occur beyond the schoolhouse or church setting as part of the classroom curriculum. They understand and appreciate that the lives of learners are valuable texts for exploration.

Critical pedagogical educators assert that the educational enterprise is forever embedded in contexts of challenges and possibilities. Each learning setting, whether secular or religious, has a particular history. It is not only the address of the property but the periphery of the situation—the background and scene—that contribute to the making of educational processes, procedures, and policies. The context has a history, but it is not unchangeable. Every context has a trajectory, even though the outlook does not negate an alternative future. In it learner-centered questions are raised: Who is doing what to whom? How are resources—from textbooks to physical facilities to lunch meals—distributed and accessed? Who makes decisions that shape students' learning

26 Garza, "A Herstory of the #BlackLivesMatter Movement."

opportunities? Where, when, and how are those decisions made? Who benefits and who pays for those benefits and resources? Context is important.

Power

Power is an important feature of critical pedagogy. "Power" refers to the material authority to direct *and* to actualize invisible capacity to influence something or someone(s). Power affects the effect.[27] It is operative in the work of public protest movements, public theology, and religious education. All education, to some degree, is political activity. Every act of critical pedagogy strives to empower learners to construct equitable communities and to challenge and dismantle unjust and unequal power relations.[28] Religious educators need to acknowledge that teaching and learning involve encounters with power. Added attention must also be given to ways power functions to ameliorate hurt foisted on certain students in schools.

Kincheloe critiques the nature of power particularly evident in schools as a means of positing a needed direction toward educational democratization.[29] "Ideological power" and "hegemonic power" are appropriate expressions to use in describing dominant views of "'others' only through the lenses of dominant (often White,

---

27 This view of power follows the thought and writings of Walter Wink. His view of power moves beyond a binary construction–the inner or outer aspect of power–to a unitary view of the term. From a unitary, integral view of power, both dimensions–inner and outer, tangible and intangible, spiritual and material–exist together. See Walter Wink, *Engaging the Powers: Discernment and Resistance in a World of Domination* (Minneapolis: Fortress Press, 1992); and Walter Wink, *Naming the Powers: The Language of Power in the New Testament* (Philadelphia: Fortress Press, 1984).

28 Kincheloe, *Critical Constructive Primer*, 9.

29 Joe L. Kincheloe, "The Foundations of Democratic Educational Psychology," in *Rethinking Intelligence: Confronting Psychological Assumptions about Teaching and Learning*, ed. Joe L. Kincheloe, Shirley R. Steinberg, and Leila E. Vallaverde (New York: Routledge, 1999), 1-26.

Western European, male, middle–or upper-middle class culture."[30] In this view, alternate or contextual-specific knowledge, thought, and reasoning are dismissed, and in fact, difference is regarded as a deficit, giving rise to the belief and treatment of persons as incapable. This treatment hinders persons, often the poor, non-White, working-class, and lower-socioeconomic-class individuals, in gaining the power needed to survive and thrive in society. The dominant power works to constrict views of human capacity and diversity while at the same time creating environments of discomfort and negative interpersonal dynamics.[31] What Kincheloe describes is literally designed to set in motion the prevailing and unjust dilemma that has come to be known as the school-to-prison pipeline for Black children and youth as well as what Michelle Alexander calls "the new Jim Crow," in which "marking Black youth *as* Black criminals is essential to the functioning of mass incarceration as a racial caste system."[32] The formation of this trajectory falls in the category of the exercise of "disciplinary power."

Disciplinary power refers to explicit manifestations of control, from expulsions from school to the institution of a militaristic state. Actually, disciplinary power and control may be as overt as screening monitors at a school entrance or as covert as assessing student readiness behind closed doors. Disciplinary power authorizes administrators to set the rules for what constitutes a classroom infraction and gives educational administrators the ability to determine the policies and to design the practices and procedures to implement educational goals and to guard against its interruptions.[33]

---

30 Kincheloe, "The Foundations of Democratic Educational Psychology," 2.

31 Kincheloe, 2–3.

32 Michelle Alexander, *The New Jim Crow: Mass Incarceration in the Age of Colorblindness*, rev. ed. (New York: New Press, 2010), 200.

33 Joe L. Kincheloe, "Postformalism and a Literacy of Power: Elitism and Ideology of the Gifted," in *The Praeger Handbook of Education and Psychology*, ed. Raymond Horn and Joe L. Kincheloe, vol. 4 (Westport, CT: Praeger, 2007), 935.

BLM stands against these forms of power–ideological, hegemonic, and disciplinary–in the day-to-day execution of its work as it struggles for restorative justice. BLM's critique of individuals and institutions that promote misogynists, haters of gays and queers, as well as those who perpetuate racism and various forms of racial bigotry are rooted in understandings of the use and misuse of power. Garza provides an example of the subtleties of ideological and hegemonic powers at work in her account of the early days of the BLM movement:

> I was surprised when a community institution wrote asking us to provide materials and action steps for an art show they were curating, entitled "Our Lives Matter." When questioned about who was involved and why they felt the need to change the very specific call and demand around Black lives to "our lives," I was told the artists decided it needed to be more inclusive of all people of color. I was even more surprised when, in the promotion of their event, one of the artists conducted an interview that completely erased the origins of their work–rooted in the labor and love of queer Black women.[34]

The forms of ideological and hegemonic power that the BLM movement contests are the same forms of power public theology addresses when it connects teachings of biblical Hebrew prophets to the political and social conditions of the day. As institutional standards regulate accreditation, they also perpetuate a particular worldview. When religious educators or public theologians pronounce ahistorical truths as universal principles, they are exerting force to diminish or ignore the particularities of human experiences, often under a call for harmony and unity. In these situations they are practicing hegemony. Framed and supported by hidden dimensions of power, their external manifestations are routinely "nonegalitarian and asymmetrical." Such misuse of power calls everyone

34 Garza, *A Herstory of the #BlackLivesMatter Movement.*

involved in an educational endeavor to engage in self-examination. When oppressed people are restricted from exercising their power to use words that are grounded in their experiences to articulate their significations of difference, justice is denied.

Praxis

A third significant feature of public theology, the BLM movement, and critical pedagogy is a distinct type of critical reflection, which Freire calls "praxis." This distinctive form of reflection is dynamic, not static,[35] and offers to transform conditions that surround the lives of disenfranchised people. As Freire states, "Human activity consists of action and reflection: it is praxis, it is transformation of the world."[36]

The BLM movement agenda is to interrogate the ideological, political, and cultural normative practices that privilege the powerful while also critiquing the practices of those who struggle to be empowered. The initiatives of the movement operate beyond the normative social, political, and cultural circles that commonly participate in legitimizing public actions. Through critical reflection, marginalized participants in the movement gain insight into the hegemonic contradictions that relegate them to positions of powerlessness. Even the movement's name–Black Lives Matter–offers opportunities for critique of the normative practices that establish and sustain domesticating structures that surround its activities and acknowledge the privileged positions that exist in relation to peoples of the African diaspora. The content and perspectives of public theology and its operatives are not immune from the misuse of power.

---

35 Peter Mayo interprets Freire's conceptualization of praxis "as the dialectical relationship between consciousness and the world, reflected in the pedagogical approach . . . a process entailing action–reflection–transformative action." See Peter Mayo, *Liberating Praxis: Paulo Freire's Legacy for Radical Education and Politics*, Critical Studies in Education and Culture Series, ed. Henry A. Giroux (Westport, CT: Praeger, 2004), 48.

36 Freire, *Pedagogy of the Oppressed*, 123.

Truly, all lives matter. But as indicated previously, language is essential and is necessarily a mediating tool of protest and dissent. Words grounded in experiences can awaken consciousness to ideologies of oppression that banish many people to the fringes of society. The BLM movement in name and action challenges those in power to surrender the ideologies that have perniciously privileged a few while the masses are constricted in their ability to pursue their hearts' desires. Critical pedagogy centers on critique and reflection that lead to transformative action.

Otherness

The fourth feature of critical pedagogy addressed in the BLM movement is its critique of ideologies that affirm and endorse particular constructions of identity while denouncing other forms by significations of difference and "otherness." Some differences are beyond human influence and control. Other differences occur through human activity.

BLM supporters understand otherness as a force of "oppositional politics in a postmodern era."[37] These supporters, informed by BLM movement guiding principles such as "unapologetically Black," "transgender affirming," and "queer affirming," refuse to permit difference to be reduced to an appearance of similarities or to discussions of essence.[38] They affirm the movement's refusal to diminish the worth of others and the need not to qualify or defend the position that is held. In short, the BLM movement is committed to "uplift[ing] Black trans folk, especially Black trans women."[39] This commitment aligns with Giroux's overall emphasis in critical

---

37 See McLaren on the postmodern character of labels. He argues that by perspectival definition labels are illusive, unstable, shifting, and transitory in nature and dependent on the context and community in which words are spoken and received. McLaren, *Critical Pedagogy and Predatory Culture*, 126.

38 Giroux, *Pedagogy and the Politics of Hope*, 42.

39 Garza, *A Herstory of the #BlackLivesMatter Movement*.

pedagogy on the embrace of differences and physical, social, and cultural border crossing as contributors to quality public life.[40] Moreover, it draws attention to language beyond heteronormativity that helps to denote persons as actors and recipients in pursuits of justice.[41]

Responses to the Black Lives Matter movement suggest that the name of the movement alone is a tour de force. Some are moved to defend their identities, which offer them places of privilege ("White Lives Matter"). Some are motivated to protect their positions of power, which afford them hegemonic authority ("Blue Lives Matter"). Still others are led to maintain their social location by reducing all issues of injustice, all matters of inequality, and other forms of social stratification that benefit some and exclude and marginalize others to the least common denominator ("All Lives Matter"). In each instance, the name *Black Lives Matter* provides religious educators and public theologians opportunities to challenge, dislodge, and hopefully instigate the deconstruction of ideologies and normative structuring policies and processes that result in unequal advantages for some at the expense of the "others."

Religious educators who engage public theology recognize learners' distinctive characteristics and teach to facilitate educational

---

40 Giroux, *Pedagogy and the Politics of Hope*, 42.

41 In their chapter, Winslade, Monk, and Drewery describe three principles in moving beyond heteronormativity, including language, positioning focuses on attention to power dynamics, and deconstruction dealing with challenging exclusionist tendencies inherent in heteronormativity. See John M. Winslade, Gerald D. Monk, and Wendy J. Drewery, "Sharpening the Critical Edge: A Social Constructionist Approach in Counselor Education," in *Constructionist Thinking in Counseling Practice, Research, and Training*, Counseling Development Series, 3, ed. Thomas L. Sexton and Barbara L. Griffin (New York: Teachers College Press, 1997), 223–45. Also see a framework for queer pedagogy set forth by Michael Seal, "Pedagogic Framework for Interrupting Heteronormativity," in *The Interruption of Heteronormativity in Higher Education: Critical Queer Pedagogies* (Cham, Switzerland: Palgrave Macmillan, 2019), 49–68.

opportunities that befit prophetic visions of human freedom. As religious educators take up the nurturing, developmental, ethical, and missional aspects of an educational enterprise, vigilant attention must be afforded to those with self-perceptions of otherness or who have been assigned to categories of "otherness." Concern for difference and otherness is important because classifications affect identity development and individual and collective life prospects. The meanings we attribute to "otherness" have important consequences for learners as well as teachers. Otherness can be celebrated and privileged, or difference and otherness can carry the scars of stigmatization, leaving learners disenfranchised from educational opportunities and its benefits.

Critical and Religious Literacy

The final feature of critical pedagogy is the role of critical literacy in public theology for achieving transformative justice. Critical literacy refers to emancipatory processes of teaching and learning in which actors engage in close readings of a text in dialectical conversation with the macroenvironment surrounding them.[42] McLaren advances this view when he writes that critical literacy is "a process whereby a person becomes empowered to unveil and decode the ideological dimensions of texts, institutions, social practices and cultural forms such as television and film, in order to reveal their selective interests."[43] Critical literacy corrects "false consciousness," whose proponents assert that knowledge is a neutral objective and exists separated from social, political, and economic processes that benefit some (the privileged powerful) at the expense of others (the oppressed and marginalized).

The BLM movement steadfastly challenges renderings of false consciousness that produce unequal access to the marginalized whether by race, gender, queer or transgendered, disability,

42 Paulo Freire and Donaldo Macedo, *Literacy: Reading the Word and the World* (Westport, CT: Bergin & Garvey, 1987), 49.

43 McLaren, *Critical Pedagogy and Predatory Culture*, 307.

incarcerated, or released from prison. It resists the myths behind labels that include some individuals and groups while excluding others and protests against and opposes the systems and structures that dismantle equal opportunities for all to achieve. It operates to expose the privileged positions of heterosexuals at the expense of sidelining queer and transgender folk, particularly when the identities of queer and transgender people are constructed and labeled in terms of "otherness," when the "other" is devalued as an object rather than respected as a subject. The BLM movement works to give voice and presence to Blacks and women who are pushed into corners of irrelevancy, and persons with disabilities and immigrants whose thoughts are dismissed and opinions ignored. The BLM movement works to correct these and other expressions of false consciousness.

The work of Ira Shor describes how critical literacy functions to turn the status quo upside down in order to chart different pathways for personal and collective growth. It does so through language that recasts the nature of the world and everyday life in ways that link political and personal, public and private, global and local, economic and pedagogical in order to replace inequity with justice.[44] The BLM movement confronts racism by asserting that Blacks matter. It presents a replacement to business as usual where teachers propagate "the public interest" when the public's interest results in people of a darker hue bearing the burdens of those in positions of power. *Black Lives Matter* is a substitute term with language grounded in experiences of the dispossessed and animated in the streets of Stanford, Ferguson, Baltimore, Staten Island, and all the places where dishonor and life-taking have occurred. It speaks to the desire to reconstruct America and the world into a more just, equitable, and loving world.

---

44 Views of critical literacy appear in Ira Shor, "What Is Critical Literacy?" *Journal for Pedagogy, Pluralism and Practice* 1, no. 4 (Fall 1999): 2–32, esp. 2–3, https://digitalcommons.lesley.edu/jppp/vol1/iss4/2/.

It is important to add here that critical literacy is not necessarily stripped of religious or theological meanings since within it, beliefs, knowledge, feelings, and experiences that underlie and motivate people's actions can appear. In this regard, then, it is appropriate to add the dimension of religious literacy. Religious literacy functions as a way people understand, guide, and make sense of human behavior including activism, protest, and other justice-seeking endeavors. Understanding this form of literacy depends on language that is not abstract. It comes out of narratives, images, rites, and histories.[45] The point here is that religion matters and cannot be excluded in a discussion of critical literacy and critical pedagogy.

Although intentionally positioning itself outside Black religious institutions, the BLM movement is, in fact, replete with religious or theological language.[46] The BLM website section on the National Church Network refers to a God who loves all people and who stands for peace and justice; a God whose power makes possible life in what is thought to be dead; a God who breathes life in every generation, thereby creating promise for tomorrow. The further claim is made that BLM organized the National Church Network to turn the dream of Martin Luther King Jr. "into a reality, one community at a time."[47] Kendrick Lamar's hip-hop lyrics, regarded as a BLM anthem, prophetically announces, "But if God got us, then we gon' be alright."[48] Moreover, among the guiding principles is the commitment of BLM to "intentionally build and nurture a beloved

---

45 These views of religious literacy appear in Stephen Prothero, *Religious Literacy: What Every American Needs to Know–And Doesn't* (New York: HarperCollins, 2007), 10–17.

46 Eleven Black leaders and academics explored the role of religion in the BLM movement in a forum introduced by Vincent Lloyd on "Religion, Secularism, and Black Lives Matter," Social Science Research Council, The Immanent Frame, September 9, 2016, https://tif.ssrc.org/2016/09/22/religion-secularism-and-Black-lives-matter/.

47 See www.Blacklifematters.org/churchnetwork.

48 Forcompletelyrics,gotohttps://genius.com/Kendrick-lamar-alright-lyrics.

community" alongside affirmation of the sacredness of everyone's life and the duty to love one another.[49]

There is also an element of critique of unjust wider societal systems in religious literacy embraced by the BLM movement as shown in the forthright assertion of BLM cofounder Alicia Garza that "violence is about poverty, . . . having access to clear water, Black girls being used as bargaining chips during wartime. . . . It's not a question of good or bad, it's a question of moral and immoral and your actions, your systems are immoral."[50] But it is also a religious literacy that is acted upon as noted in Garza's marked words: "It's about shifting the narrative from a help narrative. . . . It's about investing in and resourcing Black communities to be able to do for ourselves. . . . It's about broadening out the narrative; get free or die trying."[51] Through both critical literacy and religious literacy, the BLM movement presents a clear example of the power not simply to reconstruct identities of difference but to strive toward a prophetic vision through the use of these components of critical pedagogy.

The five features of critical pedagogy–the importance of context, understandings of the dimensions of power, the necessity of praxis, the ongoing affirmation of "otherness," and critical thinking–provide religious educators tools to help learners participate in the coming of the Creator's reign on earth. These features enhance and enrich the aims of critical pedagogy so that the utopian visions of the Hebrew prophets set forth in scripture become actualized in concrete conditions of everyday life. These components are taught and learned to engage people in reflexive thinking that weds words and actions for the purpose of transformation. They assist teachers

49 "What We Believe," Black Lives Matter, https://Blacklivesmatter.com/about/what-we-believe/.

50 Alicia Garza and L. A. Kauffman, "A Love Note to Our Folks: Alicia Garza on the Organizing of #BlackLivesMatter," *n+1 Magazine*, January 20, 2015, https://nplusonemag.com/online-only/online-only/a-love-note-to-our-folks/.

51 Garza and Kauffman, "A Love Note to Our Folks."

and learners to perceive and investigate how the content of public theologies challenges or reproduces hegemonic ideologies. Taken together, the factors function to facilitate emancipatory learning and living.

Black Lives Matter, Critical Pedagogy, and Religious Education

Pedagogically, there is a strategic advantage to teaching and learning when what is to be learned can be explicitly linked to learners' experiences and history. The connection addresses the question of relevancy. How might public protest movements in general, and the BLM movement specifically, be employed by religious educators for teaching, learning, and appropriating religious faith? What might religious educators contribute to the BLM movement currently and to public protest activities in the future?

The BLM movement and nonviolent public protests can be used to teach, learn about, and appropriate religious faith. They can provide opportunities for religious educators to examine and refine commonly held conceptualizations of educational methods. Such an analysis may result in more religious educators teaching for appropriations and embodiments of prophetic visions of justice. The BLM movement challenges conscientious religious educators to wrestle with the view that we live in a world shaped by many and varied human perspectives. Multiple views offer several options, including but not limited to the following. Religious educators can (1) ignore, deny, or reject the existence of other viewpoints and cling to their own view as "the only reality" or "truth"; (2) strive to harmonize or reconcile different perspectives, which often leads to the loss of distinction or extinction of ideas by those not in positions of authorial power; or (3) learn to live in the middle of multiple viewpoints. This latter option, I contend, requires rethinking the methods of religious education.

Religious educational methods respond to the question, What processes of learning and spiritual formation are appropriate for pursuing a prophetic vision of religious education? Religious educational methods in an ever-changing and violent world necessitate coordination of multiple perspectives at intersections of interaction. Religious educators and learners, at these intersections, must be empowered to clarify and articulate their perspective. And teachers and learners must practice hospitable welcoming, hearing, and consideration of the thoughts, beliefs, and perceptions of others. Questions are important and form a methodological frame for reflection and discovery. The following questions can assist religious educators as they join with students to analyze, understand, and appropriate insights of BLM and other public protest movements.

1. What has happened that prompts or demands response? Here, one considers the thought(s) held, the actions conducted, and on whom they were conducted.
2. How and where is the context in which the happening occurred and was carried out? This is a question of scope and boundaries forming the narrative of the event, the environment, and the perimeter of the circumstance.
3. Who is/are the actor(s) who were central in the happening and responses to it, and what feelings arise about the actors? Actors are described and defined in terms of the social construction of the identities. Such an identity goes beyond a person's "name, rank, and serial number."
4. Who is/are the actor(s) who must yet respond? In this instance, actors are described and defined in terms of the self, groups, or entities needed to carry out actions in response to answers emerging in the first three questions.
5. What are the tools, instruments, actions, conditions, and contexts for implementing the action(s)? Teachers and learners are asked to explore and consider the means for enacting and carrying out the actions, including potential risks and ways of addressing risks.
6. What is the expected outcome? Teachers and learners examine expectations in light of their action.

7. Why? Teachers and learners are encouraged to offer a description of the purpose(s), theory, theology, or religious commitments that motivate and can sustain the actions of self or identified groups or entities.

The emphasis on questioning, not telling, suggests that leaders are not wiser than the learners and that trusting relationships are needed for intentional, committed, helpful action. It is also a way of empowering learners to see and act on their role. Schein calls it "humble inquiry," in which the teacher or leader places the self on the same level as the learner.[52] Questioning is also a means of connecting educational practitioners to the contexts, heritage, and personalities of a religious tradition. They offer a method and processes for analyzing the activities and assessing the value of the BLM movement and what it has to say about the current activities and thinking of religious workers. It provides an approach to interrogating events; a method for interpreting words, texts, and actions; and a way to make meaning and decide action. It is an educational method for religious educators to use for emancipatory teaching and learning.

What Religious Educators Can Offer the BLM Movement

James Baldwin once wrote: "If the concept of God has any validity or any use, it can only be to make us larger, freer, and more loving. If God cannot do this, then it is time we got rid of Him."[53] While some public protest movements have anchored or affiliated themselves with one or more religious traditions, as indicated earlier, the BLM movement has not. It is my belief that the BLM movement is worthy of the nurture, support, and intellectual and spiritual resources public theology and religious education can extend to the movement.

---

52 A description of humble inquiry appears in Edgar H. Schein, *Humble Inquiry: The Art of Asking Instead of Telling* (San Francisco: Berrett-Koehler Publishers, Inc., 2013), 7-20.

53 James Baldwin, *The Fire Next Time*, reissue ed. (New York: Vintage, 1992), 47.

Understandings are located and meanings are constructed in particular across the varied contours of our lives. For public theologians and for the BLM movement, the various dimensions of content and the ways it is structured function to limit or enable human action.[54] Public theology and religious education can afford the BLM movement resources of religious faith traditions to analyze the current environment and to interpret the words, rhetoric, and events of social, political, and cultural situations for their critical appraisals and action. Faith traditions–their beliefs, customs, rituals, and practices–can mediate actions and infuse immanent actions with transcendent meaning.

Judaism and Christianity, two Abrahamic faith traditions, have histories that are infused with personalities that practiced critical literacy, praxis, and vigilant concern for the "other," those who are structurally and continuously left out of the boundaries of access to favor and prosperity. Hebrew prophets confronted those who perpetuated the status quo in the name of or for the benefit of Israel's religion. Jesus of Nazareth challenged and opposed the systems of domination that left women and children without adequate means for survival and the poor and vulnerable without hope. The prophets and Jesus spoke truth to ideological and hegemonic systems of power, systems and processes that legitimated the privileges of the powerful of their times. They embodied a critical literacy that rejected worship with the lips while their actions were disingenuous. Leaders of the early church took symbols and tools of their times, symbols such as a cross, and transformed them into instruments of liberation and hope.

Religious educators have the content and frameworks of public theology and the resources of critical pedagogies to form and inform the religious identities of individuals and groups. Critical pedagogies can help learners access resources for pursuing a prophetic vision of freedom, justice, and equality for all. They can help learners identify, analyze, and interpret contemporary hegemonic, domesticating practices informed by a prophetic legacy of a religious tradition. Religious educators, equipped with the knowledge

---

54 Giroux, *Pedagogy and the Politics of Hope*, 87.

and skills of critical pedagogies, can empower marginalized groups with insights and abilities to repair the brokenness of creation.

Reflections

Protest movements, like all human efforts, are flawed. The immediate outcomes are not always what is intended or desired. Those who gathered to protest under the banner "Unite the Right" in Charlottesville, Virginia, on Friday and Saturday, August 10 and 11, 2017, make this fact tragically obvious. No attempt is made here to reify or enshrine protest movements with transcendent value. Recognizing the potential for both good and harm, I have attempted to understand and articulate how the BLM movement provides an ample landscape for agents of public theology and religious education to explore some salient issues of critical pedagogy and its benefits for religious educators. The nonviolent public protests of the BLM movement, at their best, illuminate how words grounded in experience and animated by actions have the capacity–power–to reconstruct significations of difference, or "otherness," for framing and refreshing prophetic visions of teaching and learning. Black lives matter. The content and frameworks public theology can offer, and the practices critical pedagogical educators may promote, use words as tools to exert their capacity to empower marginalized individuals with creative and constructive possibilities to transform unjust institutions into agencies of liberating hope.

Religious Education and Womanist Formation

Mothering and the Reinterpretation of Body Politics

Nancy Lynne Westfield

> We are not dis-embodied, talking heads engaged in intellectual discourse and dispute. We are bodies, given life with the breath of God at creation. It is breath that connects body, mind, and soul. It is the same breath that we use in conversation for justice.
>
> –Nancy Lynne Westfield, "Christian Education as Conversation"

Womanist Formation

The politics of body and identity is permeated with issues of dehumanization, oppression, and disempowerment based on race, gender, and class. It is part of ongoing and contentious race relations, insidious gender biases, socioeconomic inequities, and daily assaults on the very being of self that African American women keenly experience. Pedagogical models of womanist formation in religious education are needed that pivot on processes whereby African American girl children and women claim their power to *be* in order to change the course of the nation and move toward healing the soul personally, individually, and communally. Central to these processes is attention to the public body and the role of maternal advocacy emerging in communication between mothers and female children. Attention will be given to the nature of womanist formation in the opening part of this chapter in advance of a specific view of the politics of body, followed by an example of womanist formation through body-centered maternal advocacy.

Through its emphasis, womanist pedagogy is not a counterpoint to traditional, male-dominated, White, essentialist pedagogies. Neither is it a new version of transgressive pedagogy delineated in the practice of freedom and engaged search for life-changing and life-affirming truth, appearing in the work of bell hooks.[1] Womanist pedagogy espouses liberation as a key want, a right, a yearning. But more than that, the aim of womanist pedagogy extends to problematizing, analyzing, making new meanings, and creating new dreams in spaces of teaching and learning. The aim is to understand and reconceive the African diaspora as normative, as critical, as life-giving, and as life-sustaining for all people.

Womanist pedagogy fully and painfully acknowledges the need for freedom and survival given the US context of captivity through the systemic hatreds of racism, misogyny, patriarchy, and economic disenfranchisement. But its sights focus squarely on creating teaching and learning agendas in which human beings engage together as equals. Womanist pedagogy brings to the center of conversation those voices whose realities were preciously made invisible, excluded from discourse, or distorted by the body politics of patriarchal racist communication. In so doing, womanist pedagogy refashions, expands, and deepens the scholarly discourse of all pedagogy. Awareness, recognition, and appreciation of the realities of African diasporan women have been misunderstood, dismissed, despised, or overlooked by mainstream pedagogies, making this endeavor challenging and especially necessary.

---

1 bell hooks, *Teaching to Transgress* (New York: Routledge, 1994).

Womanist approaches to pedagogy bring to bear upon and beyond the classroom those lived experiences, realities, and wisdom of women of the African diaspora and in so doing teach healing, unleash the power of the ancient, and beckon all into a hopeful future. The outcome is that a whole society can benefit from the brilliance, sacrifice, and artistry of African diaspora women. More specifically, without the voices of these women, the scholarship of education is deficient, and society as a whole is lacking. Womanist pedagogy does not proffer a counternarrative to White normativity but is a metanarrative of God's dream for all humanity.

All pedagogies have a politics; no pedagogy is politically neutral. The patriarchal, racist framework of education too often represents womanist pedagogy as a radical or separatist or, worst of all, a kind of "bouquet" pedagogy. This dismissive and undervaluing strategy signals not only an unwillingness to take seriously womanist scholarship but an inability to understand our emerging and ancient notions. Creating scholarly work from the reality of one's own people, mining the life experiences of kith, kin, like-minded sister-scholars, as well as with allying brothers, is the defiant genius of the womanist reflexive approach. Formation, from a womanist perspective, then, is contextual. Life experiences and contextual circumstances become the central content. Moreover, folk wisdom and literature from Africans and African Americans serve as relevant sources of content.

Learners and Teachers in Womanist Pedagogy

Womanist formation responds directly to the reality of oppression, death dealing, systemic hatred, and violence. It is constitutive of the care, nurture, and development of behaviors, habits, attitudes, practices, values, mores, clarity of purpose, and ways of making meaning for the survival and thriving of self and people as well as for equal participation in conversation about what is and what must be. These aspects of knowledge construction are the mutual responsibility of both learner and teacher. The learner is discoverer and producer of knowledge and, in the learning process, becomes a mindful participant in the lifelong journey of formation that includes revealing their own experiences and knowing and assessing the "truth" about oppressive realities. The journey requires the learner's cultivation of agency, understanding unnecessary suffering, awareness of the requirement of oppositional response for survival, a vision for the future, and abilities to rethink, reinterpret, reimagine, and act in ways that contribute to realizing the beloved community and kin-dom of God.[2] In actuality, the learner's journey centers on her empowerment as an agent of knowledge; formation of a self-defined, self-reliant consciousness; and her will to be an advocate for social transformation,[3] which includes Christian prophetic action of devising strategies that lessen Black people's susceptibility to dehumanizing and oppressive circumstances.[4]

The teacher is guide, midwife, artistic collaborator, advocate, and colearner. As guide, the teacher is forthright in engaging in race-, gender-, and class-talk and through inviting and giving direction to aspects of each one—their intersections and responses that impinge on daily life. The teacher as midwife acts as a buffer and

---

2 Martin Luther King Jr. declared that the goal is to create a beloved community, requiring "a qualitative change in our souls as well as a quantitative change in our lives." The declaration appears in Martin Luther King Jr., "Nonviolence: The Only Road to Freedom," *Ebony* (October 1966): 27–34, esp. 34.

3 Collins makes clear the importance of empowerment through knowledge that is recognizable in self-defined, self-reliant individuals. She further insists on knowledge that results in "the changed consciousness of individuals and the social transformation of political and economic institutions. See Patricia Hill Collins, *Black Feminist Thought: Knowledge, Consciousness, and the Politics of Empowerment* (New York: Routledge, 1990), 221–22.

4 See Katie G. Cannon, "The Emergence of a Black Feminist Consciousness," in *Feminist Interpretations of the Bible*, ed. Letty M. Russell (Philadelphia: Westminster, 1985), 30–40, esp. 35.

translator between the learner and the world.[5] As artistic collaborator, the teacher is a deep listener who allows the self to be led and allows the inner artist to imaginatively engage the self's and the learner's aesthetic and feeling sides by using, for example, drama, art, music, dance, and literature. This way of teaching is toward the mind, body, and spirit, or engaging a pedagogy of the soul.

As advocate, the teacher steps beyond a classroom or group meeting context and into the wider institutional or public arena as a voice of protest, vigilant observer, or social activist.[6] Furthermore, as advocate, the teacher both believes and proclaims the centrality of the Christian narrative, the message of the gospel in which all are welcome and valued, and the ethic of justice that honors the reality of God. The teacher as colearner recognizes that neither the teacher nor the learner comes as *tabula rasa* and that the stories of self are at the center of metacognitive processes. Life is a continual teacher of teachers. Likewise learners evoke in teachers what has not yet been considered or that brings forth a new perspective. Through these functions, the teacher is an active agent in the learner's development of competencies, creativities, and intelligences.[7] But the dimension of the teacher's life is also indispensably important. Alice Walker described a quality of political leadership in one of her teachers by saying that "mostly she taught by the courage of her own life, which to me is the highest form of teaching."[8]

---

5 See Dani McClain, "As a Black Mother, My Parenting Is Always Political," *The Nation*, March 27, 2019, 1-21, esp. 5-6, www.thenation.com/article/Black-motherhood-family-parenting-dani-mcclain/.

6 See Sinikka Elliott and Megan Reid, "The Superstrong Black Mother," *Contexts* 15, no. 1 (February 1, 2016): 48-53, https://doi.org/10.1177/1536504216628840.

7 See Nancy Lynne Westfield, "Christian Education as Conversation," *Under the Oak Tree: The Church as Community of Conversation in a Conflicted and Pluralistic World*, ed. Ron Allen (Eugene, OR: Cascade, 2013), 125.

8 Alice Walker, *In Search of Our Mothers' Gardens: Womanist Prose* (San Diego, CA: Harcourt Brace Jovanovich, 1983), 38.

An added point must be made about the emphasis in womanist pedagogy on engagement of both teacher and learner in conversation that is imbued with political agendas. In fact, conversation may implicitly or explicitly, through silence and negation of the voices of persons present, perpetuate the dehumanizing, alienating "normality" of oppression. Or conversation may liberate and beckon justice through risking communal speech about experiences of domination, oppression, and injustice. Conversation is a shaping force and is critical to the formation of individual and community identity.[9] In contextual womanist pedagogy, it goes beyond what oppressors or oppressive forces say is "good" for us.[10] It takes us beyond the acquisition of facts, data, and the regurgitation of a universal or essentialist truth. But neither is it the continuation and perpetuation of xenophobia and internalized oppression. From a womanist approach, formation involves engaging in conversation through which learning results in a person's resisting, refusing, and contradicting those lies of oppression that would label her as inferior, subhuman, unworthy, or a problem, while at the same time tending the growth of her own unique value and voice.

---

9 Particular emphasis on the nature of conversation that is needed in Christian education appears in Westfield, "Christian Education as Conversation," 113–33.

10 The overall message in the womanist writing of Alice Walker is that Black women desire to know, to grow, to choose, to determine for ourselves, to be in solidarity with one another, and to create hope. These views are also dominant in Walker, *In Search of Our Mothers' Gardens*; Alice Walker, *The Color Purple* (New York: Harcourt, 1982). It may be said here that history shows "systems of domination told Black women that we will not and cannot determine what is 'good' for ourselves. . . . We are intended as oppressed people, to distrust our own judgment, our own processes of knowledge." See Nancy Lynne Westfield, "'Mama Why . . . ?' A Womanist Epistemology of Hope," in *Deeper Shades of Purple: Womanism in Religion and Society*, ed. Stacey Floyd-Thomas (New York: New York University Press, 2006), 132–33.

Mothers and Othermothers as Teachers

In religious education, some might typically assume that "teacher" refers to pastors, paid or unpaid laity in congregations, or professors in higher education and seminaries, all of whom are charged with the responsibility of carrying out critical roles and functions. However, womanist pedagogy brings to the fore the vital African American community presence of the mother/othermother as teacher and the "maternal" agency of "aunties, grannies, and even adoptee mothers . . . to resist oppression and fight for change."[11] The significance of this emphasis in religious education lies in the understanding that daughters come to know, be known, and have know-how through formative conversations, observations, intuitions, and intimate engagements with their mother.

The world that is mother, and the world beyond mother, forms and informs the values, curiosities, attitudes, and beliefs of girl children. Wisdom, resilience, and moral courage are "caught" by daughters from mothers in the sacred familial bond and through daily casual but critical interactions. Equally, notions of survival, love, and worth are taught, though often indirectly, in conversations between mothers and daughters. Whether caught or taught,

---

11 Wanda Thomas Bernard, Sasan Issari, Jemell Moriah, Marok Njiwaji, Princewill Obgan, and Althea Tolliver, "Othermothering in the Academy: Using Maternal Advocacy for Institutional Change," *Journal of the Motherhood Initiative for Research and Community Involvement* 3, no. 2 (2000): 104, https://jarm.journals.yorku.ca/index.php/jarm/article/view/36305/33023. The nature of the mothering tradition in Black diasporan communities and its current presence and impact also appear in Collins, *Black Feminist Thought*, 123–37; bell hooks, *Talking Back: Thinking Feminist, Thinking Black* (Boston: South End Press, 1989), 50; Chasity Bailey-Fakhoury, "Navigating, Negotiating, and Advocating: Black Mothers, Their Young Daughters, and White Schools," *Michigan Family Review* 18, no. 1 (December 1, 2014): 57–79; and Dolana Mogadime, "Black Girls/Black Women–Centered Texts and Black Teachers as Othermothers," *Journal of the Association for Research on Mothering* 2, no. 2 (2000): 222–33.

the influence of mothers upon daughters, and vice versa, affects the formation of both through their entire lives. The mother is an active agent of knowledge, colearner, and advocate whose conversations with her daughter are informed by her own racial identity development and the truths of her experiences of racism affected by what may be referred to as the *gaze* on her Black body. Treatment of the Black body is of particular concern here, and it is to this critical reality to which this chapter now turns.

The Public Body and the Practice of Gaze

Womanist formation takes seriously the need to confront the historical and continuing corrupt and stereotypical ways Black women's bodies are viewed and situated as "specular events," called "the gaze," accompanied by the public devaluation and treatment of Black girl children and women. This negative regard for personhood has consequences for social relations and institutional actions in the public sphere. It is political because the Black body is identifiable as a visible marker of difference, and, as such, Black girl children and women are not equally accorded opportunities, care, and resources in the public sphere.[12] Black body politics has personal conse-

12 The importance of recognizing and confronting the pervasively negative views and treatment of Black bodies is accented in numerous studies and writing including the following: bell hooks, *Black Look: Race and Representation* (Boston: South End Press, 1992); Sharlene Nagy Hesse-Biber, Stephanie A. Howling, Patricia Leavy, and Meg Lovejoy, "Racial Identity and the Development of Body Image Issues Among African American Adolescent Girls," *The Qualitative Report* 9, no. 1 (2004): 49-70, https://nsuworks.nova.edu/tqr/vol9/iss1/4; Ronald L. Jackson II, "Origin of Black Body Politics," in *Scripting the Black Masculine Body: Identity, Discourse, and Racial Politics in Popular Media* (Albany: State University of New York Press, 2006); Rasul A. Mowatt and Bryana H. French, "Black/Female/Body Hypervisibility and Invisibility: A Black Feminist Augmentation of Feminist Leisure Research," *Journal of Leisure Research* 45, no. 5 (2013): 644-60, www.nrpa.org/globalassets/journals/jlr/2013/volume-45-number-5

quences that heighten awareness of the ways we come to know the world, (dis)trust the world, and find our place in the world as embodied beings. Through sight, smell, touch, hearing, and taste, as well as the internal senses of intuition, discernment, and prayer, we come to know the importance of the body in formation. African American girl children and women learn quickly that their body is more than a conduit for learning but also a targeted way to identify and label the self as inferior. In a hegemonic reality the Black women's body is simultaneously public property, and, as such, their valued human self is invisible and instead becomes hypervisible through negative portrayals. The hypervisible self as a Black body is a person under constant scrutiny, surveillance, and suspicion while the invisible self is further confirmed by the message that the person's voice does not matter and their actions, thoughts, and dreams are inferior.

The public body began at the auction block during American chattel slavery. The bodies of enslaved persons from infancy to old age were viewed and inspected before and during sale. White men, women, and children inspected the eyes, teeth, musculature, genitals, and feet of enslaved Africans. Purchase hinged on inspections of the Black body that affirmed well-to-do Whites' hopes for good stock, smart, gentle darkies who might play well with their children, work hard in their fields, and remain compliant during rape and other unspeakable violence.[13] Race, while it is not biological, was then and continues to be revealed by body "inspection." The practice of gaze is still an effective tool in the politics of the body.

-pp-644-660.pdf; Reshawna L. Chapple, George A. Jacinto, Tameca N. Harris-Jackson, and Michelle Vance, "Do #BlackLivesMatter? Implicit Bias, Institutional Racism and Fear of the Black Body," *Ralph Bunche Journal of Public Affairs* 6, no. 1 (2014): 3–11, http://digitalscholarship.tsu.edu/rbjpa/vol6/iss1/2; and Sabrina Strings, *Fearing the Black Body: The Racial Origin of Fat Phobia* (New York: New York University Press, 2019).

13 An example of the auction experience during the period of Black enslavement appears in "Slave Auction, 1859," Eyewitness to History, accessed January 22, 2020, www.eyewitnesstohistory.com/pfslaveauction.htm.

The reading of the body in current paradigms of systemic racism, hatred, and violence is thought to indicate, with a mere glance, who is vulnerable to victimization and who is bestowed with privilege. It is also thought that body appearance shows who is without social status and social power. That is, the body denotes who is the historically or socially deserving victim of systemic oppression. Those targeted to be victims of racism are persons whose skin complexion is of darker hues, with "coarse" facial characteristics and knapped hair. Similarly, those targeted as victims of sexism are persons whose genitals are female and whose features are soft and "fine." Racism and sexism combine in the form of socially stigmatizing public critiques of the unfemininity of body size and shape of Black women. With each "-ism" there is a body indicator that is determinative of social worth, value, and status.

Identifying race through gaze upon the body, then, has a kind of social warrant for relegating the body to spaces, tasks, identities, and expectations. The deleterious view of the Black physical body communicates to the Black person that his or her existence is suspect or simply wrong and that life possibilities are limited. With limited possibility based on the body, persons come to believe and practice self-hatred and find no contradiction in assisting the oppressor in oppressing those like themselves. Internalized oppression strengthens all the systemic oppressions. Belief in the lie of racism and patriarchy is soul wounding. The hegemonic mind-set that undergirds and perpetuates systems of patriarchy and racism utilize the gaze upon the human body to provide indicators of social location and the ensuing judgment of inferior or superior status. Without the practice of gaze-determination upon any body, systems of dehumanization and societal marginalization would be difficult to perpetuate.

Recollections of Body: A Personal Experience

As noted earlier, key to the development of African American girl children is the mother/daughter relationship. Alice Walker's four-part definition of a "womanist" from *In Search of Our Mothers' Gardens: Womanist Prose* references the essential communication between mothers to female children. In the first part of the definition, Walker recites a typical phrase uttered by Black mothers to their daughters who are displaying "outrageous, audacious, courageous, or willful behavior." To her daughter the mother says, "You acting womanish"–that is, like a woman.[14] The conversation between mother and daughter, the guidance of a mother to a daughter, is a pillar of formation.

I suspect my mother lived her life and died without ever being acquainted with the term *womanist*, all the while embodying all and more of what Alice Walker chronicled about and for African American women, especially the indispensable and formational relationship between mothers and daughters. I learned to be a womanist from my mother's interpretation and reinterpretation of the world around me. Learning to see the world through my mother's eyes, I learned to know the world for what it is and for what it could be.

In what follows, I recount a critical incident from my childhood, then examine the ways my mother, by reinterpreting my moments of disobedience and unpreparedness, provided life-affirming womanist formation. Specifically, I address these questions: In an age where the body is used to sort and classify the worth of human beings, what would it take to disrupt, resist, and reimagine the reality that informs the body politics of hegemonic subjugation? What if womanism, in espousing a reality of dignity and worth for African American women, is maintaining a reality unknown by most people? What if the wisdom role of mothers and the holy task of mothering are a fulcrum to the ways oppressed people survive? What acts of reinterpretation are needed to nurture agency and sacred dignity in girl children? What if reinterpretation of the messages sent by a patriarchal society is an epistemological weapon of flourishing wielded by African American mothers?

---

14 Walker, *In Search of Our Mothers' Gardens*, xi.

I offer this incident for reflection because, in retrospect, this is one of my earliest learnings of both the informing role of the body and womanist ways of knowing. My mother's teachings during this critical moment, in retrospect, was a crystallizing moment for my understanding of womanist ways, wit, and approaches. It demonstrates the nature of conversation as a central personal empowerment and justice-engendering pedagogical practice in womanist formation.

Incident Recollection—"About Face!"

In May of 1966 I turned four years old and started kindergarten in September. I could read and was tall. This combination was all it took for my mother to enroll me in George Washington Carver Elementary School in Philadelphia. The African American woman teacher, Mrs. Taylor, taught my brother the previous year. She encouraged my mother that early admissions would be good for me and told her, "She's ready." The first day of kindergarten we were told to line up by height so the class might go to recess. All the children ran to the classroom door and began to measure each other's height to see who would be in the front and who would be in the back. In short order, as the tallest girl in the class (at four I was as tall as the five-year-olds), I found my way to the back of the girls' line. The teacher informed us boys and girls to pay close attention as we traveled in the hallways because, she said with emphasis, "You might be the one to have to lead the class." The rule was that whoever was the first person in line was the leader of the line and thus had the responsibility of navigating to the gym, library, cafeteria, art room, or to the far side of the schoolyard for our fire drills.

The same procedure was set in the second grade. On the first day of class the students, when instructed to line up, raced to measure each other to see who would be where in the line. We compared shoulders, and we stood back-to-back to see whose head was higher. As the tallest girl, I was last in the line in kindergarten, grade one, and grade two. By grade three–at the age of seven–I did not measure myself with the other children's bodies. I simply went to the back of the line.

Each year the rationale remained the same. We were instructed to pay close attention in the hallways—because one day the responsibility of leading the class might fall to you. I do not remember making a conscious decision, but as the years passed, I never paid attention to how to navigate through the hallways. I knew that for me to have the responsibility of leading the class anywhere that all the children, both boys and girls, would have to be absent. Even with the analytical skills of a third-grader, I knew the likelihood of the scenario of using these skills as leader was slim to none. While walking in formation, I dutifully followed without lagging behind, but I never paid attention to the location of our route to the other rooms or spaces where our class visited.

One fall morning my class was at recess. At the appointed time, the non-teaching assistant (NTA) blew her whistle to signal my class to line up so we could go back to our classroom. Time for recess had ended. I, along with my classmates, lined up. As we stood awaiting permission to go inside, we could hear the fire drill alarm sounding inside the school. Upon hearing the alarm, the NTA who was positioned at the front of the line shouted to the class, "About face!" With this command, all the children including me whirled around to face in the opposite direction. Now, for first time in my elementary school career, I was at the head of the line. It was, of course, expected that I could lead my class to the fire drill spot that was designated for us at the far end of the schoolyard. I had no clue about the location of our spot.

Before this fateful moment, we had had regular fire drills. On all the other occasions, the drill occurred when we were in the classroom. At the sounding of the fire bell, we lined up quickly and quietly according to size and made our way outside to the designated spot for our class. There were a series of white spots painted on the ground at the farthest end of the schoolyard. The white spots had no other markings, but since all the classes had been to their spots numerous times, we had been instructed to know which was our designated spot.

Now, in this moment of "about face!" it was expected that I, as the leader of my line, would know where the designated spot is. The NTA gave the command to go to the spot. I struck out! I walked slowly toward the general vicinity of our spot. As we walked, the other classes who were at recess hurried to their spots, and classes from inside also streamed out of the building. I frantically tried to see where our class might belong. In my indecision, I began to serpentine around the school yard with the line of twenty-nine classmates dutifully following behind me. I was lost in plain sight. Finally, the shortest kid broke formation, ran over to our spot, and began jumping up and down and calling to our class. We could hear our classmate but could not see him through the lines of other children. Someone spotted him and pointed to him, and, in a wad, we all ran to where he was. We lined up in size order–with me at the back of the line. My teacher, who had witnessed the entire ordeal, looked mortified. I felt ashamed.

On the walk home after school, my brother saw fit to tell me just how much trouble I was in and how I had embarrassed him. He, as well as most of the school, had witnessed my confusion. Once home, I ran through the front door, burst into tears, and threw myself into my mother's arms. Then I told her what happened. I told her I did not know the way to the spot, but I was supposed to have known. I told her, barely able to breathe through the tears, that I was embarrassed of my wrongdoing. My mother held me and asked my brother what had happened. He, like any older brother would do, reenacted the story emphasizing, in his words, my stupidity. With my brother's telling, my mother understood what had happened.

I was sure my mother would be mad. I expected my mother to be upset at my shortcoming. She was not. I expected my mother to chastise me for my wrongdoing. She did not. I expected my mother to blame me. She did not. She asked me if I had anything else to say. I told her that I never expected "about face." I told her I never thought I would be a leader. She listened. I told her that even now I did not know where the spot was and that I was worried that it would happen again. She smiled at me and dried my tears. I was relieved that she was not angry or even disappointed.

Mom took my brother and me into the kitchen, gave us a snack, and sat down with us. Mom said it was OK for me not to have known something. After all, she said, how could I have known from the back of the line. She comforted me and told me I was not to blame and should not feel ashamed for not knowing something that was nearly impossible to know. Her words relieved my anxiety. She said it was not fair that the rules, with the command to "about face," had suddenly changed. And she continued, saying that because I was tall and placed in the back of the line does not mean I simply follow blithely behind those who lead. I must find ways, from the back of line, to know the way. The rules for us will also change as a way to make us anxious and unprepared. It's OK to make a mistake; I am not a mistake. I was shocked, amazed, and relieved. After our talk, Mom instructed my brother to take me back to the schoolyard and show me where our class's spot was so next time I would be prepared.

Unpacking the Recollection

This recollection from my elementary school classroom is both a literal account and an illuminating metaphor for the insidious ways relegation of the body is used to form and inform African American girl children for purposes of oppression and captivity. Interpretation of what happened through my mother's eyes is instructive.

What Momma Knew

What Momma knew was that if what happened to me in the classroom went unchecked and was not reinterpreted, that distortion of reality would give me incomplete knowledge of myself, my world, my community, and God. In this poignant moment, my mother refused to allow me to be erased, withered, or bent over. Momma knew that not knowing your place can get you killed.

Body relegation by height is tantamount to the way oppressions of society use body politics to label, sort, and target those deemed inferior. It is a kind of biological determinism. It is a way the mind falls victim to the neocolonial mind-set. This typical habit of organizing children in lines by height is naively practiced as an efficient way to see children while moving from space to space. The practice is said to be necessary for the safety of the children. However, if children are the same height, they are not told to walk in pairs so they can be seen. Or if a child has a growth spurt during the school year, she may not be told to move to the back of the line during the semester. While this practice is typically viewed as benign classroom management, I would suggest that it is a practice that points toward the ways children are shaped and formed about their perceived value, worth, and utility.

Body relegation is practiced throughout society and begins in elementary school. My mother recognized, as many Black women do, that the experiences of Black girl children in the racist and sexist world must not go unchecked and must be reinterpreted. My mother provided me with a different kind of knowledge about the meaning of being relegated to the back of the line.

What Momma Problematized

My mother told me I was not the problem; I was not the mistake. In so doing, my mother's conversation did not reinforce the misogynic racist narrative that would blame, shame, and criticize me for not knowing from the back of the line. Instead, my mother's wisdom instilled a narrative of dignity and worth. In his 1903 classic, *The Souls of Black Folks*, professor, sociologist, historian, and activist W. E. B. Du Bois asked the question, "How does it feel to be a problem?" Du Bois proffered that oppressed people must understand and navigate the ways the oppressor sees the oppressed. In this navigation, the oppressed learn to be of two minds or possess double-consciousness. One mind knows the cultural ways of the oppressed people, and the second consciousness knows the ways of the oppressor. My mother, a womanist, taught me that knowing the way the oppressor sees the oppressed does not mean that the oppressed believe the rhetoric of the oppressor. There are, my mother knew, other realities than the reality constructed by the lies of the oppressor. We, as oppressed, develop a double-consciousness for survival—not because the oppressor's opinion of our worth has inerrant value or truth. We learn to know the oppressor's view, but this perspective neither eclipses nor supersedes the knowledge of our own humanness.

My mother's narrative—my mother's reality—did not ignore the hegemonic reality, and equally, it did not surrender power to it. By my mother's telling, the narratives of White supremacy and patriarchy are lacking, and freedom, justice, and love prevail in other realities. My mother was the keeper of a narrative that knew Black women exist as human beings regardless of the systemic societal messaging of hatred. Her message was clear that Blackness is not a problem! This knowledge allowed my mother to instill in me that I was not the problem but that the problem was the societal values of racism, sexism, and misogyny that are housed, subtly and powerfully, in societal systems, including public education.

The radicality of my mother's perspective is that she, like her mother and grandmother before her, seized the power of a metanarrative and claimed the power of a story, which brought truth to bear on the lying claims of Whiteness. In correcting what I thought was the problem from me to the system, my mother created a healing and guiding narrative that would steer me away from internalizing oppression. When the body is relegated based on its natural characteristics, a person, a girl child, comes to learn that her way of existence is suspect, wrong, or simply inadequate. People come to believe and maintain these distorted notions without being told to. This internalized oppression is powerful. People come to believe the lie that their inherent worth is meager. Belief in this lie is soul wounding.

My mother was correcting and countering the myths, misinformation, and experiences that signaled to me that I was not capable of leading and that I was unintelligent and inattentive. This experience with my mother signaled to me that personal sense of worth comes from her, from our ways, from our narratives, and not from a prejudiced, violent society. Her metanarrative is a wisdom known in body, mind, and spirit. Rather than reinforcing the message that I was the problem, even as a childhood survival tactic, she told me that the system that would relegate me was the problem. I believed my mother. The revelation of her perspective was instantaneous and freeing.

Momma's Analysis and Meaning-Making

Embedded in the conversation with Momma is a wise analysis that gives direction to Black girl children and women's meaning-making as an essential undertaking—a necessary kind of action in life. Momma's analysis uncovers a view of meaning-making that is all about understanding the world and our place as Black girl children and women in it, as well as actions and contestations needed not simply to challenge established meanings but to form a liberated mind-set directed toward survival, possibility, and human wholeness.

Counter the Situation of Absurdity

Conforming to the absurd is a loss of possibility. In telling me my unpreparedness was not my fault, my mother honored my own suspicions that the expectation of me knowing the way from the back of the line was nearly impossible. My mother's message gave me permission to know the habits and practices of body relegation as ridiculous, while still being authoritative in my life. A womanist mother teaches her children ways of navigating the absurdity of oppression.

The messages to girl children may be subtle, but they are not vague. In this scenario, the improbability of leadership coupled with the expectation of knowing in improbable circumstances defies good teaching and common sense. And yet, this scenario is typical. So much of the construct of oppression reduces the activities of the oppressed to what my grandmother would call "a fool's errand," yet the oppressed must comply. Womanist thought counters absurdity with common sense. Hear Delores Williams on common sense.

> I define "Black common sense" as the collective knowledge, wisdom and action Black people have used as they have tried to survive, to develop a productive quality of life and to be liberated from oppressive social, religious, political, economic and legal systems.[15]

Common sense is the daily lived wit and wisdom that has kept African American people alive in the hegemonic reality of the United States. Common sense includes the knowing of the spirit as sensed through intuition, the reading of signs, the sanctified imagination, as well as the prayers to God and conversations with ancestors and babies yet to be born. Common sense is learned when mothers have conversations with their girl child about ways of knowing and being known in the patriarchal gaze.

The social formation of children in general and the girl child in particular expects obedience from the child to the parent and other adults of authority. The church, in teaching children, also leans upon the notion of obedience as a tenet of discipleship. From my mother's womanist reality, obedience for African American girls becomes learning against one's own self-interest and survival. Obedience to that which oppresses you is a twisted reality. Chains and bullwhips are not required to shackle and oppress human beings. A mind-set, a well-rehearsed reality of orderliness without new possibilities, is as shackling as any chain and as wounding as any bullwhip. This kind of obedience results in internalized racism, sexism, and self-denigration. This kind of obedience is allegiance to the lie of White normativity and unquestioned patriarchy.

---

15 Delores Williams, "Straight Talk, Plain Talk: Womanist Words about Salvation in a Social Context," in *Embracing the Spirit: Womanist Perspectives on Hope, Salvation, and Transformation*, ed. Emilie Townes (Maryknoll, NY: Orbis Books, 1997), 99.

Seeing the absurdity in standards and activities of oppression helps to unveil and realize the ways the oppressor's narratives are defended and reified. Without careful analysis oppressed people are complicit in their own oppression. Affirming a child for learning to be happy at the back of the line is a complex and self-defeating pride that would warrant African Americans to own slaves and church women to believe in and preach the inferiority of women.

The absurdity of obedience allows and rewards the cluelessness and unawareness of White people about racism and men about patriarchy. Absurdity accords incentives for oppressors not simply to be unaware but to be unsympathetic with the plight of the poor, the objectification of women and children, and the denigration of the downtrodden as a badge of their rightful existence. This kind of obedience encourages immigrant populations who too readily give up their culture, language, and social mores for the allure of Whiteness and the social goodies that accompany this identity. This obedience fuels assimilation and the global wholesale expansion of Whiteness.

Reinterpret the Prevailing Mind-Set

Reinterpretation is a formidable formational task. Reinterpretation includes the ability to see beyond what is reported by the White gaze, to know more than the perspective that would tell her she is less than, and to act on what is seen and known. The hegemonic systems of oppression are so permeated with the values of greed, empire, conquest, and individualism that African American women become victims of and fodder for this mind-set. Vigilant reinterpretation of the lies of oppression, which would teach the inferiority of some people to the superiority of other people, is a daily grind for the psyche and soul of teacher and learner alike. Reinterpretation of the inscription of subservience as the principal reason for African American women's purpose and worth requires careful reorientation and rehumanization. Teaching relies on intimate relationships between learner and teacher. The relationships in family and in community are critical to survival and actualization.

Reflections on Pedagogical Models of Womanist Formation

In this chapter, womanist formation is conceived as a religious educational process grounded in the irrefutable claim of the innate worth and dignity, given by God, of Black women. It is an ongoing, intentional process that necessarily confronts racially biased body politics through conversations that disclose the young's and women's experiences of it, deconstruct its meaning, and reframe its personal impact for the sake of affirming a valued, generative sense of self. The mother as teacher and advocate exists as a beneficial, effective, and potentially life-transforming agent in the process. The personal example of maternal advocacy offers a pedagogical model of formation that in sum consists of a particular set of roles or practices undertaken by the mother that hold import for the religious educational advocacy of mothers and other mothers (grandmothers, aunties, adoptive mothers, women teachers in the church and public sphere). The model also consists of actions or practices in which to engage daughters.

PEDAGOGY OF WOMANIST FORMATION THROUGH MATERNAL ADVOCACY

Maternal Roles or Practices	Daughter's Actions or Practices
1. Presence Being present as a holding space and comforter for the girl child's lament.	**1. Lament** Being free to release deep woundedness in response to body-shaming, assaults to the physical self, and denigration of the core of one's personhood; may come in the form of crying or wailing before any story-sharing is possible.
2. Listener Welcoming, receiving, and being wholly attentive to the contextual existential story.	**2. Recollect the Story of Travail** Releasing the detailed memory of the soul's story of travail comprising a critical incident.
3. Problematizer Inviting critical thinking by re-presenting unjust societal messaging in a contextual existential story as problematic and false and correcting the false message by offering a radical metanarrative.	**3. Unpack the Recollection** Engaging in critical thinking infused by hearing a healing and guiding counternarrative of self-affirmation and worth leading to a revelatory and freeing perspective.
4. Evocator of Imagination and Meaning-Making Using the mother's wit and wisdom formed from the self's and forebears' stories to apply an analytical framework centered on absurdity and reinterpretation as evocative guides to personhood and life-affirming meaning-making.	**4. Imagine a Way Forward** Releasing rather than conforming to the absurdity of oppression; embracing Black common sense or seeing a way of living with wit and wisdom drawn from forebears that brings about seeing and acting on possibilities in life and helping others to do the same.

The ongoing hegemonic systems of oppression and ongoing reality of body politics require vigilant responses at the personal level and the persistent and committed practice of maternal advocacy with and on behalf of young Black girls and Black women.

Religious Education and Prison Ministry

Where Public Theology and Public Pedagogy Meet

Sarah F. Farmer

> Are we willing to relegate ever larger numbers of people from racially oppressed communities to an isolated existence marked by authoritarian regimes, violence, disease, and technologies of seclusion that produce severe mental instability?
>
> —Angela Davis, *Are Prisons Obsolete?*

A Very Present Concern: Opening Considerations

The above question raised by Angela Davis over fifteen years ago remains open, and individuals and faith communities who seek to live out a response in their everyday lives engage in public theology. Public theology seeks the common good of all people, often around common issues of great public concern. Yet the work of public theology, especially within the prison context, is countercultural.

While many immediately distance themselves from any connection with the prison system, mass incarceration is a phenomenon that affects nearly every person. In this chapter, I propose a vision of public theological religious education that integrates principles of care and justice in the pursuit of persons' wholeness. I construct a macrolevel approach to prison ministry that explores core pedagogical commitments that might shape how one enters prison rather than a microlevel approach or process of engaging those within prison. My vision centers on five core pedagogical commitments: unmasking, countering, discerning, enacting, and reimagining. I argue that these commitments serve as formative actions in prison ministry and orienting movements toward a deeper engagement and transformation of the criminal justice system.

Prison Ministry: The Intersection of Religious Education and Public Theology

Faith and public life are not juxtaposed; rather, they mutually inform one another. People's commitments inform how they use their faith to engage with public life. And one's faith is deepened by critical reflection and engagement of issues that matter to the flourishing of people. It is no accident that in the last decade or so, many theological schools have become increasingly more engaged in the prison system either through contextually based chaplaincy, educational initiatives, or other forms of ministry training.[1] The criminal justice system has become a context for both ministry and theological reflection. Institutions are beginning to understand that ministers and lay leaders must know how to navigate issues related to the criminal justice system. This is especially true for faith leaders who

1 Recently, the Association of Theological Schools-hosted peer group on innovative models invited theological schools that engage with the prison to participate. Schools included Candler School of Theology, Drew, Princeton Theological Seminary, Duke Divinity School, New Orleans Baptist Theological Seminary, and New York Theological Seminary. Although each of these programs differs in how they engage the prison context, the need for theological schools to pay attention to issues around incarceration is clear.

seek to work in African American communities that have been devastated by the impact of mass incarceration.

Religious education must remain in dialogue with issues of public concern. The "public" I refer to in this chapter is primarily the criminal justice system and its process, policies, and practices. As an African American female who has both taught in prison *and* witnessed close relatives devastated by the impact of the criminal justice system, I see incarceration as an issue of public concern ripe for discourse within the discipline of religious education. Limited scholarship exists within it specifically and theological education broadly that investigates mass incarceration.[2] This chapter sits at the intersection of religious education, criminal justice ministry, and public theology. My commitment to it is grounded in my experiences of teaching and directing a program in a women's prison and interviews with ten formerly incarcerated women.

Religious education participates in how communities live out their response to Angela Davis's question by forming learners in faith communities, even those doing the work of prison ministry. Learning takes place in all spheres of life, including within and around criminal justice processes. My discussion of religious education reflects an understanding of education within the field of public pedagogy. Public pedagogy is a form of education that recognizes learning in diverse forms, sites, and processes beyond formal schooling.[3]

---

2 Some texts include Evelyn L. Parker, "A Pedagogy of Redemption with Incarcerated Girls," in *Educating for Redemptive Community: Essays in Honor of Jack Seymour and Margaret Ann Crain*, ed. Jack L. Seymour, Margaret Ann Crain, Denise Janssen, and Mary Elizabeth Moore (Eugene, OR: Wipf & Stock, 2015), 111–24; Kaia Stern, *Voices from American Prisons: Faith, Education and Healing* (New York: Routledge, 2014); James Samuel Logan, *Good Punishment? Christian Moral Practice and U.S. Imprisonment* (Grand Rapids, MI: Eerdmans, 2008); Mark L. Taylor, *The Executed God: The Way of the Cross in Lockdown America* (Minneapolis: Fortress Press, 2001).

3 Jennifer A. Sandlin, Michael P. O'Malley, and Jake Burdick, "Mapping the Complexity of Public Pedagogy Scholarship: 1894–2010," *Review of*

Within this focus on public pedagogy, I call attention to the fact that pedagogy is "a performative practice embodied in the lived interactions among educators, audiences, texts, and institutional formations. Pedagogy, at its best, implies that learning takes place across a spectrum of social practices and settings."[4] For this chapter, my approach to religious education frames the prison as the site of learning and those engaged in prison ministry as learners. People are formed as they do the work of ministry in jails and prisons, with the families of those in jail and prisons, or with the victims of crime. Further, prison ministry is an education that facilitates encounters that ultimately enable new knowledge, enhanced skills, and practical wisdom.

This chapter offers a concrete public theological vision of five core pedagogical commitments that prison ministry might adopt as it does the work of public theology in the world—unmasking, countering, discerning, enacting, and reimagining. Each of the commitments intersect with ways of engaging any issue of public concern. Even as learners are formed in these commitments, their formation affects how they perceive and engage the world. Further, these commitments are dynamic and interact with one another simultaneously, forming not just the person engaged in prison ministry but also the system in which prison ministry is done.

Unmasking Racial Injustice in the Criminal Justice System

> Between me and the other world there is ever an unasked question: unasked by some through feelings of delicacy; by others through the difficulty of rightly framing it.

Educational Research 81, no. 3 (2011): 338–39.

4 Henry A. Giroux, "Cultural Studies, Public Pedagogy, and the Responsibility of Intellectuals," *Communication and Critical/Cultural Studies* 1, no. 1 (March 2004): 61.

> All, nevertheless, flutter round it. How does it feel to be a problem?[5]

The pedagogical commitment centered on unmasking necessarily begins with attention to prevailing problems: social conditions, policies, and injustices of various forms within society that give rise to injustices within the criminal justice system. Yet underlying the problems is an overarching one centered on attitudes toward Blackness in America. "Blackness" is and has always been a problem in America. The familiar question about the problem of Blackness, which was raised by W. E. B. Du Bois in the early 1900s, finds its roots in an American soil that prided itself on conquest and domination. The experience of Blackness in America is one of imposed inferiority; Black personhood has been always held in contempt and suspicion.

Blackness is not just a social problem but a moral and theological problem. Religious scholars point to the complicated history of Whites locating the racial origins of Blacks in the myth of Noah's son, Ham, who was cursed with servitude, as biblical justification for slavery, which circulated in the American imagination.[6] This myth made a direct connection with darker skin as inferior and as chosen to be in bondage. This myth in American religious and theological discourse has severe implications for ideals about Blackness. Biblical scholar Stephen Haynes examines how Southern Whites used the stories to talk about Ham dishonoring his father, thus resulting in social death—the ultimate dishonor.[7] Further, White Southerners read the Bible as if the curse of Ham was necessary to tame Ham's

---

5 W. E. B. Du Bois, *The Souls of Black Folk: Essays and Sketches* (Chicago: A. C. McClurg & Co., 1903), 1.

6 Stephen R. Haynes, *Noah's Curse: The Biblical Justification of American Slavery*, Religion in America Series (New York: Oxford University Press, 2002); David M. Goldenberg, *The Curse of Ham: Race and Slavery in Early Judaism, Christianity, and Islam*, Jews, Christians, and Muslims from the Ancient to the Modern World (Princeton, NJ: Princeton University Press, 2003).

7 Haynes, *Noah's Curse*, 65–86.

behavior and applied this understanding to Black slaves.[8] While the curse of Ham affirmed a sense of innate immorality to Blacks, Northerners attributed immorality to Blacks based on their circumstance. They refused to see Blacks as equal in society, yet they insisted upon punishment as a way to rehabilitate them into social norms.[9] Both notions of Blackness ascribed immorality to Black bodies.

Sociocultural narratives reinforce the idea that Blackness is synonymous with evil. Black men and boys, for instance, are perceived as "thugs," which evokes fear and a need for Black men and boys to be controlled.[10] Whole schools with a concentration of Black adolescents, for instance, are criminalized because of the concentration of Blackness and the moral panic that accompanies Blackness.[11] Black women in particular have inherited gendered sociocultural narratives that continue to pervade the moral imagination of America and influence how people perceive Blackness. Images such as Mammy, Jezebel, and Sapphire permeated American society to help justify why Black women were the perfect candidates for subjugation and enslavement.[12] Common among these stereotypes is the idea that Black women are promiscuous and angry, which stands in direct contradiction to the depiction of White women as pure and servile. These narratives dictate how society expects Black women to look, behave, emote, and interact with others. When Black women and girls seem to fit one of the above profiles, they are punished.

8 Haynes, 87-104.

9 Rima Vesely-Flad, *Racial Purity and Dangerous Bodies: Moral Pollution, Black Lives, and the Struggle for Justice* (Minneapolis: Fortress Press, 2017), 6.

10 Paul Butler, *Chokehold: Policing Black Men* (New York: New Press, 2017), Kindle.

11 Sarah Farmer, "Criminality of Black Youth in Inner-City Schools: 'Moral Panic,' Moral Imagination, and Moral Formation," *Race Ethnicity and Education* 13, no. 3 (2010): 367–81.

12 Melissa V. Harris-Perry, *Sister Citizen: Shame, Stereotypes, and Black Women in America* (New Haven, CT: Yale University Press, 2011), 28–33, 87–98, 165–70.

In *Pushout: The Criminalization of Black Girls in Schools*, Monique Morris describes the Jezebel role that Black women and girls inherited, which results in more suspensions and harsher punishments for Black girls than their White counterparts.[13]

Fear exists around free Black bodies roaming without any supervision. The fact that Black people still evoke images of danger and baseness while Whiteness evokes images of purity and virtue signifies the cultural memory that exists around Black bodies. This sociocultural narrative places Black bodies in the role of potential criminal, making it more likely that Black people will be arrested, gunned down, assaulted by law enforcement, or incarcerated. "Stand your ground" culture, in other words, does not exist in a vacuum, nor do the many laws that lead to the incarceration of Black bodies.[14] Whites relied on various forms of religious and theological claims to ascribe guilt to the Black body, marking it as chattel, dangerous, sexually deviant, and criminal.[15] Ultimately, this negative identification reifies the racial stereotyping and thus legitimizes the view in America's imagination that Blackness is the problem. Overall, the sentiment that Black bodies need to be tamed, Black women need to be silent, and Black boys and girls need to be socialized is historical residue deeply engrained in the heart of America.

Since slavery, Jim Crow laws, voting restrictions, segregation, housing, and employment regulations served as a barricade against Blackness. The current situation is what Michelle Alexander calls "the New Jim Crow," which functions like a racial caste system that locks

---

13 Monique W. Morris, *Pushout: The Criminalization of Black Girls in Schools* (New York: New Press, 2016), 56–134.

14 "Stand your ground" culture refers to the social climate in which the killing of Black bodies is permitted by law. Kelly Brown Douglas, *Stand Your Ground: Black Bodies and the Justice of God* (Maryknoll, NY: Orbis Books, 2015), xiii.

15 Through social-cultural narratives, Kelly Brown Douglas creates a clear depiction of how the Black body, and Blackness, becomes a historical symbol of guilt and inferiority, which produces and sustains racial violence and death of Black bodies. Douglas, *Stand Your Ground*, 48–89.

Blacks into an inferior position through law and custom.[16] Similarities between mass incarceration and Jim Crow laws are its political origins, legalized discrimination, political disenfranchisement, courthouse restrictions, racial segregation, and a symbolic production of race.[17] Today, America's dealing with Blackness is best reflected in specified and intentional practices within the American criminal justice system. Strategies are devised about who to target and what tactics to use by reinforcing images that equate Blackness with criminality.[18] Former federal prosecutor Paul Butler makes an even more provocative claim by asserting that the injustices experienced by Black lives is not a flaw of the criminal justice system; it is exactly how the system is supposed to work.[19] Conceptualized through the "chokehold," Butler describes a state-sanctioned process in which Black lives are coerced into submission and made vulnerable to death and death-dealing circumstances.[20] In the words of Butler:

> Many people–cops, politicians, and ordinary people–see African American men as a threat. The Chokehold is the legal and social response. It contains a constellation of tools that are used to keep them down–including a range of social practices, laws, punishments, and technologies that mark every Black man as a thug or potential thug. The state–especially the police–is authorized to control them by any means necessary.[21]

Mass incarceration, in his description, is a consequence of the chokehold.[22] *Who* gets punished in the current criminal justice system reflects a history where laws were put in place to silence, criminalize,

16 Michelle Alexander, *The New Jim Crow: Mass Incarceration in the Age of Colorblindness*, rev. ed. (New York: New Press, 2010), 12.

17 Alexander, *The New Jim Crow*, 190-200.

18 Alexander, 104–5.

19 Butler, *Chokehold: Policing Black Men*, Kindle.

20 Butler, Kindle.

21 Butler, Kindle.

22 Butler, Kindle.

or exterminate the problem of Blackness. As Alexander's study of mass incarceration makes clear, laws like the war on drugs have "helped produce one of the most extraordinary systems of racialized social control the world has seen."[23]

Racism can no longer hide behind policies and laws that seek to criminalize and incarcerate Black bodies. Through a critical analysis of social conditions and policies, public theological religious education helps unmask injustice in its various forms. The commitment to unmask invites a theologically grounded critical awareness of the injustices prevalent within the criminal justice system. Those who engage in prison ministry must go in with eyes wide open so that they do not internalize distorted ways of perceiving and interacting with incarcerated persons, because it *is* possible to do prison ministry and be completely unconscious of what is actually going on in the world.

One who participates in prison ministry sits at the intersection of religious education and public theology and must have a conscious awareness of how the system really works. Unmasking is about decoding the prison context in a way that reveals injustices that might be underlying the practices and policies that take place in the system. It assumes that the prison is not value neutral; one's participation in the system either supports the status quo or counters it. Freirean pedagogy advocates for educators to "read the world" as a means of coming to a critical awareness that invites learners into their full humanity, which, for Freire, is to participate in the world.[24] Participation happens in the world when one is able to help change the world. One cannot change the world unless one has a critical awareness of the world. In this case, prison functions as a "text" that those involved in ministry must read in order to read the world accurately.

---

23 Alexander, *The New Jim Crow*, 103.

24 Paulo Freire and Donaldo Macedo, *Literacy: Reading the Word and the World* (South Hadley, MA: Bergin & Garvey, 1987), 35.

Because incarcerated populations are within a system that is broader than prison itself, I take a critical stance on the need to know how various structures affect those who are incarcerated. It is not simply about knowing what prison does to incarcerated people; it is about knowing how incarcerated people got incarcerated in the first place. It is about identifying the interlocking systems that lead to incarceration as well as the underlying ideologies that inform the practices and policies of those who work within that system. Policies perpetuate entry into a system that leads people to jail and points to an implicit curriculum that certain groups of people are disposable and should be punished by law.[25] In other words, public theological religious education adopts a critical examination of the criminal justice system in order to unmask injustices that might be operative in the criminal justice system. Once injustice is uncovered, prison ministry must seek ways to counter any false logic of law and punishment that might unjustly affect incarcerated populations.

Beyond Retribution: Countering Penal Pedagogies

> [T]here is something innate in human behavior that allows humans in a position of power to treat others inhumanely when others have little or limited power and control.[26]

The pedagogical commitment of countering draws attention to false ideals about justice, race, and identity and moves toward creating a pathway toward promise. This commitment requires a critical analysis of retributive justice that typically applies to Black people in the criminal justice system. Yet it does not stop with this analysis. The

25 Elliot W. Eisner, *The Educational Imagination: On the Design and Evaluation of School Programs* (New York: Macmillan, 1979), 90–97.

26 This phrase appears in the discussion on the theme in Tamra Ryan, "Freedom's Just Another Word—How the Criminal Justice System Works Against Rehabilitation," in *The Third Law* (Denver: Gilpin House Press, 2013), 83.

movement is beyond retribution and confronts the question, What alternatives exist to retributive penal pedagogies?

To begin, penal pedagogy is characterized by a criminal justice system that enacts punishment based on a strict adherence to retributive justice. Just-deserts retributive practices of punishment seek to pay persons back in proportion to the offense committed. The purpose, then, is for the offender to suffer for the crime because they deserve to pay for the crime. Utilitarian notions of retribution see punishment as a tool to keep people compliant with the law. Those who step out of order must pay appropriately for their incompliance with the law. Retribution is designed to keep law and order. To this end, punishment seeks to deter, rehabilitate, and incapacitate criminals or perceived criminals from committing crime.

How we carry out punishment matters. Punitive practices shape people's engagement with the world. Punishment is pedagogical, designed to teach people how they should or should not act. Punishment is intended to socialize or shape thoughts and behavior according to specific sociocultural norms. The structure, actions, and language of the criminal justice system teach an implicit curriculum.[27] In other words, whether we like it or not, punishment teaches people how to think about the world and their relationship to the world.

Public theological religious education helps respond to the question, What does the way that punishment is practiced in our current criminal justice system teach Black men and women, boys and girls about their identity, about God, about justice, and about human value? I propose that penal pedagogies teach many lessons. For Blacks, these lessons are even more poignant with more severe consequences. In this section, I will only identify three of those lessons—on justice, race, and identity.

---

27 Eisner identifies three curricula that schools teach—the explicit, implicit, and null curricula. An implicit curriculum is not stated explicitly but can be implied by the organization, structure, actions, language, and physical set-up of a space. Eisner, *The Educational Imagination*, 87-97.

Penal Lesson #1—On Justice: A System of Entanglement

Penal pedagogy teaches people that what they did is more important than why they did it. The "get tough on crime" policies constitutive of retributive punishment extend sentences with little to no discretion about the circumstances leading to committed crimes, which has the effect of negating the worth of people who commit crimes and the need to examine why crimes were committed. It doesn't matter that Black girls might have faced abuse before they ran away and were apprehended by the juvenile justice system for truancy. It is of no importance that a pimp threatened your life if you did not have sex. It is of no concern that you need counseling and other assistance to overcome addiction and the trauma that led to your use of drugs in the first place. It doesn't matter! You did not adhere to the law; therefore, you must be punished.

This approach to punishment is a system of entanglement that often becomes virtually impossible to escape. Not only does it fail to respond to the root causes of poverty, abuse, and addiction that might lead people to commit crime; it also entraps people into a justice system that renders people powerless to actually secure justice for themselves. For young people, the school-to-prison pipeline is a perfect example of how miscarriages of justice take place.[28] Disciplinary infractions that used to be punished in the school with a principal are now a direct entry into the juvenile justice system, which increases the likelihood that young people will be funneled into the adult criminal justice system. Research indicates that people of color are most affected by the school-to-prison pipeline and other forms of policing.[29] One recent study shows that African American youth are five times more likely to be detained than White youth.[30] The

28 Farmer, "Criminality of Black Youth in Inner-City Schools," 368.

29 Morris, *Pushout*, 57; Victor M. Rios, *Punished: Policing the Lives of Black and Latino Boys* (New York: New York University Press, 2011), 6-7.

30 Sentencing Project, *Black Disparities in Youth Incarceration* (Washington, DC: Sentencing Project, 2017), 1.

justice system should not be intended to trap people; rather, justice is about restoring peace to the world.

Penal Lesson #2—On Race: No Such Thing as Color-Blind

Penal pedagogy teaches that if you are Black, you are more likely to be punished for your crime, and your punishment might be harsher than your White counterpart. While laws may be designed to deter potential crimes or to incapacitate those who commit more crime, Blacks are often predisposed to be "those" people. Sociocultural narratives and unconscious biases feed into practices and policies that seem to target people of color. Race matters in penal pedagogy. Neutrality is a myth. There is no such thing as laws that are color-blind. Punishment is not value neutral. In fact, research on mass incarceration may even have you conclude that retributive justice has a color.

There is a direct correlation between the war on drugs and the mass incarceration of people of color. During the war on drugs, punishment has hardened to "get tough on crime" policies that have led judges to "lock 'em up and throw away the key." Arrests for drug offenses have caused the great increase in incarceration. Alexander provides an accurate depiction of the war on drugs from arrest to incarceration by pointing out that law enforcement can stop and search people with consent during a time when hardly anyone would refuse consent. Police receive incentives for making arrests for drug offenses. Law enforcement uses new military-grade equipment to conduct drug raids and keep the cash and equipment they confiscate. Drug raids allow gangs of people to be arrested in one sweep for nonviolent drug offenses. Those arrested are encouraged by their legal counsel to plead guilty and be charged with a felony.[31]

But who gets locked up? Communities of color are targeted with these tactics. In 2008 the Pew Center on the States released a shocking report that confirmed the racialization of the criminal justice

31 Alexander, *The New Jim Crow*, 59–96.

system. According to this report, one in nine Black men between the ages of twenty to thirty-four were behind bars and one in fifteen Black men over the age of eighteen were behind bars, while only 1 in 106 White men were behind bars. Additionally, one in one hundred Black women aged thirty-five to thirty-nine were behind bars, while 1 in 355 White women were behind bars.[32] Between 1980 and 2010, women in prison increased in number by 646 percent, exceeding the 419 percent increase rate of men during that time.[33] While these statistics have shifted recently because of the opioid and heroin addiction running rampant in White communities, the point remains–the mass incarceration of people of color in the United States is a national public concern. Race is at the heart of this concern. Further, while statistics began to shift after the Pew Report, mass incarceration remains a disproportionate reality in Black communities. We may even raise the question of whether the war on drugs is a war against Black people rather than a war against crack and cocaine. A justice system that seems to target certain racial groups makes an implicit statement about the disposability of a racial group.

Even now, in retrospect, we can see how the harshness of laws is racialized. For example, when the majority of arrests are drug offenses committed by Black people, Black people are criminal, and an all-out "war" is needed to get them under control. The crisis facilitates locking people up. The method shifts, however, when drug abuse invades White communities. Laws tend to soften and language tends to change. Drugs are a public health crisis. Instead of locking people up, the crisis facilitates resourcing communities and health clinics. Drug offenses are no longer seen as criminal but are now viewed as a public health crisis requiring governmental resources.

---

32 Pew Center on the States' Public Safety Performance Project, *One in 100: Behind Bars in America 2008* (Washington, DC: The Pew Charitable Trusts, 2008), 5–7.

33 Marc Maeur, *The Changing Racial Dynamics of Women's Incarceration* (Washington, DC: Sentencing Project, 2013), 9.

In America's retributive model, crime is committed against the state rather than the victim. With the mass incarceration of Black bodies, one cannot dismiss the implications of state-sanctioned punishment that not only Black incarcerated individuals must endure but also the communities from which they come.

Penal Lesson #3—On Identity

Social death is still the price to pay for dishonor and disorder in the face of the "fathers" of America. Black communities are ravaged by and pay a high cost for mass incarceration. The children of incarcerated parents, for instance, are more likely to grow up in poverty and experience mental health challenges, compounded by the burdensome stigma around having a parent that is incarcerated.[34] Once released, many formerly incarcerated individuals constantly remember their time spent behind bars. If that is not enough, they also face the chances that employment and housing opportunities will be denied because of their criminal record. People become dead to society through alienation and exclusionary practices.[35] Generational cycles of incarceration are proliferated. Upon release, citizens face complex challenges as they return to the community, including difficulties finding housing and employment alongside complications in family life. Penal pedagogies contribute to keeping particular disadvantaged communities from gaining access to economic opportunities that could advance the quality of their lives.

Within the United States, social death is a racial mark that incarcerated persons wear.[36] Mass incarceration is a mechanism, as

---

34 National Resource Center on Children and Families of the Incarcerated, *Children and Families of the Incarcerated Fact Sheet* (Camden, NJ: Rutgers University, 2014), 1-3.

35 Orlando Patterson, *Slavery and Social Death: A Comparative Study* (Cambridge, MA: Harvard University Press, 1982), 13.

36 Joshua M. Price, *Prison and Social Death* (New Brunswick, NJ: Rutgers University Press, 2015), 6.

Michelle Alexander argues, of social control for Black people.[37] This social death is not just a death of civil rights, but it also bears on one's identity, on one's ability to be and become. The American criminal justice system teaches incarcerated persons, especially Black incarcerated persons, *if you make a mistake, you are a mistake.*

Penal pedagogy must be challenged not just in the criminal justice system but in manifestations of other spheres in life. We can't talk about the disproportionate number of Black people in the criminal justice system without talking about the ways Christian theology has contributed to the ways we punish. Penal pedagogy is not just operative in the criminal justice system but also in the faith community. T. Richard Snyder, in *Protestant Ethic and the Spirit of Punishment*, challenges Protestant tendencies to overemphasize the doctrine of grace as only necessary to redeem humanity from sin. In overemphasizing sin, he argues, one might fail to see grace as a foundation of love found in the beauty of all God's creation. Further, to individualize sin and redemption gives grounds for the categorization of those who are sinners and those who are redeemed.[38] To be clear, I am not against redemption and think all creation needs to be redeemed. But as history has shown, Blacks have always been cast in the role of sinners in need of redemption. And now, incarcerated persons are cast as godless and in need of redemption. Thus, the question becomes, How do we form people in a way to see the fullness of God's grace manifested in individuals and systems?

Public theology and practice in religious education seek to infuse the public imagination with new narratives about who God is and how God acts in the world. These narratives include stories about God's love superseding death and punishment. Rather than God as a divine judge waiting to exact punishment on people who disobey the law, God can be imagined as one who walks with those who are negotiating the circumstances of their lives in their everyday

37 Alexander, *The New Jim Crow*, 2-4.

38 T. Richard Snyder, *The Protestant Ethic and the Spirit of Punishment* (Grand Rapids, MI: Eerdmans, 2001), 35-50.

moral decisions. According to Black theologian James Cone, God is not neutral but standing on the side of those who are suffering. He writes, "The cross places God in the midst of a crucified people, in the midst of people who are hung, shot, burned, and tortured."[39] These narratives are not just told but embodied in how individuals and communities of faith locate themselves and their activity within the criminal justice system. The question is what lessons do we as religious educators and people of faith want to teach through our practices of justice?

Prison ministry sits at the intersection of pain and promise, seeking to serve as an agent of justice in the prison. As stated earlier, it counters false ideals about justice, race, and identity by pressing toward a pedagogy that creates a pathway toward promise. Elizabeth Conde-Frazier describes the types of practical theology that work in the service of social justice: "Religious education for peace and justice should contribute to the healing places of disconnection or alienation of one from the other. It is scholarship that emerges from our embrace of both the pain of the pathos of the oppressed and the promise of the reign of love and justice."[40] We must move beyond penal pedagogies rooted in retributive justice and begin to reassess the role of punishment. If those in prison are made in God's image and possess inherent worth, they are also worthy of nurture, love, and investment of resources.

Many scholars have moved away from retributive justice to a more inclusive understanding of the nature and practice of justice. As an alternative to penal pedagogies, some scholars propose restorative practices.[41] Alternative models are names in social movements–such

---

39 James H. Cone, *The Cross and the Lynching Tree* (Maryknoll, NY: Orbis Books, 2011), 26.

40 Elizabeth Conde-Frazier, "Participatory Action Research: Practical Theology for Social Justice," *Religious Education* 101, no. 3 (September 2006): 326.

41 Christopher D. Marshall, *Beyond Retribution: A New Testament Vision for Justice, Crime, and Punishment*, Studies in Peace and Scripture (Grand Rapids, MI: Eerdmans, 2001).

as the anti-stop-and-frisk movements and Black Lives Matter movement.[42] These social movements are calling America to take into account what underlies the way it engages people of color. Further, alternative models of justice take into account the victim, the person who committed the crime, why crime is committed, as well as the families and communities who are affected by America's punishment of crime. As New Testament scholar Christopher Marshall puts it, "My premise is that the first Christians experienced in Christ and lived out in their faith communities an understanding of justice as a power that heals, restores, and reconciles rather than hurts, punishes, and kills, and that this reality ought to shape and direct a Christian contribution to the criminal justice debate today."[43]

Extending the purpose of justice, Marshall suggests that restoration rather than vengeance and forgiveness rather than punishment is the fulfillment of justice.[44] A balanced view of justice takes into account both the motive and the act, and considers justice for the victim, mercy for the offender, and concern for restoring society. This more expanded view of justice counters individualistic models of punishment that seek for one person to pay for the crime without taking any other considerations into account.[45] In other words, our response to crime should be met with care, acceptance, and an opportunity for the person who committed the crime to reintegrate back into the community rather than be met with imposed stigma and shame.[46] When one discerns God in the other, caring is made possible.

---

42 Vesely-Flad, *Racial Purity and Dangerous Bodies*, 153-94; Butler, *Chokehold*, Kindle.

43 Marshall, *Beyond Retribution,* 33.

44 Marshall, 199, 283.

45 Jack Balswick, "Towards a Social Theology of Punishment," *PSCF* 41 (December 1989): 221-26.

46 Charles Barton, "Empowerment and Retribution in Criminal Justice," in *Restorative Justice: Philosophy to Practice*, ed. Heather Strang and John Braithwaite (Burlington, VT: Ashgate, 2000), 66-67.

Discerning God's Activity in Prison Ministry

> The prison . . . functions ideologically as an abstract site into which undesirables are deposited, relieving us of the responsibility of thinking about the real issues afflicting those communities from which prisoners are drawn in such disproportionate numbers.[47]

In my personal involvement in prison ministry, I found God in the prison, not just in outsiders who came in to lead Bible studies and teach. I saw God present in those who were incarcerated. I contend that one of the greatest myths in prison work is that we have to take God to the prison. This is grossly wrong. God is already at work in the prison. What we must do as ministers is discern God's presence. Within the Certificate in Theological Studies program I directed, I heard the same comment repeatedly: "These women were nothing like I expected." The prison becomes a formative space where those engaged in the work of prison ministry can see anew. What they see and learn is that they are not going in to work with "criminals." Rather, they are going in to work with people who may have committed a crime at some point in their lives. Further, it is not unlikely that God has already encountered many of the women, sustaining them in a system that seeks to isolate and make them feel inferior.

Prison ministry is countercultural because it refuses to be *relieved of* responsibility for those who are incarcerated; rather, prison ministry seeks to stake a claim that those within prison are desired and pursued by God. It assumes that God is not outside of the prison system but actively working in it. In other words, discerning God's activity and presence in the world makes the abstract real. Prison is not an abstract site but a *real* physical location with *real* physical people who are experiencing *real* suffering. Religious education tends to the *real* stuff of life. To pay attention to those

---

47 Angela Davis, *Are Prisons Obsolete?* (New York: Seven Stories Press, 2003), 16.

in prison necessitates a responsiveness to the deep brokenness that exists in the world. It attunes one's attention to the *real*ities in prison that require God's attention. Not attending to those in prison points to a type of inattention that is not characteristic of public theology. Rather, religious education seeks to attend to those who are experiencing diverse forms of suffering, including those within prison.

Unmasking injustice with its attempts to counter penal pedagogies creates more questions than answers. It is not unusual that individuals and communities who engage in prison ministry raise questions about who God is, where God is, and whether God is even "good." This is why a core pedagogical commitment of public theological religious education in the prison is to raise the difficult questions and to set one's heart on exploring where God is at work in the prison. Helping the faith community discern God's presence and activity within the world is a primary task of religious education. Clearly, prison ministry is not about easy fixes; rather, it is about careful discernment of God's presence and activity. Particularly in prison contexts, discerning God can be hard work. Those engaged in prison ministry place themselves in a system that is filled with turmoil, conflict, and disappointment. Yet as Mary Elizabeth Moore notes, individuals and communities that mediate God's holiness embrace a "hermeneutic of reconstruction," where they actively participate in "discerning Holy nudges, analyzing sacred texts and life events, and then reconstructing community life, theology, and action in light of the emerging visions and insights."[48]

Prison ministry extends God's activity into the world. God is active through God's people—the Church. Part of discerning God's activity is knowing how one is best fit to partner with God in extending God's reign of peace, righteousness, and joy within prison ministry. Discerning God's activity requires an understanding of one's

48 Mary Elizabeth Moore, *Teaching as a Sacramental Act* (Cleveland: Pilgrim Press, 2004), 204.

own identity and vocation. Individuals and communities are formed in Christlikeness as they begin to see themselves through the eyes of Christ. To see one's identity as a partner *with* God in making the world a better place and to envision one's vocation as a means to do this work of partnering with God enriches prison ministry.

Approaching prison ministry with an eye toward God's activity in one's personal life as well as the larger system is not only important for those engaged in prison ministry but also those who find themselves incarcerated. If prison is the site where society disposes of undesirables, it is the site where God is made visible in those whom society marks as undesired. Christ is not only with those called "criminal"; Christ actually became criminal to liberate those deemed criminal. Public theological religious education calls those engaged in prison ministry to see themselves as actors in God's redemptive story. Linking a person's incarceration with a God who was both imprisoned and executed in the biblical text in an African heritage that speaks of resiliency in the midst of forced bondage invites identification with a God who is alive and active in the midst of criminal justice. Story-linking, as religious educator Anne Wimberly notes, not only helps make sense of what individuals are liberated from but also helps make sense of what people are liberated for.[49] Not only does social context form persons, but those in prison ministry simultaneously recreate the social context. Prison ministry offers an opening for those engaged in ministry to mediate the transcendent and allow transcendent power to shape the realities of prison life.[50] Prison ministry incarnates the presence of God in order to work in solidarity with those in prison toward the prospect of flourishing life.

---

49 Anne Streaty Wimberly, *Soul Stories: African American Christian Education* (Nashville: Abingdon Press, 1994), 26.

50 Jack L. Seymour, Robert T. O'Gorman, and Charles R. Foster, *The Church in the Education of the Public* (Nashville: Abingdon Press, 1984), 128.

Enacting a Public Pedagogy of Care within Prison Ministry

> Stop preaching and hire somebody. Stop preaching and let somebody stay with you. Stop preaching and find somebody somewhere to stay. Stop preaching and donate some clothes you can't fit. . . . [S]top–Be a resource.[51]

> Proximity has taught me some basic and humbling truths, including this vital lesson: Each of us is more than the worst thing we've ever done.[52]

Care is not just something you *feel*; care is something you *do*. The above instruction is aimed at the faith community by Nona, a formerly incarcerated woman who sees care as an activity expressed in tangible actions rather simply in expressed words. This woman points to an essential commitment to affirm and embrace caring as part of a public theology and practice of religious education. To care within the African American context requires a deep attention to the communal need for survival and liberation.[53] The need for survival and liberation is even more pervasive in the lives of those affected by incarceration. As Nona indicates, caring requires attention to the existential needs that incarcerated women, for instance, face right after prison. Enacting care is *being* the resource in the form of direct care for and with those affected by the criminal justice system.

The prison ministry I propose offers a counterpedagogy to the penal pedagogy currently embodied in the way the American criminal justice system executes punishment. It offers a public pedagogy of care. Rooted in relational knowing, a public pedagogy of care is a relational investment of resources from people or institutions

51 Nona, interview, January 30, 2015.

52 Bryan Stevenson, *Just Mercy: A Story of Justice and Redemption* (New York: Random House, 2014), 17-18.

53 Carroll A. Watkins Ali, *Survival and Liberation: Pastoral Theology in African American Context* (St. Louis: Chalice Press, 1999), 1-9.

that contribute to the welfare of those affected by incarceration. At the core of enacting care is a relational investment that allows concern for and with another to shape one's engagement. When we do prison ministry at the intersection of public theology and public pedagogy, we are driven by compassion for others and the desire to see broken institutions made whole. Our love of God leads us to care for others. Caring provides the basis for justice.[54]

A public theology and practice of religious education embraces the task of caring not simply for those in the faith community but for those on the margins of faith or who do not profess any faith. It recognizes and goes beyond the pivotal aspect of nurture in religious education, which is about making personal commitments to the vitality of life and to the character and dignity of another, without which life would diminish.[55] Specifically, enacting care within criminal justice ministries relies on understanding care as an act toward the flourishing of all people, especially Black and Brown people who are incarcerated. To care for incarcerated persons and their families is to care for Christ. To care for those who have faced harm resulting from victimization is to care for Christ, who was assaulted and wrongly accused. To care for a parent whose son is being demolished because of punishment meted out by the state is to care for God, who witnessed the execution of Christ. When we identify with incarcerated persons, we also identify with Christ, who was deemed a criminal and faced a criminal's death. To be a nonincarcerated Christian is, in fact, a call to identify with those who are incarcerated.

---

54 Nel Noddings, *Starting at Home: Caring and Social Policy* (Berkeley: University of California Press, 2002), 22–24.

55 See Anne Streaty Wimberly, *Nurturing Faith and Hope: Black Worship as a Model for Christian Education*, rev. ed. (2004; Eugene, OR: Wipf & Stock, 2010), xiii–xiv; and Khalil Gholami and Kirsi Tirri, "Caring Teaching as a Moral Practice: An Exploratory Study on Perceived Dimensions of Caring Teaching," in "The Moral Core of Teaching," special issue, *Education Research International* (2012): http://dx.doi.org/10.1155/2012/954274.

The startling comparison Cone makes between the cross and the lynching tree resonates with the criminal justice system. The cross, as a pedagogical symbol connected to the lynching tree, points to the paradox of suffering made evident in the lives of Black people in America. But, most of all, the cross dares people to sanitize the brutality of assault, execution, and dehumanization that was done to Christ by the hand of "good citizens" and continues to be done in the workings of the criminal justice system.[56] To witness the brutality of the cross is to be moved. The cross, in other words, calls forth a performance of public theology that invites people to care *with*.

The call to identify through caring for and with those affected by incarceration is rooted in an ethic of care. Those who are not as vulnerable to the detrimental effects of the criminal justice system bear the cross with those who are most vulnerable to entanglement in the criminal justice system. Yet caring in prison ministry is neither charity nor unidirectional. Rather, prison ministry is the mutual interchange of lives being exchanged across the border. It is life on the border where a prophetic space is created for more humane living.[57] Anne Streaty Wimberly notes:

> Persons are never fully liberated until they become aware of others' needs for liberation and accept as obligatory their responsibility for contributing to the liberation of others. This dimension of liberation entails mutual caring or the movement away from concerns and actions aimed only toward the self to concerns and actions with and on behalf of others as Jesus did.[58]

A public pedagogy of care is about solidarity. Caring is deeply relational. Our care-filled attention to the lives of women, men, and children on the incarceration continuum is formative, reminding those

56 Cone, *The Cross and the Lynching Tree*, 159.

57 Conde-Frazier, "Participatory Action Research," 326.

58 Wimberly, *Soul Stories*, 26.

who enact care of the creatureliness of humanity. Care is not only received through interpersonal relationships, but there is a role for the larger community. Communities shape how a person behaves and develops. Enacting care invites a critical practical engagement with the criminal justice system that might involve prison programming, prison education, advocacy, pastoral care, and ministry to the children of incarcerated parents.

Enacting care is not purely intellectual or imaginative; rather, it is a public theology that seeks to build a better today and tomorrow through concrete engagement with people in the world. To enact care in the context of the criminal justice system is to perform theology. As Katie Day and Sebastian Kim note in their description of the performance of public theology, "Theology is being produced even as it is being performed or expressed in the public sphere. Action challenges and informs theological understandings, even as theology interrogates the methods of activism."[59] Public theology and practice of religious education invite those engaged in the work of criminal justice ministry into deep reflection on the practice of care. Enacting a public pedagogy of care is praxis-oriented. Those engaged in justice work embody "reflection and action directed at the structures to be transformed."[60]

A praxis-of-care cycle consists of active engagement in the justice system, theological reflection on one's engagement with the justice system to make it better, and then reengaging the criminal justice system more effectively. One cares through listening and responding in compassionate ways. The relational investment that leads one to immerse the self in the prison context creates a proximity to the concerns that matter to those who are incarcerated, informing the type of care provided and deepening one's orientation toward enacting care.

---

59 Katie Day and Sebastian Kim, "Introduction," *A Companion to Public Theology*, ed. Sebastian Kim and Katie Day (Boston: Brill, 2017), 17.

60 Freire, *Pedagogy of the Oppressed*, 126.

Reimagining Prison Ministry

If Black lives are to matter, we must dream bigger.[61]

What is a vision of flourishing life for incarcerated persons?[62] The question of flourishing lies at the heart of reimagining the criminal justice system. After a systematic examination of the very criminal justice system that upholds the unjust policing of Black men, former federal prosecutor Paul Butler concludes that "if Black lives are to matter, we must dream bigger."[63] Our approaches to criminal justice not only need to be changed; they need to be completely reimagined. Learning new ways to do prison ministry that are devoid of the racial injustice and retributive penal pedagogies that structure the system requires a complete reimagining of what we call prison ministry in the first place.

Broadening Our Scope

To build more expansive and just communities requires our imagination to be more expansive, stretching to see incarceration as a process that actually begins before a person is ever incarcerated and remains with them even upon release. Thus, we must reimagine prison ministry beyond simply what we do in prison; rather, prison ministry must expand to engage the complex criminal justice system. In other words, prison ministry may be reconceived as *criminal justice ministries*—a continuum of efforts that help mitigate the experiences that people experience before, during, and after incarceration. They are efforts that go to the heart of religious education, deliberately aimed at reformation of persons, others connected to them, and structures. To be clear, I do not see criminal justice ministries occupying one physical location such as the prison, nor do I see

---

61 Butler, *Chokehold*, Kindle.

62 Questions about what it means for everyone to flourish are being pursued by Yale Center for Faith and Culture and Miroslav Volf with an aim to recenter theology around questions of joy and the good life.

63 Butler, *Chokehold*, Kindle.

criminal justice ministries as only responding to one issue. Criminal justice ministries represent a combination of activities that seek to prevent incarceration with the same tenacity as those activities that help reintegrate returning citizens back into society. To this end, prison ministry must be imagined as multifaceted, encompassing prevention, intervention, and reintegrative practices that consider both how people are funneled into the prison as well as what happens when they return to society.

Broadening our religious educational view of what prison ministry might entail challenges us to widen the prism of *who* we minister to and with and *how* we minister. To apply criminal justice ministries to only those in prison also fails to pay attention to all those affected by incarceration. Criminal justice ministries include families of people who are incarcerated, the communities that experience a vacuum due to incarceration, and those who have been victimized by crime. Criminal justice ministries engage ministry with victims and victimizers alike, since all people are made in the image of God. Victim and victimizer might be and often are one and the same. Those who commit crimes have often had crimes committed against them, which adds another layer of complexity in our responses to those entangled in the criminal justice system.

Revolutionizing Our Thinking

Conversations restricted to prison reform or making better prisons dominate prison discussions. We need to extend the conversation to examine the root causes of imprisonment and create new institutions. In her well-known work *Are Prisons Obsolete?*, prison abolitionist Angela Davis challenges people to question their assumptions about prison and explore other ways of doing justice not anchored in building and sentencing people to prison. Instead, Davis urges us to adopt "strategies of decarceration," which invest resources in education, healthcare, and restorative models of justice.[64] Really, the call is to revolutionize the role and nature of religious education. To revolutionize thinking is a call to reconsider penal pedagogies, which are often readily embraced with no critical thought about their impact. The mere fact that people cannot imagine life without prison yet fear thinking about what happens inside them indicates a gross contradiction in the way we think about prisons.[65] To reimagine life without prisons requires an opening of one's vision to possibilities not yet envisioned. The future of our young people is at stake if we fail to reimagine new modes of criminal justice in America.

Widening Our Circle

Even more than broadening our scope, we must widen our circle by convening conversations with multiple voices. Discussions about alternative forms of punishment or transformation to the criminal justice system should not only occur in boardrooms or government buildings. A wide range of voices is needed in the reimagining process, thereby making religious education an innovative collaborative advocacy endeavor. These discussions must be done with those most affected by prisons, including those in prison. Politicians from all levels of government, educators, and ministers also need to be part of the conversation. Their involvement helps connect the new vision with institutions (government, school, and faith communities) that have the capacity to create policies that build the community rather than tear it down. Parole officers, wardens, judges, and law enforcements need to be part of the conversation. Their involvement creates opportunities for them to protect rather than prosecute people and to reestablish trust in communities that have always been suspicious of those with the authority to uphold the law. Young people need to be part of the circle; their energy and passion for change will sustain the efforts throughout time. Older generations

---

64 Davis, *Are Prisons Obsolete?*, 20, 107–8.

65 Davis, 15.

need to be part of the circle; their wisdom will prevent us from making the same mistakes again and again.

Further, the voices of prison abolitionists need to be part of the circle, for they offer us a critical reminder that the very transformation we seek to make in the prison is often limited by the fact that we are working in a system that has been built to serve a purpose that contradicts our purpose. They push us toward not simply changing a system that will continue to replicate violence against Black people's personhood but to completely abolish prisons. Hearing new voices cultivates our imaginations, enlivening them with new ideas and insights toward building a better future and a theology that is wide enough to hold together all the complexities within people, places, and society.

Imagination is an essential tool for building the world we have yet to dream. Who we are and what the world can be begins to take shape in our imagination, even before words, judgments, values, and beliefs are ever formed.[66] Emilie Townes, in her keynote address on teaching and imagination, proposes "counter-memory" as imagination that responds to the caricatures we create that upholds systemic structures of evil. In the words of Townes, "counter-memories help us step outside of ourselves—and this is the best of what I find that we do in education. We challenge our students, ourselves, and the educational structures we are in to dream of more expansive and just spaces for people to live in—and not a space for a special select few. And not only do we dream it, we build it."[67] Cultivating the imagination is essential work for transforming persons and societies. The process of reimagining prison ministry invites people in the faith community to enter new social worlds that have been held at a distance. Cultivating the imagination is a task within religious

66 Seymour, O'Gorman, and Foster, *The Church in the Education of the Public*, 138.

67 Emilie M. Townes, "Teaching and the Imagination," *Religious Education* 111, no. 4 (August 2016): 369.

education that not only reimagines what we do in the prison; it reimagines theology altogether.

Reflections

Prison ministry provides an opportunity to mediate God's presence in the public sphere and transform the criminal justice system. But transformation stems from the way in which a person is formed. This chapter proposes a public theological basis for and practices of religious education that center on five core commitments in prison ministry–unmasking, countering, discerning, enacting, and reimagining–in which learners are formed. These core commitments offer a way for faith communities to press toward flourishing alongside those who are made most vulnerable because of the criminal justice system.

Religious Education and the Public Role of the Sister's Keeper

A Historical Correlational Method

Richelle B. White

> Education and justice are democracy's only life insurance. There is no substitute for learning. . . . It is the investment of our hopes and dreams for the generations that are to come.
>
> –Nannie Helen Burroughs, *Think on These Things*

Exemplars of the "Sister's Keeper" and Requirement of Public Advocacy

Distinguished activists and educators Nannie Helen Burroughs and Mary McLeod Bethune used the public sphere as a catalyst to bring quality religious education to Black girls in the early twentieth century. Through founding schools, these extraordinary Christian educators put their religious visions into action. With the opening of the National Training School for Women and Girls, Nannie Helen Burroughs's public advocacy connected to her Christian faith as she provided life-changing educational experiences for Black women and girls, persuading them to stand on their own and use their own voices. Mary McLeod Bethune organized a school for Black girls that would teach them academic basics, the importance of service to the community, and skills to earn a living. The Daytona Beach Literary and Industrial School for Training Negro Girls was a revolutionary undertaking during that time in history.

Just after the turn of the century, approximately forty years after the abolition of slavery, societal issues stood in the way of a just society for Black women and girls. Pervasive attitudes about their education included the belief that Black women were incapable of learning and that educating Black women would be an exercise in futility and therefore counterproductive. In addition, it was believed that education would turn the Black woman against her "proper" role as a servant to Whites. Moreover, the societal issues of racism, poverty, and gender discrimination confronted Black girls. However, in spite of these obstacles, Burroughs and Bethune activated their faith to make life better for Black girls through Christian religious education. This idea is essential to understanding their work, self-perception, and ways of being in the world.

Burroughs and Bethune modeled ways of being that confronted the realities of their day that hindered the growth and development of Black girls. They were their "sister's keeper." "Sister's keeper" is an expression that has been adapted from Genesis 4:9, "Am I my brother's keeper?," when Cain asks God this rhetorical question after killing his brother, Abel. "Keeper" in this context denotes responsibility for another. With this in mind, lessons can be learned from Burroughs's and Bethune's work, character, pedagogical strategies, and curricular frameworks in today's Christian religious education contexts that seek to engage and educate Black girls in the public sphere. Their historically structured and time-honored methods of delivery hold relevance for the contemporary requirement of advocacy and public theological pedagogies in educational ministries and societal engagement.

The Requirement of Public Advocacy

Postmodern thought espouses a utopian view of harmony and the elimination of social conflict. Couched in post-Western, postracial, and post-Christian terminology, racism, prejudice, injustice, and discrimination are believed to be overcome if not outdated. Moreover, the primacy of a Christian worldview gives way to the embrace of a broader spirituality framework. However, although this orientation in American life exists, it has also come under review.[1] This is clearly the case in education. Postmodern educational theory highlights the presence of racial and cultural diversity and claims the equality of all cultures. Yet this utopian view neither recognizes nor addresses present realities.[2] According to Burroughs, education and justice are the marks of a democratic society. However, systemic racism has not abated. It continues to prevent equal educational opportunities

---

1 Perspectives on prevailing understandings and critique of postmodern, post-Christian, post-Western thought appear in John B. Cobb Jr., *Postmodernism and Public Policy: Reframing Religion, Culture, Education, Sexuality, Class, Race, Politics, and the Economy* (Albany: State University of New York Press, 2002); Michael C. Dawson and Lawrence D. Bobb, "One Year Later and the Myth of a Post-Racial Society," *Du Bois Review: Social Science Research on Race* 6, no. 2 (2009): 247–49, https://dash.harvard.edu/handle/1/10347165; and Jennifer Lee, "A Post-Racial Society or a Diversity Paradox?," Russell Sage Foundation, accessed January 24, 2020, www.russellsage.org/research/post-racial-society-or-diversity-paradox.

2 Postmodernist views of education, its limitations, and direction are explored in Glenn Rikowski and Peter McLaren, "Postmodernism in Educational Theory," 1-9 and Jenny Bourne, "Racism, Postmodernism and the Flight from Class," 131–46, in *Postmodernism in Education Theory: Education and the Politics of Human Resistance*, ed. Dave Hill, Peter McLaren, Mike Cole, and Glenn Rikowski (London: Tufnell Press, 1999); and Taiwanna D. Anthony, William Allan Kritsonis, and David E. Herrington, "Postmodernism and the Implications for Educational Leadership: National Implications," *The Lamar University Electronic Journal of Student Research* (Spring 2007): https://files.eric.ed.gov/fulltext/ED495291.pdf.

for many Blacks in the public school system and affects Black girls in particular.

When surveying the educational experiences of Black girls in the twenty-first century, educational effectiveness and justice are in short supply. *Black Girls Matter: Pushed Out, Overpoliced and Underprotected Report*[3] chronicles the stories of Black girls who are leaving school because of suspensions, expulsions, or a variety of other reasons. Cynthia Greenlee adds that some of those reasons include poverty, predatory boyfriends, chaotic schools, zero-tolerance discipline policies, bullying, racialized gendered assumptions, implicit bias, and bogus offenses, including talking back, sassiness, and asking questions.[4] In short, Black girls are being pushed out of the educational system. Monique W. Morris, cofounder of the National Women's Justice Institute and author of *Pushout: The Criminalization of Black Girls in Schools*, further confirms this reality: "Too many Black girls are being criminalized (physically and mentally harmed) by beliefs, policies and actions that degrade and marginalize both their learning and their humanity leading to conditions that push them out of schools and render them vulnerable to even more harm."[5] Some schools are no longer identified as safe, protective spaces but rather contexts where Black girls are treated inhumanely.

In addition to being pushed out of schools, Black girls are confronted with policies and practices that are uniting to "save" Black boys and other boys of color while showing very little concern for the welfare of Black girls. One such initiative is former President Barack Obama's signature program "My Brother's Keeper," which is

---

3 Kimberlé Williams Crenshaw, Priscilla Ocen, and Jyoti Nanda, *Black Girls Matter: Pushed Out, Overpoliced and Underprotected* (New York: African American Policy Forum—Center for Intersectionality and Social Policy Studies at Columbia Law School, 2016).

4 Cynthia Greenlee, "'I'm Not Slow': Black Girls Tell Their Experiences of School," Rewire.News, April 13, 2016, https://rewire.news/article/2016/04/13/not-slow-Black-girls-tell-experiences-pushout/.

5 Monique W. Morris, *Pushout: The Criminalization of Black Girls in Schools* (New York: New Press, 2016), 8–9.

aimed at removing barriers to education and employment for Black boys and other boys of color. Through this initiative, the Obama Administration joined with cities and towns, businesses and foundations that are taking steps to connect young men to mentoring, support networks, and the skills they need to find a good job or go to college and work their way into the middle class.[6] The program has drawn critics who have called for gender equality, citing that Black girls are seemingly invisible and of little significance. Investment in Black boys is needed; however, it should not be to the exclusion of Black girls. The broader educational goal is to generate policy that responds to the needs of girls as well as boys. The goal for leaders–Sister's Keepers–is to develop theory and practices that support reform in teaching and learning.[7] This goal must be applied to religious education.

The Requirement of Advocacy in Religious Education

Despite the gender-based discrimination exhibited in the educational system push-out, criminalization, and marginalization of Black girls, they are both gifted and resilient.[8] However, they need a community of advocates to help them tell their stories as well as experience education and justice with the tenacity that Nannie Helen Burroughs and Mary McLeod Bethune offered Black girls in the early twentieth century. Black girls must be included in what Burroughs and Bethune call the "American Democracy."[9] Black girls are

---

6 The White House, "My Brother's Keeper," accessed January 24, 2020, https://obamawhitehouse.archives.gov/my-brothers-keeper.

7 An emphasis on the development of both theory and practice to support reform in education, teaching, and learning is highlighted in Anthony, Kritsonis, and Herrington, "Postmodernism and the Implications for Educational Leadership," 4.

8 See Venus E. Evans-Winters, "Are Black Girls Not Gifted? Race, Gender, and Resilience," *Interdisciplinary Journal of Teaching and Learning* 4, no. 1 (Spring 2014): 22–30.

9 Mary McLeod Bethune described the "American Democracy" in terms of the principles of equality, opportunity, and the fight for a new America

worthy of study, attention, and support. Burroughs and McLeod tell of the fight for democratic ideals, and in so doing, they reflect the important role of advocacy in religious education that, as indicated earlier, is the obligatory function of the "keeper." It has led to my calling and personal, vocational, and social responsibilities, including coming alongside Black girls as a "keeper" in the fight for education and justice.

Howard Thurman's essay "The Task of the Ministry" puts forth ideas on religion and Black youth that suggest a strategy for the Negro minister to serve the broader African American community as it encounters societal challenges.[10] Thurman's public theology offers the following four characteristics for the Negro minister's public engagement in ministry.

- "We must refuse to be caught in the present demand for things and must find our security in the reality of God and the spiritual tasks to which he has set our hands."[11]
- "We must put a vast faith in the contagion in the Spirit of Jesus rather than in the building of organizations to perpetuate his Spirit."[12]
- "We must seek to demolish the artificial barrier between religion and life."[13]

---

in Mary McLeod Bethune, "What Does American Democracy Mean to Me?," address at America's Town Meeting of the Air, November 23, 1939, New York City, http://americanradioworks.publicradio.org/features/sayit plain/mmbethune.html. See also "The Nannie Helen Burroughs Project: Rebuilding a Culture of Character," http://nburroughsinfo.org. This website includes Nannie Burroughs's description of the "American Democracy" in terms of "a lump of leaven which a woman took and hid in three measures of a meal, until the whole was leavened. . . . Democracy brings change. Democracy means continuous progressive readjustment."

10 Howard Thurman, *A Strange Freedom: The Best of Howard Thurman on Religious Experience and Public Life* (Boston: Beacon Press, 1998), 193.

11 Thurman, *A Strange Freedom*, 194.

12 Thurman, 195.

13 Thurman, 197.

- "We must not allow any phase of human knowledge to lie outside of our province, but we must provide a creative synthesis, in the light of which all the facts of science or what not may be viewed."[14]

Thurman teaches that we must move away from materialistic attitudes and actions and find security in the work that God calls each of us to do. Thurman admonishes God's ministers to be led by and put their faith in the authenticity of the Holy Spirit, not false gods. Religion and life must not be viewed as separate entities but as a connected whole. Finally, Thurman encourages ministers to view human intelligence in light of the world of science. In short, Thurman advocates a move from religion within a religious context to going into God's world, with God's Spirit to serve God's people. Thurman's framework is a challenge for those who serve in ministry to become students of life, namely as public theologians, being mindful of the struggles and striving of Black people and being prepared to continually assert the ethical demands of the ministry of Jesus Christ.[15] Thurman's ideas affirm my commitment to be engaged in the ministerial pursuit of providing Christian education in the public school setting as a means of developing and equipping young people with Christian values.

The following sections will explore the theme, "My Sister's Keeper: A Historical Correlation Method for African American Christian Religious Education." Part 1 will introduce the lives and educational careers of Nannie Helen Burroughs and Mary McLeod Bethune, school founders whose primary mission was to offer Christian religious education to Black girls and bring that education to the public sphere. I will also share implications of their work for Christian religious educators today. Part 2 will explore contemporary pedagogical strategies that connect with the historical practices of Burroughs and Bethune as means of informing present and future

14 Thurman, 198.
15 Thurman, 198.

practices of African American Christian religious education. Part 3 will share stories of how the historical correlation method informs the work of Christian religious education with Black girls in the public sphere.

Part One: The Lives and Educational Careers of Nannie Helen Burroughs and Mary McLeod Bethune

The lives and educational careers of Nannie Helen Burroughs and Mary McLeod Bethune are critical to understanding advocacy in religious education and meanings of public theology and praxis in religious education. Each of these prominent historical leaders uniquely contributes to this understanding.

Nannie Helen Burroughs

Nannie Helen Burroughs, educator and social and moral change agent, was born in Orange, Virginia, on May 2, 1879. At the age of five, her mother took her to live in Washington, DC because there were better educational opportunities for Blacks.[16] She attended the historic M Street High School. Although segregated, M Street High School boasted a highly qualified educational leadership team, including Dr. Anna Julia Cooper and Mary Church Terrell, who were leading African American educators and social activists and models for Burroughs's life.[17] The curriculum demanded that students use reason rather than solely depending on memorization

---

16 Opal V. Ester, *Nannie Helen Burroughs*, Studies in African American History and Culture (New York: Routledge, 1995), 25. Also see Jone Johnson Lewis, "Nannie Helen Burroughs: Advocate for Self-Sufficient Black Women," ThoughtCo., March 7, 2019, www.thoughtco.com/nannie-helen-burroughs-biography-3528274.

17 Sharon Harley, "Nannie Helen Burroughs: The Black Goddess of Liberty," *The Journal of Negro History* 81, no. 1 (Autumn 1996): 62–71, www.jstor.org/stable/2717608?seq=9#metadata_info_contents.

for learning.[18] Burroughs studied business and domestic science. She graduated with honors, but she could not find work as a domestic science teacher in Washington, DC. She accepted a position as an associate editor for the *Christian Banner*, a Baptist newspaper, as editorial secretary for the National Baptist Convention's Foreign Mission Board.

Burroughs was no stranger to working in the church. Her father was a minister, and Burroughs herself was active in Sunday school and young people's organizations. In 1900 she attended and spoke at the National Baptist Convention. Her theme was "How the Sisters Are Hindered from Helping," wherein she expressed the discontent of women and their desire to work alongside men in the work of evangelism around the world.[19] Her speech led to the establishment of the Women's Convention Auxiliary of the National Baptist Convention. During that time, she persuaded the women to establish the National Training School for Girls and Women to prepare them to become missionaries, Sunday school teachers, and domestic service workers.[20] In 1909 the school opened in Washington, DC with urban poor African American students for whom racial discrimination in housing and daily living demanded response. The philosophy and curriculum consisted of the three Bs—the Holy Bible, the Bathtub, and the Broom. The Bible was the guide to everyday Christian living (clean lives). The Bathtub symbolized personal cleanliness (clean bodies). The Broom symbolized environmental cleanliness (clean homes).[21]

Burroughs was a consummate teacher who believed in and preached lifelong learning. She argued passionately and eloquently for the education of Black girls and Black women as "vital agents" in uplifting the race and maintained "that preparation of our women

---

18 Ester, *Nannie Burroughs*, 26.

19 Ester, 28.

20 Ester, 32.

21 See Lewis, "Nannie Helen Burroughs: Advocate for Self-Sufficient Black Women."

for domestic and professional service, in the home and communities ranks next in importance to preparing their souls for the world to come."[22] She committed to the holistic growth of young people, women's leadership development, and women's need to move beyond the church's walls and engage in community efforts to uplift the Black race. Moreover, she modeled this commitment in her social activist and advocacy roles by pushing for the desegregation of public transportation in DC and by making clear in her statement, "The Negro must be ready to die for justice."[23] The specifically stated aim appearing in a Circular of Information of the school was "the full development of true womankind. The training is, therefore, designed to make its pupils keen in vision, alert in action, modest in deportment, deft of hand, and industrious in life."[24]

As an agent of social and moral change, Burroughs utilized a teaching praxis focused on transforming practices that circumscribed the lives of Black students. Her pedagogy was political and revolutionary. She required her students to learn Black history and pass both written and oral exams in it.[25] She strongly believed that Black students had a responsibility to learn their history in order

---

22 Karen A. Johnson, *Uplifting Women and the Race: The Educational Philosophies and Social Activism of Anna Julia Cooper and Nannie Helen Burroughs* (New York: Routledge, 2000), 91.

23 Linda Gordon, "Black and White Visions of Welfare: Women's Welfare Activism, 1890-1945," in *We Specialize in the Wholly Impossible: A Reader in Black Women's History*, ed. Darlene Clark Hine, Wilma King, and Linda Reed (Brooklyn, NY: Carlson Publishing, Inc., 1995), 466.

24 National Training School for Women and Girls, "Special Aims," *Circular of Information for the Seventeenth Annual Session of the National Training School for Women and Girls Incorporated* (Washington, DC: Lincoln Heights, 1925-1926), 13. Reprinted from the Collections of the Manuscript Division, Library of Congress. The document also appears in R. R. S. Stewart, "Designing a Campus for African American Females: The National Training School for Women and Girls 1907-1964" (master's thesis, University of Minnesota, 2006), appendix.

25 Daphne Spain, *How Women Saved the City* (Minneapolis: University of Minnesota Press, 2001), 66.

to have a sense of pride. Her perspective on women's racial uplift through the education of women and girls was not exclusionary of men but based on the premise that women and girls had a special responsibility to their communities that only they could fill. Burroughs was a staunch proponent of fostering and enabling agency within her students in order for them to become mature agents in the progress of the Black race. The legacy of Nannie Helen Burroughs shown in her life's work and educational pursuits influences the lives of contemporary Black women and girls. A similar legacy is found in the life and work of Mary McLeod Bethune.

Mary McLeod Bethune

Mary McLeod Bethune is regarded as the most influential Black woman in the United States. She served as a school teacher, advisor to President Franklin Roosevelt, activist, and college president. Born on July 10, 1875, in Mayesville, South Carolina, this woman of humble beginnings was the fifteenth of seventeen children.[26] Her family lived a life centered on God despite the social, educational, and economic challenges that were pervasive in America during that time. As a young child, she wanted to learn how to read and write. This desire was prompted by an interaction with a White girl who told her of her inability and impermissibility to read. Bethune knew she had a right to read; she was determined and learned to read. Attending school led to the development of Bethune's spiritual life as well as a passion for education. As a teenager, she became aware of a need for missionaries in Africa, and she knew training was needed to serve. She received a scholarship to Scotia Seminary, where she completed seven years, followed by two years of missionary training at Moody Bible Institute in Chicago. Upon graduating from Moody, Bethune's request for a missionary position was denied because

26 Beverly Johnson Miller, "Mary McLeod Bethune: Black Educational Ministry Leader of the 20th Century," *Christian Educational Journal* 3, no. 2 (November 1, 2006): 330.

she was Black.[27] This disappointment shifted her focus from Africa to America and to her appointment as an eighth-grade teacher at Haines Normal Institute in Augusta, Georgia.

Bethune's lifelong passion for equal opportunity and education of Blacks, particularly Black girls, led to her desire to establish her own school. Bethune was determined to fulfill this desire in a destitute area of Daytona Beach, Florida. The school would be her mission field. With faith in God, $1.50, and no guarantee of a salary, Bethune opened the Daytona Literary and Industrial Training School for Negro Girls on October 4, 1904, to help Black girls "earn a living" and address the systematic need for training and education.[28] The specific aims were to "uplift Negro girls spiritually, morally, intellectually and industrially; offer a broad, thorough practical training; develop Christian character and a trained mind, heart and hand being the idea of a complete education."[29] The curricular offerings of English, industrial arts, and biblical studies correlated with the concepts of head (English), hand (industrial), and heart (biblical).

In her insightful article on Dr. Mary McLeod Bethune, Kim Cliett Long identified her as "equal parts educator, politician, and social visionary."[30] Undergirding all of her efforts were a deeply ingrained God-consciousness, commitment to service, and understanding of Christian principles, as reflected in her statement: "Faith is the first factor in a life devoted to service. Without it, nothing is possible. With it, nothing is impossible."[31] Her practical theological perspective moved her toward the role as educator who "enabled African Americans to move beyond the oppression and degrading

---

27 Audrey McCluskey and Elaine M. Smith, eds., *Mary McLeod Bethune: Building a Better World, Essays and Selected Documents* (Bloomington: Indiana University Press, 2001), 42.

28 Miller, *Mary McLeod Bethune*, 335.

29 McCluskey and Smith, *Mary McLeod Bethune*, 76–77.

30 Kim Cliett Long, *Dr. Mary McLeod Bethune: A Life Devoted to Service* (Baton Rouge, LA: Forum on Public Policy, 2011), 3, https://files.eric.ed.gov/fulltext/EJ969859.pdf.

31 Long, *Dr. Mary McLeod Bethune*, 10.

conditions of servitude toward spiritual, economic, and political liberty."[32] Like Burroughs, her educational role extended to that of public advocacy as developer and leader of the National Association of Colored Women, the National Council of Negro Women, the Federal Council on Negro Affairs, and the Division of Negro Affairs of the National Youth Administration set by President Franklin D. Roosevelt.[33]

July 1923 marked a transition for the Daytona Literary and Industrial Training School for Negro Girls when it merged with Cookman Institute, a coed Methodist school for Blacks. This merger caused a shift from Bethune's commitment to educating Black girls in a single-sex environment to a coed environment. Bethune served as president for almost twenty years. Through faith, determination, perseverance, and fortitude, Mary McLeod Bethune built a better world for others, in particular for Black girls.

Unique Contributions of Burroughs and Bethune

Nannie Helen Burroughs and Mary McLeod Bethune's work as Christian religious educators was not limited to their personal religious convictions and practices or relegated to the four walls of the church; rather, their work found a significant place in the public sphere. Public life was shaped according to their visions of and advocacy for education of Black people, particularly Black girls, that would affirm positive cultural and self-identity, develop responsible leadership, and open the way for social change in Black life. Burroughs and Bethune experienced the triple sources of oppression: gender-based discrimination of Black women, economic discrimination of the poor, and social discrimination based on humble family backgrounds. Nevertheless, these women knew the power of education and advocated for and dedicated their lives to racial uplift,

---

32 Long, *Dr. Mary McLeod Bethune*, 9.

33 Beverly Johnson Miller, "Mary McLeod Bethune," Series on Christian Educators of the 20th Century, Biola University, www.biola.edu/Talbot/ce20/database/mary-msleod-bethune.

social justice, and gender equality. Their engagement in public life was propelled by their vision of "uplifting the women and the race."[34] Through active involvement in the public sphere, specifically in the field of education, Burroughs and Bethune overcame what Burroughs termed the *wholly impossible*. Their work provides lessons for contemporary Christian religious educators desiring to embrace a public theology and live out a public faith. We can learn three lessons from these Christian educator-activists:

1. Christian religious education is an intentional practice.
2. Instilling racial pride is a nonnegotiable practice.
3. Activism is not an option but rather a mandatory practice.

Holistic Christian Religious Education Is an Intentional Practice

Both Nannie Burroughs and Mary McLeod Bethune demonstrated profound intentionality in their Christian religious educational endeavors, which had an impact on the daily lives of students. Nannie Burroughs's curricular efforts included biblical studies along with practical learning to bring about personal growth and cultural uplift. Mary McLeod Bethune's contributions to Christian religious education were rooted in her daily life of religious and public service. She promoted a whole-person philosophy of Christian religious education through the establishment of the school for Negro girls. The school offered practical training in Christian character (head, heart, hand). Students under Bethune's tutelage were immersed in the Christian faith as a means of experiencing a full and wholesome life.[35]

It is important to add here that along with founding her Christ-centered school for Negro girls, Bethune also established numerous Sunday schools, which provided important Christian religious instruction for her students. Her educational approach emphasized praxis-based heart, mind, and hands experiential learning through its integration of intellectual stimulation, application of

34 Johnson, *Uplifting Women and the Race*, 7.

35 Newsome, "Mary McLeod Bethune in Religious Perspective," 164–65.

biblical principles, and involvement of service that moved beyond the church's doors on Sundays.[36] Bethune's Christian religious education revealed a practical public theology for making disciples that centered on Jesus as the religious standard and American democracy as the ideal to act in the public sphere.[37] These aspects in her practice of Christian religious education were intentional, concrete, and transformative, and were demonstrated through her school, community outreach, and servant leadership initiatives. Bethune was a public theologian, actively involved in the public sphere on a daily basis. Clearly, her life was not compartmentalized in sacred and secular spheres.

Instilling Racial Pride Is a Nonnegotiable Practice

Both Burroughs and Bethune were committed to improving conditions in the Black community. Their activism became lifelong journeys of uplifting Black girls, women, and the race. For Burroughs in particular this effort extended to self-help, social reform, institution-building, community organizing, and instilling racial pride and an understanding of Black history in the students at the National Training School for Women and Girls. All students were required to take Black history classes, pass exams, and participate in Black history essay and oratory contests. The impartation of Black history and Black pride were essential components of Burroughs's curriculum.

Within the Women's Convention of the National Baptist Convention, and among the public, Burroughs emphasized pride and uplift through her speeches. Her speech at the 1927 meeting of the Association of the Study of Negro Life, "The Social Value of Negro History," emphasized this theme as "the duty Negroes owe themselves to learn their own history and the duty of Whites to learn the spiritual struggles and achievements of the despised but not inferior Black race."[38] Burroughs believed and fought for the common good of all

36 Newsome, "Mary McLeod Bethune in Religious Perspective," 225–26.

37 Newsome, 217–19.

38 Ester, *Nannie Helen Burroughs*, 108.

people and believed that developing a positive racial identity was a step in the right direction. The West African principle of *Sankofa*, which symbolizes learning from the past to understand the present and move toward a better future, can be applied to Burroughs's commitment to racial pride.

Activism Is Not an Option but Rather a Mandatory Practice

Nannie Helen Burroughs and Mary McLeod Bethune were committed and dedicated to the education of their students. Education was viewed as a conveyance of empowerment and liberation. Because of the oppression they faced, they were awakened to a sense of responsibility to utilize their knowledge, skills, and education for the enhancement of future possibilities of Black people.[39] Their roles were not only to educate their students but also to become involved in resistance struggles in order to combat oppression. This struggle moved Burroughs and Bethune beyond classroom boundaries into the arena of public activism. Both women's lives embodied the need for religious persons and institutions to make a difference in society. Burroughs said, "Every church should attempt a definite program that projects itself into the community. No church should be allowed to stay in a community that does not positively influence community life."[40]

Burroughs also believed that a regular practice of studying scripture led to changes in people and society. She often used scripture in her speeches and writing to make arguments for racial uplift and social justice.[41] Bethune's activist activity included gathering Black

---

39 Cynthia Neverdon-Morton, *Afro-American Women of the South and the Advancement of the Race, 1895–1925* (Knoxville: University of Tennessee Press, 1989), 7–8.

40 Nannie Helen Burroughs, *Nannie Helen Burroughs: A Documentary Portrait of an Early Civil Rights Pioneer, 1900–1959*, ed. and annotated by Kelisha B. Graves (Notre Dame, IN: University of Notre Dame Press, 2019).

41 Rosetta E. Ross, *Witnessing and Testifying: Black Women, Religion, and Civil Rights* (Minneapolis: Fortress Press, 2003), 280.

women to organize for group goals. Her mission, undergirded by her belief that Black women's leadership paved the road to racial progress, was to organize and elevate women.[42] Her goal was to get the broader society to recognize the plight of Black women. Through her activism, Bethune's work led to democratic change by redefining Black women's status and visibility in civic affairs.

In the spirit of Nannie Helen Burroughs and Mary McLeod Bethune, I want to advocate here for a curriculum and teaching methodologies that minister to the whole person. To move in that direction, I expand on the three life and vocational practices by exploring contemporary pedagogical strategies that connect with students of color. This builds on my own recognition of the need to advocate for these practices in current Black Christian religious education in light of very real challenges that are not unlike those faced in Burroughs's and Bethune's time. Part 2 of this chapter will explore pedagogical models that connect with the learning styles and social, familial, and cultural experiences of Black girls and other girls of color; it will identify how those practices connect with the time-honored strategies and methods of Burroughs and Bethune. This emphasis on the work of contemporary educators clearly correlates with the work of Burroughs and Bethune by emphasizing hope, girlhood celebration, self/other awareness, cultural and contextual reality, and Christian wisdom formation.

Part Two: Public Theology and Culturally Relevant Pedagogical Practices

In this section, I highlight five teaching and learning models that signal the importance of culturally relevant education for Black youth that correlates with the pedagogical praxis of Nannie Helen Burroughs and Mary McLeod Bethune.

---

42 McCluskey and Smith, *Mary McLeod Bethune*, 39.

Hope Model

I begin here with the assertion that hope must be at the center of current Christian religious education that is intentional. Hope must guide efforts to instill racial pride and is insinuated in activism as a mandatory practice. Dr. Anne E. Streaty Wimberly provides some insights on the nature of hope that can give direction to these practices. She articulates a Black Christian pedagogy of hope centered on a historic theme of hope that continues in Black Christian faith and life. Hope as a past, present, and future construct is based on two assumptions according to Wimberly: "Hope has and must continue to transform the lives of Black people through experience and action," and "for Black Christians to know and grasp the power of hope, religious education must draw from experiences of hope building on the past and present."[43]

Wimberly's insistence on hope bears resemblance to Mary McLeod Bethune's view. Bethune was convinced of the power of hope. Her life and career as a prominent educational leader was anchored in the confidence she had in her people to overcome adversity and live a more secure life than in past generations. Bethune suggested that the history of Black people as slaves was built on a legacy of hope. In spite of the reality of enslavement, Black people retained their dignity by using their gifts, skills, and talents to build a better world.[44] Bethune affirmed that the sacrifice of Black ancestors would establish life more abundantly for future generations.

Wimberly's teaching and learning model introduces an educational methodology that teaches Black people how to hope. Her model emphasizes a historical, relational, and hermeneutical Christian religious educational framework. The pedagogy uses biography, reflection, interpretation, imagination, and decision-making

---

43 Anne E. Streaty Wimberly, "A Black Christian Pedagogy of Hope: Religious Education in Black Perspective," in *Forging a Better Religious Education in the Third Millennium*, ed. James Michael Lee (Birmingham, AL: Religious Education Press, 2000), 159.

44 McCluskey and Smith, *Mary McLeod Bethune*, 39.

that results in "rebiographing," or Black participants' reframing their lives toward wholeness by focusing on the hope of God.[45] The Black Christian pedagogy of hope engages persons in Black historical biographies revealing hope. Black Churches also serve as a key habitus for biographical encounters that include "teaching" by example, or how one lives, because people learn from what they see and hear.[46] This strategy takes teaching and learning beyond Sunday. From Wimberly we learn that the curriculum of hope is a lived biography from which lessons are taught and learned about movement forward in life with optimism and confidence. Bethune's legacy of hope closely connects with Wimberly's pedagogy of hope. Both emphasize the importance of teaching Black girls the meaning of seeing life and living life in hopeful terms.

Girlhood Celebration Model

Saving Our Lives Hearing Our Truths (SOLHOT) is a Black girl-centered experience created and implemented with Black girls by Dr. Ruth Nicole Brown. A pedagogical strategy creates narratives of Black girlhood that recognize Black girls' worth, power, and value.[47] Nannie Helen Burroughs and Mary McLeod Bethune were celebrants of the goodness, capability, and merit of Black girls in the early twentieth century. Both knew they had a special mission to educate Black girls as a means of uplifting women and the race. They helped girls develop their voices as a symbol of self-help and achievement, and as a result, girls and young women were empowered to stand in the truth of their selfhood. Brown delineates this vision with SOLHOT in that girls are encouraged to explore and speak in a community that values who they are and what they bring to what may be called "the table," constituting the communal ethos and the teaching/learning agenda.

---

45 Wimberly, "A Black Christian Pedagogy of Hope," 159.

46 Wimberly, 177–78.

47 Ruth Nicole Brown, *Black Girlhood Celebration: Toward a Hip-Hop Feminist Pedagogy* (New York: Peter Lang, 2009), 1–2.

Brown defines an original critical hip-hop feminist pedagogy, including multimedia musical ritual experiences, to celebrate Black girlhood and educational practices focused on democratic ideas that lead to transformation and social action. Her contemporary SOLHOT model and Bethune's and Burroughs's historic legacy of activism testify that personal advocacy is an expectation of growing into womanhood. Organized by Black girls, Black women, and those who love and care for them, SOLHOT is a space composed of dancing, singing, writing, and discussion about important issues as well as improving the community through support and action. The pedagogical praxis of SOLHOT includes developing confidence, creating and reciting poetry, and sharing truth. It is a place where Black girls can be themselves and where girls and women learn from one another. A significant practice of SOLHOT is challenging erroneous narratives about Black women and girls in books and media and finding language that accurately describes who Black women and girls really are. Connecting with Burroughs's and Bethune's legacy of uplifting women and the Black race, the girlhood celebration model offers a vision of what Black girls might contribute to the growth and development of society when given support, teaching, mentoring, and a safe space to speak their truths.

Self/Other Awareness Model

Dr. Dianne Johnson introduces a self/other awareness model that incorporates a pedagogical strategy utilizing African American children's literature as a means of teaching art and morality. She argues that children's books are powerful agents of socialization, politicization, and formal education with messages about life and living.[48] Johnson suggests engaging youth with African American children's literature as a teaching and learning strategy in order to instruct them in their history and culture as African diasporic people. Education and inspiration are the outcomes of this literature-based

48 Dianne Johnson, *Telling Tales: The Pedagogy and Promise of African American Literature for Youth* (New York: Greenwood Press, 1990), 1.

framework. Johnson is interested in literature written by African Americans that represents, interprets, and envisions the real and imagined lives of African American people. By literature, Johnson includes periodicals, fiction, poetry, history, historical fiction, and picture books.[49] This kind of exploration of African American literature instills racial pride in Black youth. It is analogous to Bethune's and Burroughs's belief that interaction and examination of historical and cultural materials is nonnegotiable in the positive development of Black youth.

Burroughs's teaching and leadership also emphasized the necessity of engaging in self/other awareness through literature. Although Burroughs drew on and wrote Christian religious literature for moral and spiritual uplift of persons in churches, schools, and Black community life, these materials connect with Johnson's idea that broad-based literature should provide self-help and spur critical thought and reflection on life and current affairs. Both Burroughs and Johnson also believe that ongoing uses of materials from the past in the present, or "passing it on," is necessary to ensure the future survival of Black communities.

Cultural/Contextual Reality Model

Reality pedagogy is the brainchild of Dr. Christopher Emdin. It is a culturally relevant pedagogical model that is mindful of the culture of students in the educational process, as well as the space, place, and contexts where they live. Reality pedagogy is created with urban America in mind. It is an approach to teaching and learning that has a primary goal of meeting each student on his or her own cultural and emotional turf.[50] He cites traditional models of education as being out of date and proposes culturally relevant strategies like hip-hop and call and response that connect with urban youth.

---

49 Johnson, *Telling Tales*, 10.

50 Christopher Emdin, *For White Folks Who Teach in the Hood . . . and the Rest of Y'all Too: Reality Pedagogy and Urban Education* (Boston: Beacon Press, 2016), 27.

Using culturally relevant educational strategies in the Black community, however, is not new. In 1926 Mary McLeod Bethune articulated a philosophy of education for Negro girls.[51] Bethune's philosophy set forth a vision of what Black women might contribute to uplifting and advancing the Black race if they were provided with intellectual training that was relevant to who they were and what they were called to do. Bethune's cultural and contextual philosophy and Emdin's reality pedagogy are similar because both advocate for uses of the customs and settings where students engage life. This form of advocacy and activism provides opportunities for urban youth to construct knowledge and utilize ways of communicating in their own voice. Although Emdin's reality pedagogy situates relevant educational practice in today's urban public school classrooms, it has relevance in Christian educational settings within and beyond churches.

To support this view, Emdin offers the reality pedagogy framework to address the unique learning needs of urban youth. The framework consists of a set of tools he calls the "5 C's" that help educators gain insights into student realities and gives students the space to express their true selves in the classroom.

1. *Cogenerative dialogues*: Teachers and students discuss the classroom, and both suggest ways to improve it.
2. *Co-teaching*: Students get opportunities to learn content and then teach the class.
3. *Cosmopolitanism*: Students have a role in how the class operates and what is taught.
4. *Context*: It is necessary for teachers to understand the backgrounds of their students in order to better understand how to engage them.
5. *Content*: The teacher has to acknowledge the limitations of his or her content knowledge and work to build his or her expertise with students.

---

51 McCluskey and Smith, *Mary McLeod Bethune*, 84–86.

Reality pedagogy focuses explicitly on engaging both the student and the teacher with the understanding that before teachers can teach anything, they must understand the realities of their students. In short, being conscious of the sensibilities and worldviews of the students connects to the pedagogical strategies of Bethune and Emdin.

Christian Wisdom Formation Model

Christian wisdom formation is a process of discipleship, which I explore more fully in my book *Repertory with Roots: Black Youth, Black History, Black Culture, Black Music, and the Bible.*[52] Being formed in wisdom is essential to the discipleship process because it equips persons with an awareness and understanding of who they are as followers of Jesus Christ. Wisdom formation is a key element of both contextualized education and the development of one's voice.[53] Christian wisdom formation is an avenue for youth to grow in their understanding of what it means to be a disciple through intentional reflection and engagement with Black history, Black culture, Black music, and the Bible. Christian wisdom formation is explored through the *Repertory with Roots* pedagogy.

The pedagogy is defined as a "designated ontological niche wherein lie sources for African American youth's identity formation."[54] I begin with the foundational belief that Black youth identity should be "unashamedly Black and unapologetically Christian" and suggest that religious education should be an everyday practice encountered in the daily journey of life. This "unashamedly Black and unapologetically Christian" identity was prominent in the work of Nannie Helen Burroughs at the National Training School.

To foster a strong Black and Christian identity, students learn Black history and racial pride. Burroughs's ideas are instrumental

---

52 Richelle B. White, *Repertory with Roots: Black Youth, Black History, Black Culture, Black Music, and the Bible* (Maitland, FL: Xulon Press, 2016).

53 White, *Repertory with Roots*, 63.

54 White, xxi.

in building a strong Black and Christian identity. *Repertory with Roots* further develops Burroughs's concepts on fostering positive youth identity. The model in it identifies four "roots" or sources of identity formation—Black history, Black culture, Black music, and the Bible. Each of these sources comprises a teaching and learning framework that fosters Christian wisdom formation. Christian wisdom formation is a process of discipleship that continually calls for exploration and acknowledgment of the teachings and ministry of Jesus Christ in order for them to be "perpetually" reborn in a person's life.[55] The framework includes seven curricular movements of inviting, listening, connecting, engaging, exploring, emerging, and honoring that invite participants to dig deep into Black history, culture, music, and the Bible while exploring and claiming who and whose they are.

The hope, girlhood celebration, self/other awareness, cultural or contextual reality, and Christian wisdom formation models bear important linkage with the educational practices of the past and, in fact, merge with the contextual, societal, and cultural realities that confront Black youth today. Advocacy for both past and present models are worthy of consideration in Black religious education in this postmodern era. In part 3, brief narratives demonstrate how the historical correlation method informs my current practice of Christian religious education with Black girls in the public sphere.

Part Three: My Sister's Keeper Program

My Sister's Keeper is an after-school program created for Black girls and other girls of color in grades three through six in a small Midwestern city. Creating My Sister's Keeper has been my way as a religious educator of engaging the public sphere through ministry and education that connects to young people beyond the walls of the

55 See Anne E. Streaty Wimberly and Evelyn L. Parker, eds., *In Search of Wisdom: Faith Formation in the Black Church* (Nashville: Abingdon Press, 2002), 12–13.

church. Since much of young people's time is spent in the school setting, I thought it was important to become aware of the cultural or contextual climate of the public schools and seek out ways to become involved. Leading and facilitating an after-school program for girls was an area of need. My Sister's Keeper was initiated to empower Black girls and other girls of color to construct positive identities, namely through the areas of leadership development, self-esteem, character education, and identity formation. These four aspects build on the previously mentioned hope, girlhood celebration, self/other awareness, cultural or contextual reality, and Christian wisdom formation models of teaching and learning while also emphasizing self-esteem, empowerment, and cultural uplift of girls so pivotal in the work of Burroughs and Bethune. Following are four brief stories that demonstrate how the historical correlation method of African American Christian education provided a framework for teaching and learning within the context of My Sister's Keeper.

Building Leaders

The girls gathered in a circle. I showed them a diagram of a rectangle with circles surrounding it. This diagram symbolized a boardroom with a table and chairs. I asked them, "Who is sitting at your table?" I immediately shared leadership principle #1: leaders need support. I instructed the girls to create a list of who supports them, how they support them, and why they chose that person. After completing their lists, students were encouraged to gather in groups of three to share their responses. The dialogue that followed was remarkable. They did not sit and listen passively but asked each other questions about what they shared. This was a girlhood celebration where the girls were encouraged and empowered to use their own voices. It was solely their decision who would sit at their leadership table, and they thought critically about why. It was an opportunity to share their truths and learn a leadership lesson that was also a valuable life lesson. Everyone needs support.

Strengthening Self-Esteem

Strengthening self-esteem is more than thinking about oneself in a positive light. It is also thinking of others in light of the self by sharing compliments. It was important to teach the girls how to give and receive compliments yet at the same time highlight how jealousy and insecurity play a role in the process. My inspiration for this activity was the Christian wisdom formation model, which serves as a way of forming positive identity.

We sat in a circle. I explained that we would say nice things about each other as a way of complimenting each other with the goal of making each person feel good about themselves. The girls were grouped in pairs. The process included addressing their partner by name and sharing a compliment. The partner would say "thank you" and then give a compliment in return. The process continued until everyone had the opportunity to share.

When asked how it felt to give and receive compliments, they shared responses such as "It made me feel good about myself," or "It felt special when my sister noticed me." Following the activity, I passed out a journal prompt where they could respond to the following questions: What is the best compliment you received? How did it make you feel? What is the best compliment you gave? How did it make you feel to give it? Examples of comments were: "She liked my smile." "It made me want to smile more." "I told my sister that she makes me feel better when I am sad." "It felt good to encourage her because she always encourages others." This exercise in strengthening self-esteem encouraged the girls to explore the positive effects of giving and accepting compliments and how they affect self-esteem and relationships.

Transforming Character

One girl had been spreading gossip about another girl for a couple of weeks. Stories about this permeated our after-school group, and I knew I needed to address it very soon. At our next meeting, I wrote "GOSSIP" on the whiteboard and told the girls to get into groups of three and write a definition of gossip. The three group definitions were (1) spreading rumors that are not true, (2) saying mean things about others to hurt them, and (3) talking about someone or being mean and hurting their feelings. All of these definitions possessed elements of truth. I wanted to clarify the meaning of gossip and continued by saying, "Gossip is talking about the personal lives of other people." Upon request, a volunteer joined me in the front of the group where I had a tube of toothpaste and a small plate. After asking her to squeeze out an amount of toothpaste, she did so and stopped. I told her that she squeezed too much, and she had to put it back in the tube. She looked surprised and said, "I can't put it back." Without elaborating on her response, I asked the question, "How is gossip like this tube of toothpaste?" After a couple of responses, one girl said, "Once you say it, you can't take it back." I repeated the response and briefly addressed the issue of gossip and what it was doing to our sisterhood. Then I introduced the West African folktale *Why Mosquitoes Buzz in People's Ears.*[56] After reading we talked more about the effect and hurt of lies and gossip and how it affects the community. I ended the lesson with the following comment: If it's not your business, don't spread it.

Dr. Dianne Johnson's emphasis on the transforming power of story brought both self and other awareness to this session. Through the use of African folklore, the girls gained knowledge and skill in what it means to "be nice and respectful of others." In addition, the cultural or contextual reality model provided insight into how students lived day to day and interacted with others.

Pursuing Identity

Each girl was given an identity box outlined on paper. The drawing consisted of two boxes: an outer box and an inner box. The outer box stood for what others (the world) think about you. The inner box stood for what you think about your own identity. I shared

56 Verna Aardema, Reteller, *Why Mosquitoes Buzz in People's Ears: A West African Tale* (New York: Puffin Books, 1975).

the following directions: In the outside box write words and draw images that represent what others think about you. In the inside box, write words and draw images that represent what you think about yourself. I gave the girls five to seven minutes to write. Afterward, I asked them to share the words and images in their outer and inner boxes. In every instance, they shared negative words and images. I then read the following affirmation for the group, which I indicated we would say at each session:

- I am in pursuit of identity.
- I am a boldly believing beautiful creation.
- I am striving to be my best self, my authentic self.
- I don't care about the world's opinion.
- I am becoming the best I can be.
- I am discovering my purpose on the planet.

After reading, I invited the group to stand and read the affirmation together. Then we all sat and explored the affirmation line by line, putting it in conversation with the words and images in their identity boxes. As an example, one student shared a statement from her outer identity box: "People always talk about how dark I am." I asked her to share what she might say about herself based on the words in the affirmation. It is important to note that she was in no way hesitant in stating, "I am beautiful just the way I am. I am a boldly believing beautiful creation, and I don't care about the world's opinion." In follow-up to the time of sharing, I presented a decorated shoebox, which I called the "Identity Box." It contained cards with Bible verses, quotations, and affirmations. I indicated that anyone is free to pull from the box and read the card(s) when they needed an "identity boost." Through this invitation, I was engaging the girls in the practice of seeing themselves in a new way, and of building a positive rather than a false identity. But it was not simply for their personal selves; it was also so they could see and affirm the beautiful creation of others, which ultimately goes to the heart of being and becoming "My Sister's Keeper."

Reflections

The four areas of leadership development, self-esteem, character education, and identity formation have been explored through the pedagogical lens of Nannie Helen Burroughs and Mary McLeod Bethune. Their time-honored educational practices emphasize that advocacy in these areas is critical for self-identity and empowerment in difficult, degrading, dehumanizing circumstances. In light of ongoing turbulent times, they provide a necessary foundation for African American Christian education. The intent of this chapter has been to advocate for teaching and learning strategies for use in African American Christian religious education in the current postmodern era. The strategies may take place in public locations or in congregations for the transforming preparation of girls for positive, hope-filled, self-affirming everyday life in a continuing difficult public sphere. The models presented here are further intended to create a pathway by which girls can envision and act on their own personal understanding of being "My Sister's Keeper" as they live out a public life of faith.

Religious Education for Making It Out of "Da Hood"

Spiritual Retreat Encounters for Youth and Young Adult Resilience and Spiritual Formation

Cynthia P. Stewart

> It is important to release the gifts of personal agency within people; it is equally important to address those forces in culture that recruit persons into negative stories, plots, and images that destroy personal agency and full participation in society.
>
> —Edward P. Wimberly, *African American Pastoral Care and Counseling: The Politics of Oppression and Empowerment*

Facing Up to "Da Hood" and a Way Out

"Da Hood" is a slang label for an inner-city neighborhood. It is a place often circumscribed by adverse conditions or a space covered (or hooded) by seemingly inescapable daunting odds stemming from inequality in education, employment, health, and other resources. It is where money for everyday needs is in short supply, poor housing poses safety risks, violence occurs, gangs and drugs are apparent, community relations with police are difficult, and racial hostilities are real. In that everyday public space, time behind bars is an unsurprising option for far too many youth in a school-to-prison pipeline ethos, the sirens of paramedics often ring out, and death is real. The lyrics of the 1993 rap song "Da Hood" further describe an environment where the feeling lingers that there is no option but to remain with nowhere else to go. The song opines that good does leak out where "everything is gloomy and grey," but survival is the mode of existence that adjoins the mantra, "It's just another day in the hood."[1]

On the streets of inner cities, pejoratively named "Da Hood," African American adolescents also tend to be portrayed as the "other." They are stigmatized as outsiders and judged as being lesser or inferior beings in the wider social sphere because many come from broken homes and incarcerated parents, and are deemed participants in gang-infested communities of misfits, dropouts, hopeless causes, and "thugs" to be feared. Let there be no mistaking the imperative need for advocacy that confronts and reverses unjust, inefficient, and nonexistent structures or systems that help to perpetuate deleterious conditions in places that have come to be known as "Da Hood." However, advocacy is required for opportunities leading to releasing and affirming within "bowed down" people the tremendous value of oneself given and seen by God, resilience in the face of adversity, and ways to envision and act on possibilities for one's life. This chapter is about this latter form of advocacy.

---

1 The 1993 rap song "Da Hood" provides a vivid description of the environment from the perspective of the song's composers. It was written and performed by the rap group called Da Youngsta's from Philadelphia. The group consisted of brothers Taji "Taj Mahal" Goodman, Qu'ran "Q-Ball" Goodman, and their cousin Tarik "Reek Geez" Dawson. "Da Hood," MP3 audio, track 10 on Da Youngsta's, *The Aftermath*, East West, Atlantic, 1993. The song lyrics appear on www.lyrics.com/lyric/2762994/Da+Youngsta%27s/Da+Hood.

Here at the outset, let me begin with the saying "it takes a village" to highlight a way of life in African American communities, where neighbors, church members, family, friends, educators, and community leaders are surrogate parents to many African American adolescents. Kimberly Gordon Rouse discusses the importance of supportive environments in the public sphere outside the home in nurturing resilience:

> Children in impoverished and stressful situations need other adults besides their parents to offer advice and assist with their lives. Their parents may or may not be able to assist them in all situations. They especially need emotional support, another trusting relationship, and information and advice about the future. This other adult may be tied to an educational or spiritual setting, or they may be members of their extended family.[2]

Certain factors within the African American community affect resilience. Thornton highlights the importance of researchers who do not simply bring awareness to instances of instability and disorganization of Black families but who highlight the very real fact that these families and young people within them have survived in the face of racial hostility and discrimination, and have learned how to adapt to adverse conditions.[3] Outside the family, resilient children find emotional support in the community. They have at least one friend and a network of relatives, neighbors, peers, and elders for counsel and support whenever they encounter a crisis. Education plays an important role in the lives of youth as well. In educational

---

2 Kimberly Gordon Rouse, "Resilience from Poverty and Stress," *Human Development and Family Life Bulletin Review of Research and Practice* 4, no. 1 (1998): www3.uakron.edu/schulze/401/readings/resilience.htm.

3 Michael Thornton, "Indigenous Resources and Strategies of Resistance: Informal Caregiving and Racial Socialization in Black Communities," in *Resiliency in African-American Families*, ed. Hamilton I. McCubbin et al. (Thousand Oaks, CA: Sage, 1998), 49–66.

environments, youth have at least one teacher who is a role model, friend, and confidante. Extracurricular activities are also related to their resilience status. These activities help bond them to their school and teach them important skills such as leadership and teamwork. Some find emotional support from a church leader. Spiritual faith gives their lives meaning and helps them feel that they have control over their fate. The key here is that structures within which these activities can occur are vital.

This chapter focuses on a particular example of a support structure called the Agape Scholars Program (ASP), a nonprofit college readiness scholarship program for low- to middle-income African American high school students in Chicago. The program provided not only an academic environment but also a spiritual development component. My awareness especially of the spiritual component occurred during a period of more than ten years when I was the retreat facilitator. This particular aspect of the program may be appropriately described as an effort of taking the church and religious education into the public space of the urban community and a means of making it possible for young people to refocus their lives and envision contrasting ones to that of "Da Hood." In what follows, attention will be given to ASP as an advocacy endeavor, the importance of spirituality and religion as protective factors and resilience-builders, a theology of spiritual formation, and stories of transformation.

The Agape Scholars Program—An Advocacy Endeavor of Taking Church into the Urban Community

ASP retreats started in the early 1970s and have continued except for a few changes. The provision of spiritual development is a unique phenomenon. Most college readiness programs provide services designed to counter negative school and community influences by helping students seek, prepare for, and obtain college degrees. These programs typically offer a series of interventions that emphasize academic preparedness, help students develop college aspirations, and assist students in setting realistic college expectations.[4] ASP was started by a Catholic priest and has a Catholic foundation. Scholars who are accepted into this four-year college readiness program are not required to be Catholic, but they must attend a Catholic or private high school within the Chicagoland area. As a pivotal and intentional program addition to fulfill spiritual formation requirements, scholars attend teen masses and annual spiritual retreats all four years of high school. While the teen masses were important, my focus for this research project was only on the impact of the spiritual retreats.

ASP implemented a mandatory spiritual retreat for all participants, which focused on the Black social and cultural experience, particularly regarding the Black family and female-male relationships.[5] According to a staff leader whom I will call Father Nash,[6] spirituality was foundational to the scholarship program because of its connection to Catholic parishes and high schools within the Chicagoland area, specifically within impoverished communities. During his face-to-face interview, he explained to me how the spiritual retreats were initially implemented in the program. It all started when he attended an Archdiocese-sponsored retreat called Teens and Christ.[7] Father Nash's description of how the first retreat came to fruition is as follows:

> I had sent a few kids from the parish not in ASP to one of those Teens and Christ retreats. They came back all excited

4 Yvette Gullatt and Wendy Jan, "How Do Pre-Collegiate Academic Outreach Programs Impact College Readiness among Underrepresented Students?" Pathways to College Network, accessed January 26, 2020, http://citeseerx.ist.psu.edu/viewdoc/download?doi=10.1.1.483.7094&rep=rep1&type=pdf.

5 Agape Scholars Program, newsletter, Fall 1974.

6 The name has been changed for the confidentiality of research participants.

7 The name has been changed for the confidentiality of the program.

> and said, "Father, you have to see this." So I decided I would make one of these just as a participant. And it blew me out of the water, and I was like, "I will be damn [*sic*]. This is good." It was a three-day thing, Saturday, Sunday, and Monday. And the sharing that went on as part of this. This was new to me, this kind of sharing about their personal lives and the context of the other group. And the emotion and the tears, you know, this was not phony; this was real. And I was impressed by this, I was like, "I will be damn [*sic*]." So, what I decided was, we are going to do our own retreat.
>
> So, I required the seniors, required just like I made summer school a requirement doing one of those retreats. And the retreat was done in Des Plaines; they had their own special place where they were running these things. I would have the kids meet at the rectory and take them out there on a Saturday morning and pick them up on a Monday night. Then we would go out to eat and I would debrief them. What happened? What do you think? What impressed you, blah blah? I had a whole bunch of questions. And we spent a good part of the evening right after this debriefing them over a McDonald's or a Wendy's whatever it was. Listening to them tell their stories of what happened. So, then I realized we are going to institutionalize this. So, we became part of the Archdiocese's retreats and we were to bring Blacks, which they did not have any Blacks at all. This was like a resource for them. "Umm, are you sending any kids this week?" Ahh, yeah, whatever. So, every kid as a senior had to make it.

The conversations with Father Nash revealed a transformative quality of spiritual retreats that needed to be replicated. Father Nash continued to talk about how other retreats were formed, not just for the seniors in the program but also for freshmen, sophomores, and juniors. This is key to understanding the dynamics that facilitated the anomalous implementation of spiritual retreats into a college readiness program. I know of only one other (former) college readiness program in Chicago that included annual spiritual retreats for its scholars. However, because the other program had fewer than thirty students, the retreats were held once a year and were for all the students in the program. It was not broken down by class group as was ASP.

The scholars[8] were required to participate in monthly teen worship services and annual spiritual retreats over their four years of high school. This chapter focuses solely on the retreats, the component of the program for which I, as a contract employee, had the most involvement. The spiritual retreats provided a sacred space for the scholars to gain trusted relationships with peers and adults. Due to the attendance of many of the scholars at different Catholic or private schools throughout the Chicagoland area, many were not in constant contact with their peers.

I have maintained a lifelong relationship with many of the alumni who are currently young adults between the ages of twenty-four and thirty-five. When I first met them, they were adolescents entering their freshman year of high school. From their freshman year to senior year of high school, I conducted their spiritual retreats. Therefore, I was able to see their spiritual, physical, emotional, and intellectual development flourish throughout their adolescent development period, or what G. Stanley Hall calls "storm and stress."[9] I became witness to the fact that many have made it out of "Da Hood."

In conversations and group discussions with retreat alumni, I explored what social scientists call "protective factors." I wanted to know their stories and whether the retreats fostered resiliency in them. The narratives of four alumni revealed their lives in impoverished communities and attending predominantly White, Catholic high schools. Some experienced racism, many resided in

---

8 The terms *scholar* and *ASP alumni* will be used interchangeably to identify the participants of this study who participated in the spiritual retreats.

9 Paulo Freire, *Pedagogy of the Oppressed*, trans. Myra Bergman Ramos (New York: Continuum Publishing, 1970).

single-parent households, a few had parents with substance abuse problems, and many were first-generation college students. They were in fact part of a larger group that graduated from college, with a few receiving graduate and advanced-level degrees. Many are also working in a professional career. They affirmed their resilience as a result of participating in annual spiritual retreats through ASP and the effectiveness of spirituality and resilience as protective factors. What the graduates shared is also important because their voices are not often heard. Fuller attention to their narratives appears later.

Spirituality and Religion as Protective Factors and Resilience Builders

Interest in the topic of spirituality has grown considerably in recent years. However, more research is needed regarding inner-city African American adolescents and young adults. Both internal and external factors contribute to the success of African American youth who live in adverse environments. External factors include family, peers, education, church, and mentors. The internal factors are the adolescents' values, morals, and beliefs. The intent of ASP was to promote students' spiritual development during their four years of high school and attendance at annual spiritual retreats and their becoming resilient while living in adverse environments.

Spirituality and the Black Church as a Protective Factor

Among peoples of African descent, spirituality—that is, an acceptance of a nonmaterial higher force that pervades all of life's affairs and a core of religious beliefs that guide everyday life—has been identified as a common cultural value.[10] Beginning in the era of slav-

10 A. Wade Boykin, "Harvesting Talent and Culture: African American Children and Educational Reform," in *Schools and Students at Risk, Context and Framework for Positive Change*, ed. Robert J. Rossi (New York: Teachers College Press, 1994), 116-38; Jerome Schiele, "Afrocentricity:

ery, spirituality as a core aspect of religious life has been known to bring about human agency that Black people exercised in actions of resistance. Blassingame wrote that in the throes of abject cruelty, spirituality provided "ultimate purpose . . . , communal fellowship and personal worth, and reduced suffering from fear and anxiety."[11] Beginning in that era, spirituality and religiosity, or people's religious practices, were formed and nurtured in the Black Church and have been historically proven, culturally relevant ways in which African Americans have coped with an ambivalent life reality filled with social injustice and compromised health conditions.

The Black Church has been central in African American life. It was described to Wendy Haight by adult informants as a haven in which children could learn about their heritage from other African Americans who valued and nurtured them. Through the (Black) Church, children have been exposed to the hopeful, loving, and egalitarian message of the Christian gospel.[12]

In the current era, Hale-Benson characterizes the spirituality of African Americans as a key factor in coping with stressful events. Spirituality is perceived as a protective factor. It is a lifeline, informing eternal life through belief in Jesus, but also a healthy way of managing the trials of everyday life.[13] Emmy Werner observes that

---

An Emerging Paradigm in Social Work Practice," *Social Work* 41 (1996): 284–94.

11 John Blassingame, *The Slave Community: Plantation Life in the Antebellum South* (New York: Oxford University Press, 1972), 206, quoted in Gayraud Wilmore, *Pragmatic Spirituality, The Christian Faith through an Africentric Lens* (New York: New York University Press, 2004), 51–52. Elisions in Wilmore.

12 Wendy Haight, "'Gathering the Spirit' at First Baptist Church: Spirituality as a Protective Factor in the Lives of African American Children," *Social Work* 43, no. 3 (1998): 213–21.

13 Janice Hale-Benson, "The Transmission of Faith to Young Black Children" (paper, Conference on Faith Development in Early Childhood, Henderson, NC, December 1987); and Haight, "'Gathering the Spirit' at First Baptist Church," 213-21.

resilient children from a variety of backgrounds and communities have in common religious beliefs that provide stability and meaning to their lives, especially in times of hardship.[14] With specific regard to African Americans, Robert Coles describes spirituality as an important tool on which these children relied to survive racial hatred during forced school desegregation.[15] Research undertaken by Kaye V. Cook has also shown that active participation of inner-city Black youth in the religious life of the Black Church results in less stress and psychological difficulty, less likelihood of joining a gang or yielding to peer pressure, and greater possibility of having a strong sense of self-worth.[16]

In short, the Black Church has been about human agency from the hegemonic evils of racism, classism, sexism, and other oppressive factors from African enslavement forward. Joseph Washington states, "In the beginning was the Black Church, and the Black Church was with the Black community, and the Black Church was the Black community. The Black Church was in the beginning with the Black people; all things were made through the Black Church, and without the Black Church was not anything made that was made."[17] This statement details the importance and meaning of the Black Church in relation to the community for which it is formed and located. Yet, in the continuing culture of violence, urban African American adolescents and young adults need renewed coping mechanisms and

---

14 Emmy Werner, "Protective Factors and Individual Resilience," in *Handbook of Early Childhood Intervention* (New York: Cambridge University Press, 1990), 97-116.

15 Haight, "'Gathering the Spirit' at First Baptist Church," 213-21; and Robert Coles, *The Spiritual Life of Children* (Boston: Houghton Mifflin, 1990).

16 Kaye V. Cook, "You Have to Have Somebody Watching Your Back, and If That's God, Then That's Mighty Big: The Church's Role in the Resilience of Inner-City Youth," *Adolescence* 35, no. 140 (Winter 2000): 717-30.

17 Joseph Washington, "How Black Is Black Religion?" in *Quest for a Black Theology*, ed. James J. Gardiner and J. Deotis Roberts (Philadelphia: Pilgrim Press, 1971), 28.

ways to make meaning as they see and hear on a daily basis death of another Black body, usually a Black male body.

The Black Church should provide these coping mechanisms; however, some Black Churches lack these resources. Current injustices call for remedies that appreciate present circumstances and how youth and families of African American descent think and feel. There is need to hear the stories of young people and provide guidance on how to manage racial injustices, hostilities, and "myriad subtleties" while making thoughtful rather than reactive life choices.[18] ASP became a mechanism to address this need.

Culture, Spirituality, and Coping

Shawn Utsey, Mark Bolden, Otis Williams, Angela Lee, Yzette Lanier, and Crystal Newsome propose a model for African Americans wherein spiritual well-being is hypothesized as a mediator between cultural-specific coping and quality of life. According to this model, both external and internal coping resources are based on a strong spiritual orientation and on supportive social networks.[19]

A study by Daly, Jennings, Beckett, and Leashore found that African Americans preferred coping strategies that were group centered (e.g., family, community, and social support networks) and/or relied on religious or spiritual approaches to dealing with adversity (e.g., prayer and meditation). Other researchers have found that African Americans prefer coping strategies that include forming affiliations with others, seeking guidance from elders in the community, praying, and using rituals.[20] Although these behaviors are not

---

18 Howard Stevenson et al., "Development of the Teenage Experience of Racial Socialization Scale: Correlates of Race-Related Socialization, Frequency from the Perspective of Black Youth," *Journal of Black Psychology* 28, no. 84 (2002): 84-106.

19 Stevenson et al., "Development of the Teenage Experience of Racial Socialization Scale."

20 Stevenson et al., "Development of the Teenage Experience of Racial Socialization Scale"; Alfrieda Daly, Jeanette Jennings, Joyce O. Beckett,

exclusive to African Americans, they represent a cultural worldview common among persons of African descent.[21]

The first concept of the model is a cultural-specific coping mechanism. Utsey, Adams, and Bolden incorporate in this concept the notion of cognitive and emotional debriefing, which helps African Americans manage environmental stressors. It serves as a cultural value and practice that places the group's interest above that of the individual.[22] African Americans rely on group-centered activities for managing stressful situations. Spiritual-centered coping enhances resilience by providing a basis for optimism and a cognitive framework for understanding stressful situations.[23] This concept can include a ritual-centered cultural practice of coping that relies on the performance of rites and rituals as means of acknowledging the role of ancestors in an individual's life, celebrating events, and providing structure to spiritual expression.[24]

---

and Bogart R. Leashore, "Effective Coping Strategies of African Americans," *Social Work* 40, no. 2 (1995): 240–48; Shawn O. Utsey, Eve P. Adams, and Mark Bolden, "Development and Initial Validation of the Africultural Coping Systems Inventory," *Journal of Black Psychology* 26, no. 2 (May 2000): 194–215; Jacqueline S. Mattis, "Religion and Spirituality in the Meaning-Making and Coping Experiences of African American Women: A Qualitative Analysis," *Psychology of Women Quarterly* 26 (2002): 309–21; and Anita P. Jackson and Susan J. Sears, "Implications of an Africentric Worldview in Reducing Stress for African American Women," *Journal of Counseling and Development* 71 (1992): 184–90.

21 See Shawn O. Utsey et al., "Spiritual Well-Being as a Mediator of the Relation between Culture-Specific Coping and Quality of Life in a Community Sample of African Americans," *Journal of Cross-Cultural Psychology* 38, no. 2 (2007): 123–36.

22 See Utsey, Adams, and Bolden, "Development and Initial Validation of the Africultural Coping Systems Inventory," 194–215.

23 See Oscar Barbarin, "Coping and Resilience: Exploring the Inner Lives of African American Children," *Journal of Black Psychology* 19 (1993): 472–98.

24 See Utsey, Adams, and Bolden. "Development and Initial Validation of the Africultural Coping Systems Inventory."

The second concept of the model is spiritual well-being. Several scholars have suggested that the concepts of spirituality and religiosity are interrelated and that religion provides a forum for expressing spirituality.[25] Spirituality is distinguishable from religiosity, however, in that the latter typically involves an affiliation with an organized institution, the practice of group-specific rituals, a system of worship, and doctrines that drive an individual's beliefs about God or a higher power.[26] Spirituality is said to involve a search for meaning and purpose in life, unfolding mysteries of the universe, harmony, peace, wholeness, and transcendence.[27] Empirical evidence shows that African Americans engage in prayer and other spiritual practices more frequently than their White counterparts.[28] Moreover, as indicated earlier, spirituality has been found to strongly influence the health benefits and practices of African Americans.[29] Overall, evidence suggests that for African Americans, spirituality positively correlates with increased health and well-being, greater life satisfaction, and a higher life quality.

---

25 Peter Hill and Kenneth I. Pargament, "Advances in the Conceptualization and Measurement of Religion and Spirituality," *American Psychologist* 58 (2003): 64–74; Kelly Newlin, Kathleen Knafl, and Gail D'Eramo Melkus, "African American Spirituality: A Concept Analysis," *Advanced Nursing Science* 25 (2002): 57–70; and Ruth A. Tanyi, "Towards Clarification of the Meaning of Spirituality," *Journal of Advanced Nursing* 39 (2002): 500–509.

26 Kristy McNulty, Hanoch Livneh, and Lisa M. Wilson, "Perceived Uncertainty, Spiritual Well-Being, and Psychosocial Adaptation in Individuals with Multiple Sclerosis," *Rehabilitation Psychology* 49 (2004): 91–99; Tanyi, "Towards Clarification of the Meaning of Spirituality"; and Newlin, Knafl, and Melkus, "African American Spirituality."

27 Tanyi, "Towards Clarification of the Meaning of Spirituality"; and Mattis, "Religion and Spirituality."

28 Jeffrey S. Levin, Linda M. Chatters, and Robert Joseph Taylor, "Religious Effects on Health Status and Life Satisfaction among Black Americans," *Journal of Gerontology* 50 (1995): 154–63; and Jo Kim, "Spirituality, Quality of Life, and Functional Recovery after Medical Rehabilitation," *Rehabilitation Psychology* 45, no. 4 (2000): 365–85.

29 Utsey et al., "Spiritual Well-Being as Mediator."

The last concept of the model is quality of life as it relates to strength and resiliency among African Americans. Quality of life is defined by the World Health Organization (WHO) as an individual's perception of their position in life in the context of the culture and value system in which they live and in relation to their goals, expectations, standards, and concerns.[30] Racism, poverty, poor psychological and physical health, and a lack of access to healthcare have been found to infringe significantly on the quality of life of African Americans.[31] These empirical findings were based on studies conducted with African American adults, but they could be applied to African American youth and young adults as well. Although specific attention was not given to physical health in ASP, emphasis was given to group-centered activities and rituals for youth that were directed toward God, self, others, and purpose in life.

Spiritual Development and Resiliency of African American Adolescents

As a Christian educator, I expand on the concept of spirituality and religion as a protective factor that promotes resilience in the lives of urban African American adolescents and young adults. Recall my focus on ASP, a college readiness scholarship program that provided annual spiritual retreats and teen masses for scholars across all four years of high school. The spiritual component of the program provided spiritual formation, identity and emotional development, and socialization within annual retreats for Black scholars,

---

30 WHO Quality of Life Group, "Development of the HOQOL: Rationale and Current Status," *International Journal of Mental Health* 23 (1994): 24–56.

31 Shawn Utsey et al., "Assessing Quality of Life in the Context of Culture," in *Handbook of Multicultural Assessment*, 2nd ed., ed. Lisa Suzuki, Joseph Ponterotto, and Paul Meller (New York: Jossey-Bass, 2000), 191–212; and Clovis E. Semmes, *Racism, Health, and Post-Industrialism: A Theory of African American Health* (Westport, CT: Praeger, 1996).

which Westfield calls "concealed gatherings."[32] The retreats offered a sacred space for these scholars to gather and to share, reflect, and refocus on oppressive environments of some of their homes, schools, and communities. These events provided an essential understanding of how to work with African American adolescents who live in adverse urban communities.

Religious and spiritual involvement has been found to be a buffer or resiliency factor for African American children at a high risk for poor adjustment.[33] Resilience is determined by an individual's sense of meaning and purpose about his or her life and a sense of hope for his or her future, which from a theological perspective is a form of spirituality. Spirituality is formed by one's sense of connection with God, others (family, friends, mentors, etc.), and nature. It is through relationships with others—whether individual or collective—that one develops a sense of safety, peace, support, validation, and identity development.

Central to spirituality as a protective factor for African American adolescents is a focus on resilience built from assets and not the negative aspects of their lived experiences. My particular interest has been to capture how spiritual development and resilience complement academic and personal achievement as an asset. This interest counters resilience studies that focus on the negative effects of risk, trauma, or stress, and instead emphasizes "good" outcomes

---

32 The retreats emerged from the vision of White Catholic leaders and functioned as special events of a Catholic-based college readiness program in which the majority of the participants were Black students. Westfield refers to these types of gatherings as "concealed gatherings" because, she states, "they came together out of the ears and eyes of 'White folks.'" See Nancy Lynne Westfield, *Dear Sisters: A Womanist Practice of Hospitality* (Cleveland: Pilgrim Press, 2007), 34.

33 Gene H. Brody, Zolinda Stoneman, and Douglas Flor, "Parental Religiosity, Family Processes, and Youth Competence in Rural, Two-Parent African American Families," *Developmental Psychology* 32 (1996): 696–706.

among those exposed to high risk or those who experience high levels of stress.[34]

Margaret Beale Spencer, Steven Cole, Davido DuPree, Alvin Glymph, and Phaedra Pierre state that "character formation for many minority youths occurs in a hostile environment and the media continues to perpetuate such images by portraying African American youth and their communities as dens of violence, psychopathy, and aggression."[35] The social sciences have not fared much better than the media. For decades, African Americans have been studied in relation to Whites or have been relegated to research on dysfunction and aggression. As an example, much more interest is shown in children who come from "broken homes" rather than "supportive homes" and in the way in which such an upbringing would manifest later in life.[36]

ASP's mandatory spiritual retreat offered an important and unique opportunity to focus directly on Black social and cultural experiences and ways in which resiliency could be formed and nurtured in the lives of students who came from neighborhoods regarded as "Da Hood" in the Chicagoland area.

Structure and Theological Guides to Spiritual Formation and Resiliency in the Spiritual Retreats

As the retreat facilitator from 1995 through 2008, I was responsible (along with my colleagues) for planning and facilitating the spiritual retreats. ASP class size averaged eighty students, beyond the

34 Ann Masten, "Commentary: The Promise and Perils of Resilience Research as a Guide to Preventive Interventions," in *Resilience and Development: Positive Life Adaptations*, ed. Meyer D. Glantz and Jeanette L. Johnson (New York: Plenum Press, 1999), 251–57.

35 Margaret Spencer et al., "Self-Efficacy among Urban African American Early Adolescents: Exploring Issues of Risk, Vulnerability, and Resilience," *Development and Psychopathology* 5, no. 4 (1993): 721.

36 Oscar Barbarin, "Coping and Resilience: Exploring the Inner Lives of African American Children," *Journal of Black Psychology* 19 (1993): 472–98.

capacity of the local retreat center. Therefore, freshmen, sophomore, and junior year retreats involved half the students at a time. However, during the senior year, all students came together for the final retreat at a location outside Chicago.

Each spiritual retreat had a theme and a scriptural reference based on an undergirding theology of empowerment and theological themes. Theologically, the retreats were deemed spaces where Black youth would experience God's empowering presence and activity that animate resilience within them. The underlying view is of a God who empowers the powerless and emboldens persons' affirmation of their somebodiness.[37] Through use of biblical principles, resilience-forming empowerment occurs as youth define their reality in light of the communities in which they live, their discovery of God's activity in their lives, possibilities for their lives, and their agency in responding to God and making life decisions. Below, I have listed the themes and theological significance by class.

Freshman Retreat (Friday and Saturday)—Who Am I?

> For surely I know the plans I have for you, says the LORD, plans for your welfare and not for harm, to give you a future with hope. (Jer. 29:11, NRSV)

The purpose of this retreat was to help freshmen gain an understanding of who they were in Christ and to know that God had a purpose and plan for their lives as they transitioned into adolescence. Each student was given a personalized name card with their name, the meaning of their name, and a scripture reference. This helped the students gain an understanding about their identity in Christ. Theologically, this theme posits the truth espoused in the work of Rosner that amid the tough stuff of life, persons are known by God.[38] This

37 Views of God's empowering activity is explored in Daniel Migliore, *The Power of God and the Gods of Power* (Philadelphia: Westminster, 2008).

38 Brian S. Rosner, "Known by God: C.S. Lewis and Dietrich Bonhoeffer," *Evangelical Quarterly* 77, no. 4 (2005): 343–52; Brian S. Rosner and Loyola

being known and born with a promised purpose is attested to in the book of Jeremiah in the throes of a people's chaotic and wounding situation of exile.

Sophomore Retreat (Friday and Saturday)—Choices and Consequences

> I appeal to you therefore, brothers and sisters, by the mercies of God, to present your bodies as a living sacrifice, holy and acceptable to God, which is your spiritual worship. Do not be conformed to this world, but be transformed by the renewing of your minds, so that you may discern what is the will of God–what is good and acceptable and perfect. (Rom. 12:1-2, NRSV)

The purpose of this retreat was to help sophomores gain an understanding about making their own decisions as they reached the legal age to drive and do things for themselves without their parents. Each student was given a journal to teach them the importance of writing down their feelings and emotions as they encountered certain situations in their lives. The theological premise is that scripture provides a platform on which choices and actions, called *ethical decision-making*, reflect Christ's character centered on the well-being of self and others.

Junior Retreat (Friday through Sunday)—Family

> Love is patient; love is kind; love is not envious or boastful or arrogant or rude. It does not insist on its own way; it is not irritable or resentful; it does not rejoice in wrongdoing but rejoices in the truth. It bears all things, believes

---

McLean, "Theology and Human Flourishing: The Benefits of Being Known by God," in *Beyond Well-Being: Spirituality and Human Flourishing*, ed. Maureen Miner, Martin Dowson, and Stuart Devenish (Charlotte, NC: Information Age, 2012), 65-83; and Brian S. Rosner, *Known by God: A Biblical Theology of Personal Identity* (New York: HarperCollins, 2017).

> all things, hopes all things, endures all things. Love never ends. (1 Cor. 13:4-8a, NRSV)

The purpose of this retreat was to help junior scholars gain an understanding of the importance of family, communal relationships, and the love of Christ as they were beginning to transition into adulthood. The juniors were given letters written by adults in their life—family members, sponsors or mentors, ASP staff, and teachers. The letters allowed adults to write positive things about the students and how they were proud of them. Students were given a cross as a symbol of their relationship with Christ. They also took part in a Saturday service project either at a homeless shelter or nursing home. In addition, they attended a Sunday church service at a Catholic church near the retreat center. A relational theology of love undergirded the theme and highlighted an ethic of responsibility and actions that contribute to and foster what is right, honest, and just in one's own life and the lives of others, based on God's love.

Senior Retreat (Friday through Sunday)—Transitions

> Finally, be strong in the Lord and in the strength of his power. Put on the whole armor of God, so that you may be able to stand against the wiles of the devil. For our struggle is not against enemies of blood and flesh, but against the rulers, against the authorities, against the cosmic powers of this present darkness, against the spiritual forces of evil in the heavenly places. Therefore take up the whole armor of God, so that you may be able to withstand on that evil day, and having done everything, to stand firm. Stand therefore, and fasten the belt of truth around your waist, and put on the breastplate of righteousness. As shoes for your feet put on whatever will make you ready to proclaim the gospel of peace. With all of these, take the shield of faith, with which you will be able to quench all the flaming arrows of the evil one. Take the helmet of salvation, and the sword of the Spirit, which is the word of God. Pray in the Spirit at all times in

> every prayer and supplication. To that end keep alert and always persevere in supplication for all the saints. (Eph. 6:10–18, NRSV)

The purpose of this retreat was to help the seniors gain an understanding about what was required of them as they transitioned from high school to college and to know that they were equipped with the full armor of God. Their whole senior class was together for the first time for a retreat. They went to a retreat center that was approximately two and a half hours away from Chicago, which was the farthest from home that many of the students had ever been. They were given a Bible as a symbol of the word of God to take with them wherever they go. The session was theologically guided by an understanding of God's empowerment of their somebodiness and abilities to move with resilience into the coming stage of their lives based on their seeing it, owning it, and acting on it.

Meet the Alumni: Narratives of Transformation and Movement beyond "Da Hood"

What follows here are background information and narratives of four of the fifty-one alumni, obtained through interviews and a survey. Their profiles uncover the phenomena of resilience and spirituality emerging amid present realities in the home, school, and community, as the result of participation in ASP. Pseudonyms are used to protect the participants' identities.

Tiffany Mason's Story: "Agape Scholars Program Helped Me Experience God"

Tiffany was raised by her maternal grandmother in the inner city of Chicago. She identified as growing up in a Christian household. Within her household were her aunt and her mother, who was in and out of the house. Her father was in and out of her life but came back more regularly when she was ten years old. While Tiffany was growing up, both of her parents were substance abusers. During her interview, she stated, "My mother was a substance abuser, but she was clean while I was in high school. She had been clean for quite some time, but still it was the aftereffects. My mother could be a calm person for one second and then go crazy next, and you can be like, 'What just happened?'" She described her dad as being a substance abuser; however, when she was in high school he was no longer taking drugs but rather drinking alcohol. He was only allowed limited visits, which her grandmother oversaw and which could only take place in the living room.

She recalled that there was never a time for her to bond with her father, because she was not allowed to spend time outside of the house with him. Even though she was not able to bond with her father, during her interview she discussed how participating in ASP created an opportunity for her to bond with other minorities who came from similar situations. It gave her the ability to connect with them, especially because she was attending a predominantly White, all-girls Catholic high school. She felt that she was not able to bond with a single person at her high school, but ASP allowed her to stay connected with others and build lifelong friendships.

She recalled, "Other ASP students were going through similar circumstances such as single-parent homes, substance-abuse parents, low-income families, and no matter what was going on they all had the goal to be successful and make something of themselves." When asked about the highlight of participating in ASP, she responded:

> ASP gave me an opportunity to experience more with God. I will start with the church services. They gave us an opportunity to create a spiritual experience for the students and their families. It allowed us to not do church traditionally, even though I went to my own church regularly. It felt like a FUBU [For Us By Us] moment because the teens were able to plan the services, pick the music, choose the guest speakers, plan skits, and so much more. Most important were the ASP retreats–loved those. It gave us an opportunity to come

> together and bond. I remember having to come back as a retreat leader and the gift of a journal, which was passed out the first night of the retreat. You all taught us the importance of putting our feelings down on paper. I continued writing in my journal until I ran out of pages and I remember calling asking where I could I purchase another one. To this day, I still keep a journal. The retreats allowed us to be open, be ourselves, come out of our comfort zone, be open to Christ. Those retreats prepared me to be open to God and more free and fluid. I learned that your spiritual experiences are shaped by your environment, your family, friends, and everyone around you. Going into college, my faith was tested, but I continued to read my Bible, listen to Christian music, pray, read a devotional, and realized that I needed God more in my life than ever before.

Tiffany was asked to share whether she considered herself to be resilient. She defined herself as resilient because she is someone who remains steadfast or peaceful during stressful situations. She has always had an awareness of her circumstances and has known what extra work she needed to do to come out of a situation and be successful. Living in a household with a substance-abusing mother and her GED-educated grandmother as her guardian, Tiffany knew it was a challenge to attend a predominantly White, all-girls Catholic high school and matriculate to a predominantly White, top-tier university as a first-generation student.

In her survey, Tiffany recalled inequalities at her school. Her high school classmates were seemingly more advanced than she was in mathematics. Indeed, Tiffany's grandmother received notification from her math teacher that Tiffany was not advanced enough for the honors class and should be placed in a regular math class. Tiffany took matters into her own hands and informed her grandmother, "I got this." She stated, "I purchased note cards, learned what an 'all-nighter' was, and I spread the dining room table with note cards, old tests, worksheets, etc. I studied and practiced my way from a D to an A." Her motivation to succeed was her faith, family, and ASP. Tiffany graduated with a bachelor's degree from a top-tier university and is currently a senior implementation specialist for a major healthcare company.

Malcolm Gaston's Story: "I Was a Retreat Leader, and It Changed My Life"

Malcolm grew up with his stepfather and mother in the inner city of Chicago. He identified as growing up in a Christian household, even though his family did not attend church on a regular basis. During his interview, he recalled his neighborhood as a place where he witnessed dope dealers, gangs, and violence, but it felt strange to him to state that he knew all the 'hoods and everyone within his community. He attended a predominantly White, all-male Catholic high school. He felt that it was hard to juggle attending a Catholic school and living in a rough neighborhood. He felt like he was never validated and that he was always looked down upon because of negative elements of the neighborhood. He knew that he needed these guys and needed them to be OK with him because otherwise things would not go well for him. He felt safe in his neighborhood because he knew the guys who hung out there. As he reflected on his teenage years participating in ASP, he stated:

> I would not have gotten through high school without it. I made some good contacts as far as mentors that I can have for the rest of my life, and it was the beginning of my Christian experience with the retreats. I would not have had that without ASP. The retreats offered me an environment where I could vent or think differently about things and stuff that I was going through.

When asked to expound on his Christian experience while participating in ASP, he recalled, "A lot us lived in bad neighborhoods and some of us went to church, but we may not have had retreats at our church. We did not have an opportunity to get with friends and talk about what we were going through or our life circumstances and have God at the center of those things." Malcolm became a bit emotional as he shared a spiritual experience that occurred while he was a retreat leader his junior year of high school. He stated:

> I was a retreat leader and it was Sunday and we was at St. Angela, and I had spoken that day on or maybe it was the day before that, Saturday or Friday night. I did a talk on forgiveness of my father, basically forgiveness of my father. And I had told my story and the students responded well to it, they related to it. We got to church and I think Fr. Peter said something about if there is something you want to let go or someone you need to forgive come up to the altar. I cannot remember for what, other than just looking back I cannot remember for what it was, just get up, walk the aisle, and walk to the center, and show the world, and show God physically in action and behavior that you identify that there is something that you need to give up and you need the help to give it up. And so, I was sitting there, I was like saying to the students, "Alright y'all, go on up there, get your little tails up there [*laughs*]. All y'all said you had something going on, gone on up there," and that is not something that you cannot tell people that is something they need to do if they do not feel it. So, I was sitting there with my head down, just kinda like reflecting, and my best friend Mason came and tapped me on the shoulder and was like, "What did he say? You know you need to be up there too." Instantly I started crying and bawling and snooting. So, I walked up there. I think there were two people or maybe one in front of me. I think he [Fr. Peter] was like giving out hugs [*laughs*], but anyway, I had my head down when I was walking up there and you know St. Angela has that big ol' Black Jesus with the hands out like this [*he demonstrates*] and remember when I finally looked up, whenever I looked up and saw that and it was like over [*demonstrates*] Father Peter, and when I looked up and when

> I saw that it was not like I was about to faint, but I remember my legs almost gave out. I had never experienced anything like that before, it was so, it was so, I want to say faint, but I do not think "faint" is the right word, but I know that I looked up and looked down again, my legs almost gave out and I did that a few times, every time I looked up I felt like I was going to fall to my knees. I cannot remember if I fell into Fr. Peter's arms or if he just embraced me. That was pretty life changing; that was one of those, like, this is real, and that I was a retreat leader and I was not even in a retreat and I was there to help impact and not to be impacted [*laughs*]. I guess that was the secondary part of the job description. But, yeah, that was a life-changing experience, and I would say that was one of the top five spiritual experiences that I have ever had in my life. Just knowing that God is real and these experiences are they happen and they are not like stories and they are truthful and that sort of thing.

Later in his interview, Malcolm talked about his stepfather, an alcoholic who passed away when Malcolm was a sophomore in high school. He shared the financial challenge he witnessed his mother experience as a single parent and the strained relationship they had as mother and son. But what kept him afloat was attending the ASP retreats all four years of high school. When asked to explain whether he viewed himself as resilient, he stated, "I guess to completely go against the environment in which you grow up in, I think I am resilient. I always had the desire and ought to keep working hard at something even while attending a predominantly White high school, which was filled with prejudices and prejudgments. I wanted to succeed, and I did not want anything to stop me." Malcolm received his bachelor's degree from a predominantly White, Midwestern college and recently received his master's degree from a Southern university.

Brian Hicks's Story: "Show Kids from the Inner City—Don't Be a Follower"

Brian grew up with his parents and oldest sister in the inner city of Chicago. He identified as a Christian while growing up but states that currently he is "spiritual, meaning I am open to other religious beliefs." He described his neighborhood as predominantly Black. There were a few White people who attended his local Catholic grammar school. He recalled his parents telling him about how the neighborhood had been when they moved there in the 1960s: well esteemed and with thriving Black businesses. However, over time, violence, drugs, fewer fathers, lower education, and less guidance all led to an influx of crime in the neighborhood. Brian began to fear for his life more than he had when he was younger, but he knew all the guys in the neighborhood because they played sports together. However, many of his friends were killed due to gang violence and drugs. Brian attended a predominantly White, all-male Catholic high school, and his mother worked for a top-tier university a few blocks away.

He recalled one time in which he was walking with friends to the "L" (the train in Chicago) to go home after skipping track practice. As usual, a group of males from the local public high school started a ruckus on the train platform. He remembered about thirty young men circling him and his friends to start a fight. He knew he had done nothing to incite a fight, and therefore he decided that he would separate himself once the train arrived. The next day, he thought that everything was OK, but when he went to sit with his friends during lunch, they all got up and walked away. This tore him up inside; he had thought that these were his friends. After school that day, he decided to meet his mother at her job. He stated that it was a blessing and a godsend to have his mother close because he did not want to go home alone that day.

His mother consoled him and encouraged him that everything would work out. This incident allowed him to refocus his life and do his own thing. However, at a party a few months later, a young man approached him and hit him in the face unexpectedly. This young man was friends with the young men from the incident at the platform, whom Brian referred to as his "so-called friends." This young man felt that Brian had not stood up for his friends. The next month, Brian realized that this young man was a year ahead of him and was also an ASP scholar. A few years later, while visiting family during a college break, this young man was killed because of gang violence. At this point in the interview, Brian remembered being an ASP retreat leader and was thankful for the structure the retreats gave to his path in life. He felt that the retreats laid a foundation and were a journey for him. He stated that the retreat facilitators instilled wisdom in him and helped him learn how to march to the beat of his own drum. He realized that it was OK to be different and that he could go down his own path. He felt that he had found his voice while being a retreat leader because he could lead his peers. For him, it is essential for young kids living in the inner city to see what is possible in life and that they can make a change. The retreats as well as his attendance at Catholic grammar and high schools were foundational for Brian's belief in God because he could figure out his own truth. When asked to share whether he saw himself as resilient, Brian used the metaphor of scar tissue. He stated:

> The idea of you being able to be beat, battered–not only physically, but any sort of emotional trauma, verbal trauma, mental trauma–those are the things that shape who you are. But resiliency is being able to move forward no matter who tries to chop you down or tell you to stop trying to be an Oreo [a Black person who is viewed as a sellout]. The goal is to see something within yourself that is bigger and better than you are. You have a choice about your own life to move forward.

Brian received a half million dollars in college scholarships and graduated with a bachelor's degree from a top-tier university. He interned for a top media company during his undergraduate years, was hired after college, and worked there for three years. He took a leap of faith, quit his high-paying job, and became an entrepreneur, traveling the country.

Sasha Jones's Story: "It Was the Best Day of My Life; I Felt Whole Again"

Sasha, from the inner city of Chicago, was raised until the age of six by her mother. Her father is from Africa. She grew up in a Christian household. Her maternal aunt was her guardian while her mother was detained in another country for ten years. She lived with her aunt, her cousin, and her aunt's boyfriend in a low- to middle-class neighborhood. During her face-to-face interview, she did not share why her mother was detained in another country. However, she did share that her aunt had a live-in boyfriend who was mentally, emotionally, and physically abusive. She recalled being the recipient of mental abuse from him. Her dad was around during this time, but she feared informing him because she did not want to be taken away from her mother's side of the family. She had a hatred for her aunt because she was not getting the love she should have received while her mother was away. She stated in her survey that she endured a lot of emotional abuse from her aunt, whose words were very hurtful. In addition, her aunt hid in her room many nights out of fear of her abusive boyfriend.

It was not until Sasha was a sophomore in high school that her mother was able to return to the United States. Sasha stated, "It was the best day of my life; I felt whole again." She recalled her prayers for her mother to come back home, which were now answered. Even though Sasha was overjoyed to have her mother back home, she was sad that she had to leave her friends and move to the south suburbs. Sasha felt as if her aunt immediately kicked her out of the house when her mother returned. She recalled her aunt saying, "Your mother is back home now; go deal with it. You all figure out how you both will work it out."

Sasha talked about how her attendance and the staff at the ASP retreats helped her to process what was going on in her life at that moment. She continued to talk about how the retreats helped her to become less shy and more vocal. The retreats taught her what it meant to write things down in a journal and not hold on to her emotions. She recalled being a retreat leader, which helped her grow in her faith and understand who she was as a young woman. When asked for five words to describe resilience in her life, she said *strong, patient, unbreakable, flexible*, and *understanding*. Sasha grew up in an emotionally abusive home, but this upbringing did not make her a statistic, a person who comes from a broken home and thus does not deal well with adversity. She made the decision to not feed into those statistics and to not want that for herself. Sasha attended a predominantly White, all-girls Catholic high school and matriculated to a small, private, Midwestern college where she received a bachelor's degree. She is currently a district trainer for the second-largest pharmaceutical company in the country.

Reflections

ASP revealed the importance and outcomes of advocating for a space to empower resilience in the lives of African American adolescents who come from adverse environments. The program offered an opportunity for Black youth to build resilience sufficient to beat the odds and overcome stereotypes of African American adolescents from what is pejoratively called "Da Hood." Their experiences affirm that engaging young people in spiritual development can enable them to overcome oppressive systems. The program helped them discover their ability to achieve academically as well as grow spiritually and affirm their somebodiness given by God. The retreats pointed to advocacy for and implementation of the following:

- Seeing and reaching out to young people in the public sphere
- Developing and implementing spaces that invite youth into what one called FUBU (For Us By Us) moments that allow for bonding and personal story-sharing moments

- Opening the way for empowerment and resilience-building by unapologetically offering young people opportunities to experience God and explore scripture and meanings of both in the real stuff of their lives
- Creating structured experiences through youth discovery and concretely expressing their voice, choices for their intended path, their leadership, the nature of their resilience, and God's role in their lives
- Receiving and affirming the stories of youths' onward journey

This kind of advocacy is needed so that Black youth are afforded supports needed to avoid a life of crime, depression, early onset sexual activity, and substance abuse. This action is key for those who work with African American adolescents in inner-city or urban contexts.

Epilogue

Religious Education, the Black Church, and the Future of Public Ministry: A Village Encounter

Annie Lockhart-Gilroy

> So make no mistake about it. There are still so many causes worth sacrificing for. There is still so much history yet to be made.
>
> –Michelle Obama, "Remarks by the First Lady during Keynote Address at Young African Women Leaders Forum"

Sometimes, once my seminary students have taken their first religious education course, I overhear them sharing that the course was not what the name had led them to expect. They had expected the course to be centered on tools and tips for teaching Sunday school and Bible study and for putting together a Christian education program in their congregations—all important endeavors but all activities that are focused within the walls of a congregation. Some seminarians come to their first religious education class with the false belief that religious education happens solely within the church building. Church-related projects that happen outside of the walls of the congregation are important and necessary aspects of *other* functions of church life but not of religious education. These students find these beliefs challenged when they take part in a religious education course centered on conversations revolving around liberation, social justice, religious education as an act of freedom, and the work of the religious educator in the public sphere. From the breadth of different public spaces presented within this book, it is clear that I am far from alone in my understanding of the role of religious educators. As I bring this book to a close, I will share my reflection on the importance of Black religious educators as public theologians and how it has been further informed by themes within this text. I will then venture to explore some ideas as we think about the future of public theology.

My vocational understanding of the Black religious educator as public theologian began as a practitioner. Before becoming a seminary professor and even before becoming a seminarian, I served as an educator and youth worker in a predominately Black congregation with a faith-based social service entity. At first, I thought the same way as my seminary students. I was very interested in outreach but saw that as separate from religious education. That Black congregation taught me to see my role differently and showed me that a religious educator was also a public theologian. Over the course of my ten years of serving that congregation in my role as religious educator, I worked with many different publics. Sometimes I was responsible for a program for youth adjudicated by the courts. Sometimes I worked with adults, helping them get jobs and transition off public assistance. Sometimes I planned youth group activities and retreats. Sometimes I planned Sunday school lessons. And sometimes I worked with women, teaching job and life skills. This congregation taught me that *sometimes* my job was about creating education opportunities *about* the religious, but my job was *always* to create education that *is* religious. This education is religious because it is powered by a faith that sees the oppressions of Black people within public spaces and sees these oppressions as hindering Black people from being truly free to be the children of God they were created to be—a faith that sees God as a liberator, sees education as an act of freedom, and therefore sees the job of the religious educator as providing educational opportunities that free people to be the children of God they were created to be. To paraphrase John Wesley, who said, "I look upon all the world as my parish," Black religious education sees the whole world as its classroom. The broader world is where the people of God are, so that is where we need to be.

Religious Education as Countering a Problematic Public Curriculum

Religious educators are needed as public theologians because whether explicitly or not, public spaces present their own curriculum. Throughout this book several authors have highlighted what US society has tried to teach Black people. Society teaches one how one ought to act, behave, and be in public spaces. Nancy Lynne Westfield's chapter especially interrogates how people are taught to be complacent and to participate in their own oppression because of the identities we embody. Public spaces and the many factions thereof present their own explicit, implicit, and null curriculum.[1] While these terms were originally reserved for formal educational settings like schools and classrooms, they can be applied to any space that teaches—and all spaces teach. Society's curriculum is distributed through many different avenues including but not limited to school systems, advertising, media reporting, and actions by law enforcement toward Black bodies. The explicit curriculum about Black bodies has been taught throughout history through legalized chattel slavery, Jim Crow laws, the celebration of lynchings, and racial massacres. The lesson was made clear: Black bodies and Black lives have less value than White bodies and White lives. We see this message stated today as law enforcement all over the

1 Elliot Eisner presented the view of education spaces having three types of curricula—explicit, implicit, and null. The explicit curriculum is what the educational space advertises it does. The implicit curriculum is a hidden one; its goals are not explicitly stated but can be deduced by organization, structure, actions, language, and physical set-up of a space. The null curriculum refers to what these spaces leave out and do not address. Elliot W. Eisner, *The Educational Imagination: On the Design and Evaluation of School Programs*, 2nd ed. (New York: Macmillan, 1985).

United States staunchly declares that race has nothing do with fatal shootings even though American Blacks are 2.5 times more likely to be killed by the police than their White counterparts and Whites are more likely to be armed when killed by the police.[2] Society's implicit curriculum is taught through microaggressions, like the annual Halloween conversation about the appropriateness of Blackface, and the ongoing need for apologies from politicians for what some simply call racial missteps. These are implicit because they convey what many no longer feel free to say in public spaces explicitly, but the message is the same. The null curriculum can be seen through a lack of representation of Black bodies in films, TV, corporate boardrooms, and other spaces of societal power. Despite some recent improvement, much more work remains to be done. In many places of power, few Black voices are heard or projected, so our voices and presence remain null. These curricula come together to try to teach Blacks to stay within the confined spaces society has set for them; these curricula constantly teach Blacks that it is within these confined spaces that they belong.

It is the role, then, of religious education to provide a countercurriculum—a curriculum that counters society's curriculum by first calling it out for the lie that it is, lamenting the messages we have internalized, and then countering with public advocacy centered in religious education. That happens best in the same public space where the miseducation is happening—in the public sphere. The chapters within this edited work present wonderful examples of countercurricula. Joseph Crockett's chapter, for example, explores the pedagogy present in the Black Lives Matter movement, a movement that directly counters the public curriculum that states that Black bodies and Black lives do not matter. Sarah Farmer's chapter explores the implicit curriculum in the penal system and counters

---

2 Frank Edwards, Hedwig Lee, and Michael Esposito, "Risk of Being Killed by Police Use of Force in the United States by Age, Race-Ethnicity, and Sex," *Proceedings of the National Academy of Science* 116, no. 34 (August 2019): 16793–98, https://doi.org/10.1073/pnas.1821204116.

this with her exploration of a public pedagogy; this pedagogical framework centers her work in the understanding that learning can take place in many different forms and spaces. Dr. Farmer names the many things that penal pedagogy teaches and then presents a countercurriculum. This book as a whole presents countercurricula.

Note that I did not suggest that we are to present counter*narratives*. A counternarrative presents a different story or an alternate ending, but it accepts the underlying premises of the story. A metanarrative presents a different kind of story. A metanarrative rejects the entire premise of the story being told. The countercurricula presented in this book are grounded in a metanarrative of transformation and justice, and declare that Black bodies are made in the image of God and should be treated as such. Recognizing that as truth also leads us to ask, What does it mean to free people to be children of God? In a society that seeks to constrict people to particular roles because of their embodied identities, a religious education is freeing when it teaches what it means for human beings to bear the image of God.

These countercurricula are rooted in a metanarrative that sees God as a liberating God who wants all people to be freed to be children of God that are made in the image of God. When people learn from the problematic public curriculum and believe that their Black body is of less worth, they believe that they are of less worth and they are less able to see the image of God within them. The body that is made in the image of God cannot be worth less than another body. It is the role of Black religious education to infuse the public with this metanarrative. Within this text, we see the different ways this happens and the different public spaces where this happens. Yet one text cannot possibly cover the entirety of ways that religious education intersects with public theology and corrects a problematic public curriculum. While this volume presents key ideas and concepts to remember and act on, much remains to be envisioned, taken seriously, and put into action in advocacy and activism that is sustained by an intentional and thoughtfully articulated theology for the sake of a more justice-centered and promising future for Black people. So where can we go from here?

Younger Generations and New Spaces

When considering the future of public ministry, one place to start is to look at younger generations, specifically Black millennials (born between 1981 and 1996) and members of Gen Z (born from 1997 to the present).[3] There is much to learn from these generations, the public theology work they are doing, and the spaces in which they are performing this work. As millennials are currently on the cusp of becoming the largest adult population group, it is clear that they are aging out of being "the young people," as all generations do, but what these generations have contributed and are contributing to different understandings of public theology allow us to see the continuing relationship between Black religious education and public theology as well as the new places and spaces it is expanding into.

Much has been written about the relationship (or lack thereof) between millennials and the Church since the Pew Research Center released the findings of its 2014 religious landscape study. The findings show a trend of a drop-in church attendance, a decline in those that call themselves Christian, and a rise in "spiritual nones"—those who do not identify with a religious tradition. However, what has been less discussed is that affiliation with historical Black denominations suffered a loss of less than 1 percentage point. These data suggest that as of 2017, Black Americans between the ages of eighteen and twenty-nine (this sample contains younger millennials and

3 Different sources present different birthdates for these generations. Because I rely on research done by the Pew Research Center, I use their demarcations. Designating cutoffs for these generations is not an exact science. Unlike the Baby Boomers, a generation named after an actual period of history where the baby boom can be mapped, other generations tend to be brought together by looser events that may define them. In essence, millennials are members of the generation that came of age around the new millennium. Gen Z is the generation that follows them.

the older members of Gen Z) are not leaving the Church in the way that their White counterparts are; the majority of Black millennials and older members of Gen Z are still affiliated with an ecclesiastical body and identity with a particular faith tradition. This is a subsection of the study that is often ignored when speaking of these generations and their relationship to the church. Much remains to be researched about the racial differences and the relationship to the Church and religion by millennials and Gen Z. And with this differentiation, that Black youth and young adults feel a connection that is often overlooked. This connection to the Church, religious identity, and God provides fertile ground for further research on the future of public theology.

In the article "'I Speak to God in Public': Are Young Black Millennials Reclaiming a Theology of Resistance?" Joshua L. Lazard points to a Black millennial aesthetic that is not ashamed to claim their belief in and relationship with God in public spaces and one that connects their theology to their social action.[4] The title of Lazard's article is taken from the lyrics of a song by recording artist Chance the Rapper. Lazard argues the artist's success may be because of his public display of his faith and not in spite of it, for he speaks to a Black generation that seeks to combine their passion for justice with their understanding of God. Noting the amount of religious material that is shared through virtual spaces, he concludes, "The opportunity is ripe for Black millennials en masse to construct their own practical public theology of anger and resistance."[5] These generations are also seen as a generation of activists. Joseph Crockett's chapter highlights the work of the Black Lives Matter movement and a religious education response. Black millennials and Gen Z'ers have not only been on the front lines of the Black Lives Matter movement

4 Joshua L. Lazard, "'I Speak to God in Public': Are Young Black Millennials Reclaiming a Theology of Resistance?" Religion Dispatches, April 14, 2017, http://religiondispatches.org/i-speak-to-god-in-public-are-young-Black-millennials-reclaiming-a-new-theology-of-resistance/.

5 Lazard, "'I Speak to God in Public.'"

but have also played key roles in the March for Our Lives, which seeks an end to the numerous school shootings, and movements of ecological justice. Black millennials and Gen Z'ers are continuing in the tradition of fighting for justice on a larger societal scale while connecting it to the fight for personal survival. They are doing this, however, while creating new public spaces and forms of leadership that are shaping the future of public theology. And, indeed, these theological practices are already in the works as these generations lead. As they lead, we are seeing new areas of leadership, communication, and activism that can teach us a lot about what needs further study. Chance the Rapper, for example, is a musical star without a label whose album *Coloring Book* is the first streaming-only album to win a Grammy. As an artist whose work lives solely in virtual spaces, Chance the Rapper is the epitome of a Black millennial aesthetic. To follow the leadership of Black millennials and Gen Z, more attention must be paid to virtual space as its own kind of public sphere.

Millennials are often described as digital natives, and Gen Z has also been referred to as iGen (in reference to the smartphone). These qualifiers show the creation and usage of a growing public space that is tied to the identity of those within these generations. This virtual public sphere is diverse in that it includes blogs, websites, podcasts, online streaming, and social media, just to name a few. The growing importance of this space can be seen by news reports that are based on statements made on social media platforms and what is trending. It is clear that growing virtual spaces that are dimensions of the public sphere deserve further conversation. Certainly, all aspects of this public virtual space cannot be seen as equal, for example, those that are used solely for entertainment and voyeurism. However, more conversation and research are needed on how these spaces contribute to the future of public ministry.

These virtual spaces are contributing to the ways we see corporate worship. While there has long been opportunity to participate in corporate worship from afar through radio broadcasts and televised worship services, this growing virtual space allows for corporate worship that does not center on an in-person congregation but entire virtual congregations with virtual pastors fully realizing the old adage that the church is not the building but the people. People can also be spiritually fed and theologically informed by podcasts, videos, and Facebook Live videos that allow those watching to type in their "Amens." These spaces are ripe for religious educators to take more advantage of, as these spaces are challenging what it means for us to be together.

This growing public space is also changing the notion of leadership in areas of advocacy. Because the bar to entry is lower than more traditional published spaces, virtual spaces are more egalitarian. This opens the notion of activist leadership. People have been referred to as leaders of movements because they created a hashtag. This reality has brought further critique as to the efficacy of these movements—another great space for future research. However, the egalitarian nature of virtual spaces gives space for young leaders to make their voices heard and for various oppressed individuals to bring forth a coalition or more readily know when a coalition is forming or has been formed. Of course, some people are kept out of this public space because of economic hardship and lack of regular access to the internet. Additionally, some rural areas around the country still do not have reliable wireless connection. This space is not universally accessible, but the rise of social media is increasing the ability to participate in various issues of public discourse and activism and allowing more people to have a voice.

They are using their voices in a variety of ways, and as activist generations, one of the ways that Black youth and young adults are using these platforms is to bring attention to the violence perpetuated against Black people. While violence against Black people in the United States has been perpetrated for longer than there has been a United States, social media puts faces and names to these violated bodies—sometimes in real time. Just as television brought the reality of the Vietnam War into American living rooms, puncturing comfortable myths about the war's severity, social media can bring reality into the palms of one's hands. Camera phones and social media are the foremost tools of civil rights today. These tools have been used to bring awareness, which has led to action.

Some have critiqued participation in virtual spaces and questioned whether hashtags amount to lazy protesting. Some have questioned to what extent social media uproar translates to change in the physical world. While a few studies have been done on this, there is much more to study. However, it is important to realize that as a public space, the virtual world does not have to be personified into a concrete public space. The virtual public space is sufficient and acts as a space unto itself.

Moving forward, Black religious educators need to take greater advantage of social media and other virtual spaces. In what ways can these spaces serve as communities of learning? How does the conversation change about leadership in a more egalitarian space where just about anyone can have a platform? How does interacting with bodies mostly in virtual spaces affect changes in an understanding of embodied pedagogy? Many questions and areas remain to be explored. And the different public spheres of the virtual world provide not only spaces to interact but spaces for practical theologians to study. Examining tweets, hashtags, trends, and so on is a place of ethnography for the practical theologian. The future of public ministry is in these spaces, and these spaces should be studied in ethnographic studies. As we continue to move from lament to public advocacy, this virtual public sphere is of utmost importance, for indeed, the revolution will not be televised; it will be livestreamed.

Contributors

Joseph V. Crockett is chief executive officer, Friendship Press, Inc., Chester Heights, Pennsylvania; elder, The United Methodist Church.

Sarah F. Farmer is assistant professor of practical theology and community development, School of Theology and Ministry at Indiana Wesleyan University, Marion, Indiana.

Annie Lockhart-Gilroy is assistant professor of Christian education and practical theology, Phillips Theological Seminary, Tulsa, Oklahoma.

Cynthia P. Stewart is assistant director and academic internship program manager for the Center for Experiential Learning, Loyola University, Chicago, Illinois.

Nathaniel D. West is chair of the master of arts in Christian education program at the Samuel DeWitt Proctor School of Theology, Virginia Union University, Richmond, Virginia.

Nancy Lynne Westfield is director, the Wabash Center for Teaching and Learning in Theology and Religion, Crawfordsville, Indiana.

Richelle B. White is professor of youth ministry and director of ministry leadership internships, Kuyper College, Grand Rapids, Michigan.

Anne E. Streaty Wimberly is executive director, Youth Hope-Builders Academy (a theological program for high school youth) and the Connecting with Hope Innovation Hub, Millennials Ministry Initiative; professor emerita of Christian education, Interdenominational Theological Center, Atlanta, Georgia.

Mary H. Young is director of leadership education, Association of Theological Schools, Pittsburgh, Pennsylvania.

CPSIA information can be obtained
at www.ICGtesting.com
Printed in the USA
LVHW110858050121
675767LV00009B/202